DEVELOPMENT and DISPLACEMENT

Edited by Jenny Robinson

The Open University

in association with

OXFORD
UNIVERSITY PRESS

OXFORD
UNIVERSITY PRESS

Great Clarendon Street, Oxford OX2 6DP
Oxford University Press is a department of the University of Oxford.
It furthers the University's objective of excellence in research, scholarship,
and education by publishing worldwide in
Oxford New York Auckland Bangkok Buenos Aires
Cape Town Chennai Dar es Salaam Delhi Hong Kong Istanbul
Karachi Kolkata Kuala Lumpur Madrid Melbourne Mexico City Mumbai
Nairobi São Paulo Shanghai Singapore Taipei Tokyo Toronto
and an associated company in Berlin
Oxford is a registered trade mark of Oxford University Press
in the UK and in certain other countries

Published in the United States by Oxford University Press Inc., New York

Published in association with The Open University
The Open University, Walton Hall, Milton Keynes, MK7 6AA
First published 2002.
Copyright © 2002 The Open University

Edited, designed and typeset by The Open University.
Printed and bound in the United Kingdom by The Alden Group, Oxford.

British Library Cataloguing in Publication Data
Data available

Library of Congress Cataloguing in Publication Data
Data available

ISBN 0 1992 5507 5
1.1

DEVELOPMENT AND DISPLACEMENT

WITHDRAWN

Books are to be returned on or before
the last date below.

This book is published by Oxford University Press in association with
The Open University

It is the companion volume to *Poverty and Development into the 21st Century*,
edited by Tim Allen and Alan Thomas

These publications form part of an Open University course U213 *International
Development: Challenges for a World in Transition*. Details of this and other
Open University courses can be obtained from the Course Information and
Advice Centre, PO Box 724, The Open University, Milton Keynes MK7 6ZS,
United Kingdom: tel. +44 (0)1908 653231, e-mail ces-gen@open.ac.uk

Alternatively, you may visit the Open University website at
http://www.open.ac.uk where you can learn more about the wide range of
courses and packs offered at all levels by the Open University.

To purchase this publication or its companion volume, contact
Oxford University Press, Great Clarendon Street, Oxford OX2 6DP,
website http://www.oup.com

To purchase other components of this course contact Open University
Worldwide Ltd, The Open University, Walton Hall, Milton Keynes MK7 6AA,
United Kingdom: tel. +44 (0)1908 858785; fax +44 (0)1908 858787; e-mail
ouwenq@open.ac.uk;
website http://www.ouw.co.uk

Contents

Authors and production team

ACADEMIC STAFF

Joanna Chataway, *Co-Course Chair and Senior Lecturer in Development Management*

Jenny Robinson, *Co-Course Chair and Lecturer in Geography*

Gordon Wilson, *Co-Course Chair and Senior Lecturer in Technology and Development*

Simon Bromley, *Senior Lecturer in Government and Politics*

Will Brown, *Lecturer in Government and Politics*

Pam Furniss, *Lecturer in Systems*

Tom Hewitt, *Senior Lecturer in Development Studies*

Hazel Johnson, *Senior Lecturer in Development Studies*

Bob Kelly, *Staff Tutor, Social Sciences*

Maureen Mackintosh, *Professor of Economics*

Judith Mehta, *Lecturer in Economics*

Stephen Peake, *Lecturer in Design and Innovation*

Sandrine Simon, *Lecturer in Systems*

Alan Thomas, *Professor of Development Studies, University of Wales Swansea*

Richard Treves, *Staff Tutor, Technology*

David Wield, *Professor of Innovation and Development*

Helen Yanacopulos, *Lecturer in Development Studies*

BBC STAFF

Jenny Bardwell, *Series Producer July 2000–May 2001*

Gail Block, *Audio Producer*

Giselle Corbett, *Production Manager*

Phil Gauron, *Series Producer*

Julie Laing, *Series Personal Assistant*

Andrew Law, *Executive*

Jenny Morgan, *Freelance Director*

Claire Sandry, *Audio Producer*

Mercia Seminara, *Audio Producer*

SUPPORT STAFF

Carolyn Baxter, *Course Manager*

Sylvan Bentley, *Picture Researcher*

Kevin Brown, *Picture Researcher*

Philippa Broadbent, *Print Buying Controller*

Daphne Cross, *Print Buying Coordinator*

Tony Duggan, *Learning Projects Manager*

Carl Gibbard, *Graphic Designer*

Richard Hoyle, *Graphic Designer*

Peta Jellis, *Course Manager July–November 2000*

Lori Johnston, *Editor*

Roy Lawrance, *Graphic Artist*

Cathy McNulty, *Course Secretary*

Katie Meade, *Rights Editor*

Jenny Nockles, *Graphic Designer*

Pauline O'Dwyer, *Course Secretary*

Janice Robertson, *Editor*

John Taylor, *Copublishing Manager*

Pamela Wardell, *Editor*

Rob Williams, *Graphic Designer*

EXTERNAL ASSESSORS/CRITICAL READERS

Dr K Bezanson, *Institute of Development Studies, University of Sussex*

Abdou Maliq Simone, *University of the Witwatersrand, Johannesburg*

CONSULTANTS

Vandana Desai, *Department of Geography, Royal Holloway, University of London*

Giles Mohan, *Department of Geography, University of Portsmouth (Currently Lecturer in Development Studies, The Open University)*

David Turton, *formerly Director, Refugee Studies Centre, Oxford*

Preface

The displacement of people through war, famine, conflict and poverty, and indeed, through development itself, is increasingly central to the work of development and human rights agencies. More than this, it is becoming increasingly apparent to development scholars and practitioners that their own advice and actions can contribute to displacement. Writers and observers have estimated the number of displaced people during the last decade of the twentieth century at over 200 million – and at least half of these displacements resulted from development interventions. Such development-induced displacements have received most attention in relation to the construction of dams, but many other interventions, including urban regeneration, infrastructure provision and rural development projects, often have similar consequences, albeit perhaps on a smaller scale.

This book is one of very few attempts to present the experiences and consequences of displacement in relation to development studies for an undergraduate audience, but we hope that it will also be of interest to scholars and practitioners. While development studies has increasingly come to embrace the profound issues posed by displacement, forced displacements have remained the primary concern of this field. This book, though, places the experiences of forced displacement in the context of a wider field of displacements, which can range from forced to voluntary, but which resonate with similar analytical issues concerning the importance of place and the experience of resettlement.

Displacement brings into question some of the long-established orderings of the contemporary world. These include: the borders of states; the legitimacy of the inter-state agencies which manage and set the legal environment in which human movements are regulated; and the restrictive forms of sedentary democracy which protect the privileges of those living in wealthy, mostly Western, states. The concepts explored in this book together contribute to challenging a view of development which has been rather content to reinforce the national order of things; instead, some new directions for innovation in the field of development are suggested. Drawing directly on the analysis of displacements and, by implication, of places, the authors argue that development studies needs to be as attentive to flows of people and resources as it is to the plans and fortunes of places.

The book is part of an Open University course on development studies, *International Development: Challenges for a World in Transition*. This book comprises one of the five themes which students are encouraged to explore, while a companion volume, *Poverty and Development into the 21st Century*, forms the core of the course. *Development and Displacement* can be read on its own (we offer some support through marginal notes in the text for students who have not yet studied a core course in development), or it can be studied in association with the companion volume and other related course material. The chapters in this book are all quite long, each covering a wide range of material on complex topics which are individually worthy of much lengthier treatment, and we therefore recommend that students reading this text break their study of each chapter into two or three components.

Developing the ideas involved in writing this book has been a challenging task. Bringing together experiences generally thought of as being unrelated, such as those of refugees and traders, or resettlers and consumers, has not been easy. But thanks to the rigorous demands of the OU course team, their collective attentiveness and critical eyes, we feel that we have been able to draw together a range of arguments and analyses which add up to a new kind of lens through which development studies can consider the phenomenon of displacement.

The result is a book whose subject matter ranges from the devastating impacts of forced displacement and development-induced displacement to the potentially enabling role of transnational networking in stimulating creative responses to emerging forms of global governance. We look at the developmental consequences of diasporic networks and communities, and explore the ways in which the many different kinds of flows and networks making up cities add up to a territory of growing significance to development agendas. We hope that the text will make some kind of contribution to the task of reframing development for the twenty-first century, a task which the initial course text, *Poverty and Development into the 21st Century*, set for itself. Our overall aim is to shift development studies from its attachment to territories. But, and building on the many observations that suggest that territories like the nation-state remain vital and relevant to contemporary life, we develop an analysis which sees places and displacements as strongly interrelated.

The authors all anticipate that such a reframing in the light of a consideration of displacement could support the growth of alternatives to the development agendas of corporations and international agencies which currently dominate the field. But this book not only brings into view aspects of development which are associated with various forms of displacement; we also suggest that some key concepts need to be rethought in a field of development whose focus has shifted beyond the national or the local. In Chapter 6 we explore the ideas of deterritorialized governance, and social capital 'out of place'. Furthermore, we suggest that bringing both displacements and places into view within the field of development studies offers yet more evidence against the idea that development can be associated solely with 'Third World' or 'Southern' countries. Instead, we suggest that displacement encourages a more mobile account of the geography of development, one which tracks across national borders, and appreciates the challenges of inequality and poverty in all parts of the world.

It only remains for me to thank all those who have contributed to bringing this book into being, and who have made the process such a productive and intellectually engaging experience. We especially thank the Course Team Chairs, Gordon Wilson and Jo Chataway, for their encouragement and organization, and Gordon for his diligent reading of many drafts of our chapters. We thank the two editors who worked on our theme: Janice Robertson, who prepared the material for the introduction to this theme (published separately as part of the *International Development* course material and available from the Open University); and Lori Johnston, who took on the very large task of editing this book. We are very grateful to them, for their professionalism and patience, and for their work beyond the call of duty with images and the detail of the text. Thank you! Vandana Desai, who helped to write the introduction to the theme (not published here), was a helpful collaborator early in the book's development and Maliq Simone, our external reader, offered us some very helpful pointers. The support staff in the course team office, Cathy McNulty and Pauline O'Dwyer; the picture researchers, especially Kevin Brown; Jenny Bardwell, Julie Laing and Mercia Seminara of the BBC who worked on the audio-visual material associated with the course; and my own secretarial assistance from Sylvia Lay-Flurrie in the Social Science Faculty were all equally important to the completion of the project. We hope very much that the final product is something that students and teachers alike will find interesting and helpful.

Jenny Robinson, January 2002

1 Introduction
by Jenny Robinson

Contents

Introduction to development and displacement

At the beginning of the twenty-first century diverse experiences of 'displacement' – including those of refugees, migrants, sojourners, travellers and tourists – have a high profile in public debates, and have become central to how the current age of globalization is imagined. The aim of this book is to explore these displacement experiences, together with the related phenomenon of growing interconnections of all kinds across the globe, specifically in relation to development studies.

Travelling, moving and communicating across vast distances are by no means new phenomena, but their ease and accessibility, and aspects of their social and political significance, are distinctive to the contemporary era. With reference to development studies, however, these flows and networks have received little direct attention. It is the nation-state and the locality which have been the primary foundations for most development-related thinking and practice – and there are good reasons for this. However, even as these territories continue to be relevant to development, there is increasingly a need to address how the dynamics of displacement also affect development.

The association of development with people on the move has been long and varied. One of the most significant development-related movements of modern times has involved the displacement of rural people to urban areas as the economic opportunities in industrializing countries became concentrated in large cities. This process of urbanization continues apace today, most especially in the poorest countries in the world. Historically some of the largest flows of people have also been associated with attempts to promote economic development, or respond to its absence – whether it be the mass deportations of African people in the course of the slave trade, used to lay the foundations for the Caribbean and North and South American economies, or the indentured labourers from India and China who played a similar role in parts of Africa and South-east Asia. European migrations to the Americas, Australasia and other colonial settlements, while largely unforced, were often also a response to poverty and the hope of a better life in a 'new world'.

In addition to journeys in search of a better life, contemporary experiences of human displacement equally involve forced migrations. As I write, forced displacements dominate the media, with millions of people around the world experiencing great hardship as they flee from political conflict, whether in Chechnya, Kosovo, Afghanistan, Rwanda or East Timor. These events pose vast challenges for the people who find themselves refugees, and for the humanitarian and development agencies who respond to the complex emergencies which both generate and result from mass movements of these kinds. Agencies first involve themselves in meeting urgent needs for food, shelter and health care, but often also need to address longer-term developmental needs, and the political complexities of repatriation or settlement in new countries.

Less newsworthy, and therefore more hidden from public consciousness, are those forced displacements undertaken in the name of development itself: development-induced displacements. Many such displacements are quite hidden and go unremarked – rural development schemes all over the world have involved the relocation and disruption of local communities and livelihoods. More dramatically, large-scale infrastructural investments, such as dams, mines, ports and major industrial expansion all induce human displacements (in this case, the displaced people are usually referred to as **resettlers**). Over the last decade of the twentieth century these kinds of developments caused the displacement of almost as many people as political conflict did (about 10 million people per annum). Although there are international guidelines for how these resettlements should be undertaken, in different countries around the world there is quite variable attention to the needs of resettlers, who are often members of marginal and disadvantaged groups.

The cases of refugees and resettlers both alert us to a key theme of this book. *The phenomenon of displacement does not diminish the significance of territories or places.* For both refugees and resettlers, it is usually the nation-state which not only causes displacement, but which also assumes responsibility for attempting to reduce the undesirable effects of its consequences. However, the future of the nation-state, a profoundly sedentary, territorialized entity, is also brought into question by the persistence and size of both kinds of flows.

But so long as the current international system of the nation-state persists, for all forcibly displaced people the costs of losing access to their territorially based rights accorded through the nation-state are considerable, and the loss of physical access to the place where they had been settled also has many consequences. It may involve a loss of livelihood, loss of land rights or housing, or a loss of social networks. Impoverishment commonly follows forced displacement. Whatever the cause, though, moving from one place to another is a profound human experience with substantial consequences for livelihoods and rights. The experience of displacement, perhaps somewhat ironically, highlights the continued importance of place in sustaining livelihoods and facilitating development.

We should bear in mind, however, that although the experience of displacement involves dramatic and often disruptive changes, it does not follow that places, or territories, are static and stable entities by comparison. In a world increasingly connected through information and communication technologies, staying in one place does not mean isolation from the sometimes disorienting, sometimes stimulating, experience of displacement. Indigenous people in settler societies, for example, experienced vast dislocation, although they themselves had not moved anywhere. The spread of global consumer culture and the rise of global corporations might be seen as threatening similar dislocations to local cultures and livelihoods. Moreover, xenophobic conflicts over growing migrant communities in wealthier countries highlight the broader significance of displacements even for those who may not physically move anywhere.

Technological change during the last decades of the twentieth century has presented the public with an image of the world as a global village. For firms and individuals, technological innovations in communication and travel have arguably made the globe a smaller place, with more information available from and about different places, easier contact with other parts of the world, and more opportunities to travel. The consequences for development are substantial. There are opportunities for the nature and distribution of foreign investment to change, for organizations of all kinds to operate across a greater spatial reach, and for people who move to keep in close touch with those they have left behind. We will be exploring how each of these offers scope for new kinds of development interventions and for new kinds of agents of development to emerge.

Box 1.1 What is displacement?

The figure of the refugee is perhaps the most evocative and distressing image of displacement experiences, and the refugee experience portrays the challenges of displacement most starkly. But in this book we suggest that the condition of displacement is also experienced by a range of other individuals and groups. Who, then, might fit into the category of displaced people? And how is the experience of displacement related to development?

At first the word displacement suggests a range of *involuntary* movements. Apart from refugees, one might consider: captured slaves transported across the Atlantic; deported convicts removed from the UK to Australia in the eighteenth and nineteenth centuries; illegal immigrants returned home; council tenants removed for the demolition of a tower block; homeowners whose property has been expropriated for a passing highway; villagers removed to make way for a dam which will flood their homes and land. The line between forced and voluntary movements quickly blurs though. Perhaps the council tenants were pleased to move to a newer estate? Perhaps some of the villagers moved because of the dam now have access to regular jobs? Evidence does suggest, however, that forced relocation is more likely to be damaging to poor people's livelihood prospects than it is to improve them. And what of people who move of their own accord to try to improve their chances of earning a living – perhaps they had little alternative but to seek opportunities elsewhere. Some people, for example, consider that they will earn more money in a large city or abroad, and therefore choose to migrate regularly for work whilst maintaining their homes and families in their 'home' town or village.

As the line blurs into more *voluntary* migrations, other types of human mover come into view: illegal border crossers; people who live between two locations over a long period of time; sojourners who stay a while, even indefinitely, but plan to return home; élite business travellers; poorly paid and temporary migrant labourers; informal traders who travel to collect goods to sell or to trade in different markets.

Finally, we would suggest that the term displacement also draws into its ambit apparently sedentary figures such as the cosmopolitan consumer, whose relationship with other places is mediated perhaps by commodities or the media; local activists who link their struggles electronically with groups elsewhere; or city neighbours from different parts of the world who learn about other places and cultures in their daily routines.

Figure 1.1 UNICEF aid worker with refugees.

1.1 The aims of this book

Throughout this book, we will be working with a broad sense of what displacement means, including both human movements (involuntary and voluntary: see Box 1.1) and the flows of information, ideas and resources which are transforming people's lives everywhere. This is because we consider that forced displacement, while dramatic and certainly a traumatic form of human mobility, requires the same analytical treatment as other kinds of movements, and presents similar challenges for the conceptualization and practice of development.

Central to our exploration of development and displacement, then, is the human experience of movement from one place to another, or of interaction with others and other cultures 'at a distance'. Some observers, such as Giddens (1990), insist that there has been a change in social relations, from the dominance of close, face-to-face interactions in an earlier period, to the predominance of social relations stretched across space in the modern era of efficient global communications and greater mobility. Following other writers, though, we might be advised to reserve our judgement on whether the global economy and global culture are really so very different now than they have been in earlier periods of international interaction (Hirst and Thompson, 1996). More importantly, we will be suggesting through the various case studies presented here that whatever the extent of change has been, place and location, or territories, remain significant features of the contemporary political and economic landscape. We hope to *deterritorialize development studies*, encouraging practitioners and thinkers to bring into focus the flows and networks which play such a large part in contemporary views and experiences of globalization. But we suggest that in order to do this we need to explore and understand *places* as much as *displacement*, *territories* as well as *flows*.

Following Tsing (2000), we suggest that flows and networks, as they stretch across defined borders and reach into familiar communities, have an impact on these places and territories. More than that, it is places and territories which generate or enable many of these flows in the first place. As we have noted already, conflict against or over a territorially circumscribed state, or action by such territorial states, is frequently the cause of the forcible displacement of people, both refugees and resettlers. Displacement has an impact both on the places people are forced to leave and on the communities and countries where they settle. So, just as the displaced refugee brings into sharper focus the territorial entity of the state, the broader experience of displacement also directs our attention to the social and economic significance of places.

*Territorialization: We can interpret this as the making of territories. Here we are thinking about how a certain way of dividing up the Earth's surface has been made significant in development studies. We are suggesting that approaches to development have reflected the borders of the nation-state, when we might instead have chosen other divisions, such as cities, or villages, or regions, or sub-continents, or flows and other kinds of cross-border interactions.

These are important issues, and go to the heart of what this book is trying to address. Development practice and development studies have previously built on the nation-state and local places as the primary bases for interventions and analyses. Meanwhile the architecture of the world's political, economic and social relations has been shifting, becoming increasingly deterritorialized. In the face of such substantial changes, we feel that the territorialization* of development thinking around local areas and states needs to be challenged.

This book fills the disjuncture that has been created, addressing quite directly the consequences for development studies of this era of globalization, where displacements are as important a feature of the human condition as places; where flows across borders are as crucial to consider in development planning as the future of a national territory; and where social and economic networks of all kinds reach across the globe and shape and contest development policies as much as local community actions or national organizations.

This is a substantial ambition – to reframe development studies, to redirect its vision away from borders, territories and settled communities, and to bring into focus the flows and networks which play such a large part in contemporary social life (McGrew, 2000). It will be necessary to consider a range of vocabularies and approaches which are currently quite unfamiliar to development studies: accounts of space, place and mobility; questions of cultural hybridity; and an attention to social relations which cut across scales or levels of analysis. These concerns, we hope, will bring into view new agendas and new agents for development in the context of displacement.

Summary

The aims of this book are to:

- account for the diversity of experiences of human displacement;

- shift the focus of development studies from its association with the bounded territories of nation and locality – and thus to consider the possibility of a development practice more in tune with the experiences of displacement and mobility which, together with places and territories, shape contemporary social and economic life;

- explore the intertwining of places and displacement, of territories and flows, in shaping development;

- encourage the stretching of the ambitions of development interventions beyond the nation-state and the locality towards wider concerns with diasporic flows and transnational networks;

- support more effective responses within the development field to the sometimes devastating but sometimes enabling experiences of human displacement.

1.2 Displacement: disaster or opportunity?

The terms we have been using so far to describe the focus of this book – place, displacement, territories, flows – are, like all human phenomena, not innocent of values, politics and power relations. Forced displacements of people, for example, seem profoundly disruptive experiences and are commonly portrayed as having negative consequences. Does this suggest that we should value place, settlement and stability above mobility and displacement? Conversely, the apparent significance of rapid technological change at the end of the twentieth century has led many commentators to make a positive assessment of the broader phenomenon of displacement. Flows of people and of information and resources potentially disrupt, or dislocate, existing forms of social organization and, it is argued, could stimulate innovation. For those concerned with social change and addressing entrenched forms of power and inequality, outside forces or new influences can present opportunities for positive transformation.

Of course, they could also do exactly the opposite, and reinforce pre-existing social hierarchies, or undermine the claims of marginalized people. But the view persists, as we will see in the example of Tanzanian refugees below, that displacement as a form of openness to change can be thought of as a positive virtue.

Our analysis in this book, though, does not simplistically advocate the virtues of displacement over place; or flows over territories. Rather, we suggest that we need to ask ourselves some difficult questions about when and where displacements can have a positive influence (as we will see in Chapters 3 and 5), and when they undermine or limit the potential for development (as Chapter 2 discusses). Similarly, the evidence on the demise of territories such as the nation-state is hotly debated. We suggest that, far from becoming increasingly irrelevant in a world of flows and networks, nation-states are important agents in shaping these wider flows (as we see in the discussion of the International Refugee Regime in Chapter 2). Moreover, other kinds of territories, like cities (explored in Chapter 4), are emerging as significant agents of development in a globalizing world.

The argument of this book is that *both* territories and flows are important; that they are closely entwined with each other, and that, on the whole, there is no intrinsic basis for valuing one above the other. What we are proposing, then, is that both flows and territories, or displacements and places, should be brought into view within the field of development. Moreover, we would suggest that displacement and place are both conditions which can just as easily carry opportunity as disaster.

Box 1.2 Refugees in Tanzania

The discussion below draws on the experiences of refugees in Tanzania, and explores contrasting values and meanings attached to displacement, and, by implication, to places. Some specific questions are raised, which you might like to consider as you read the following section:

1 What aspects of the places that the refugees had been forced to leave behind were valued?

2 What aspects of the experience of displacement could be considered positive?

3 What implications do experiences of displacement (both positive and negative) have for the practice of development?

We will return to these questions in Box 1.3.

Refugees in Tanzania

Displacement and place are closely related: to be *dis*-placed, a person logically has some relationship to a place or places – usually that person is no longer there, but they are assumed to have some (intrinsic or prior) connection to it. Furthermore, the particular meaning that we ascribe to displacement – often as a traumatic or problematic condition – rests on a very particular view of 'place', as somewhere to belong, or where life is settled and, therefore, better. This is particularly heightened in the case of refugees, whose displacement often occurs across national borders, putting them outside the jurisdiction of the state and leaving them without formal citizenship entitlements.

Malkki (1997), however, has made the argument that it is not the condition of displacement per se which is a problem, but the way in which it is framed by an overarching political system which organizes rights and entitlements on the basis of territorial states. Malkki observes that it is 'our sedentarist assumptions about attachment to place [that] lead us to define displacement not as a fact about socio-political context but as an inner, pathological condition of the displaced' (p.64). It is only in the light of these assumptions about the intrinsic right of the territorial nation-state to define belonging, Malkki says, that displacement can be judged a problem, or more strongly, be seen as pathological. Malkki makes these observations in the context of a study of refugees from Burundi in Central Africa , and the assumptions about attachment to place which she is particularly interested in are those which concern the 'nation'. The status of refugee as a problematic condition, she suggests, is only possible to identify in a world of nation-states, where there is a naturalized, or taken-for-granted, assumption concerning the relation between people and place, in this case between the citizen and the territory of the state. Refugees may be 'out of place', but only in relation to this international system of states.

Malkki goes even further, suggesting that within this context, and despite the traumatic conditions of being forcibly displaced, the condition of displacement, of not belonging somewhere, may have positive political value. Malkki contrasts the situation of two groups of Hutu refugees from Burundi: one group had been settled in a closely supervised refugee camp, Mishamo, in eastern Tanzania for over 15 years; the other group of refugees lived in a nearby town, Kigoma. For the camp refugees, the vision of returning to Burundi had been kept strongly alive through a rich oral retelling of the history of the nation, in which the virtue of the Hutu nation's claims to dominance in Burundi was reiterated in allegorical and religious narratives. Ongoing conflicts with the Tanzanian authorities kept alive their memories of the traumatic genocidal conflicts of 1972, when the Tutsi-dominated military put down a Hutu rebellion and over 100 000 people, or 3.5% of the country's population, were slaughtered. Far from challenging the idea of the nation-state, exile in these camps had reinforced a commitment to the territory of Burundi, and to the idea of the Hutu's intrinsic right to rule there.

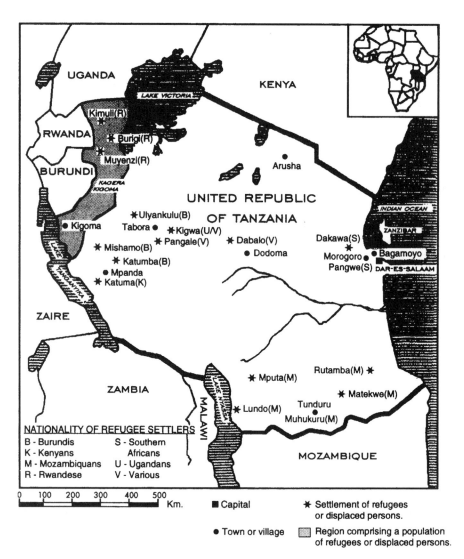

Figure 1.2 Map of the main refugee settlements/transit camps in Tanzania. Source: Armstrong, A. (1987) *Developing New Refugee Settlements: An Evaluation of Mishamo's Establishment and Operation*, for the Tanganyika Christian Refugee Service.

For the town-based refugees, avoiding the camp meant breaking Tanzania's laws concerning the rights of refugees to remain in the country. Survival had come to depend on hiding their identity, claiming to belong to local ethnic groups or constantly shifting between different activities and languages so as to obscure their background. Malkki describes them as inhabiting 'multiple, shifting identities', and showing little desire to return to Burundi – although in the pursuit of their livelihoods a number of these refugees travelled back and forth to Burundi quite frequently, something which the camp refugees did not do. Many had found local partners and adopted elements of local identities and customs, not too difficult in a town with a range of language groups and cultures, some not dissimilar to those of the Barundi (people from Burundi).

While the camp refugees held on to, and indeed reinforced, their commitment to their ethnic group and to their home country, the town refugees dissipated their sense of being Hutu, or even belonging to Burundi, and had developed a more pragmatic attitude to their sense of identity and nationality. Malkki's point (which David Turton will be exploring in some detail in Chapter 2) is that the international system for dealing with refugees (camps, repatriation, controls on settling in the new country) reinforces national identity and refuses to embrace the challenge which the status of refugee presents to the nation-state system. In this case, the nationalist projects of the Hutu were fostered by the refugee camp system, with the potential danger of later re-igniting the ethnic conflicts in Burundi which had initially led to the mass displacements.

The condition of displacement experienced and mobilized by the town refugees posed a challenge to the nation-state model of belonging and, Malkki argues, represents a more agreeable political alternative. Malkki interprets the town refugees' experiences, and their embracing of the opportunities of not belonging to one specific nation-state, as a challenge to the territorial foundations of the contemporary political order. Displacement, in Malkki's view, has more positive political potential than the maintenance or even reinforcement of the concept of the nation-state which is implied in the usual international responses to refugees – and which, as we saw for the case of the Hutu refugees, had shored up the importance of the nation-state.

Figure 1.3 Tanzania was also host to Rwandan Hutu refugees who fled conflict there in 1994, although most have since returned home. Here, tens of thousands of Rwandan Hutu refugees are returning home over the bridge at the Tanzania–Rwanda border, 1996.

Malkki's analysis is part of a growing enthusiasm, both politically and theoretically, for forms of identity and belonging which involve mobility, change, flexibility and cultural hybridity (Chapter 3 will be exploring these in more detail, in relation to diasporic communities). In this view, displacements of all kinds can be harnessed to social change and progress, especially in an era when communication and interaction are more likely than ever before. Old forms of identity and belonging, around states and localities, can be seen as a way of resisting positive changes – holding on to these can provoke conflicts with newcomers and involve attempts to defend privilege (as Chapter 2 explores). In the case of the Hutu, rather than move beyond the ethnic identity and national aspirations which had sparked the civil war in 1972, the group of camp refugees held fast to these identities, as did their Tutsi foes. These came into play again with renewed mass killings in Burundi in 1993 following repatriation from Tanzania and a short-lived Hutu political victory. Many Hutu found themselves refugees once more.

Territorial and national conflicts, centred on states and organized around fixed identities entrenched through the nation-state system, can certainly have devastating political consequences. The alternative argument, though, that displacement, or deterritorialization, is a solution to these consequences of territorial politics – as in the experiences of the town refugees in Kigoma – is harder to sustain. Malkki has been criticized for making light of what was an extraordinarily difficult and dangerous mode of existence for Kigoma-based refugees, on the edges of the law. Barundi living in Kigoma were not always welcomed by the local people, and were constantly in danger of repatriation or relocation to a refugee camp with far fewer livelihood opportunities. Kibreab (1999) has responded to Malkki by suggesting that the strategy of fitting in, or 'invisibility', was a matter of necessity for these people. The experience of the Kigoma refugees, of not belonging or fitting in anywhere and juggling multiple identities, was, in his view, not one to be celebrated as an alternative to a legal right to settle somewhere. Kibreab redirects our attention to the continuing role of national territory and local communities as places where rights are accorded and defended and access to land and livelihoods enabled. He observes that:

> Cosmopolitan identity cannot be wished into existence in societies where identities are determined and rights are apportioned on the basis of territorially anchored identities. In almost all African countries, self-settled refugees are people without secure and enforceable rights.
>
> (Kibreab, 1999, p.399)

So although the pitfalls of a territorial state system may be highlighted by the displaced figure of the refugee, the continuing significance of territories and places in the lives of refugees and citizens makes a celebration of the experience of displacement more than a little premature. As Morsink (1996) notes, for displaced people and for humanitarian and development agencies the consequences of displacement, 'mental suffering, the destruction of customary institutions, the forced abandoning of established modes of livelihood, and the collapse of social networks … all pose formidable challenges'. In being forced to leave their place of abode many refugees are forced also to abandon livelihoods and networks which are centred on that place. It is clear that the places where people were living were important to them, to their material well-being and to their sense of who they are.

The potentials and pitfalls of the territorial form of government embodied in the nation-state will be picked up in Chapter 2, where the developmental potential of the state will be contrasted with the ways in which the sedentary, territorial form of its sovereign power has left refugees and resettlers with few or no rights of redress. The disjuncture between the needs of the displaced refugee and the organization of political rights around the sedentary state presents long-term challenges to the development imagination. Ultimately, this provokes questions about the morality of maintaining current state boundaries along with the limits they set to redistribution and to the enforcement of human rights. The alternative could be to support claims to human rights and redistribution on a global or transnational scale.

Box 1.3

We can now look again at the questions we posed in Box 1.2:

1 What aspects of the places that the refugees had been forced to leave behind were valued?

Displaced people may long for their homeland as a meaningful place where they can more fully belong to the local and national community, with rights which they may be denied in any other country. More personal and practical losses, of family, relatives, language, land, homes and livelihoods, also figure highly.

2 What aspects of the experience of displacement could be considered positive?

The experience of displacement offers an opportunity to redefine and experience an alternative foundation for belonging beyond that of the territorial nation-state or ethnic or national identity. Malkki suggests that refugees in Kigoma had found creative (if difficult and often dangerous) ways to forge an identity and a range of livelihood strategies based on the diversity of groups, languages and activities present in the town.

3 What implications do experiences of displacement (both positive and negative) have for the practice of development?

In this example, development interventions to help displaced communities would benefit from appreciating the condition of displacement as an alternative to settled national communities, without underestimating the difficulties involved in this experience.

> Repatriation and continued settlement outside the country of origin
> would both be valid in development responses to the long-term needs
> of displaced communities. Displacement per se is not an easier or
> more valuable mode of existence than being settled in one place or
> country. Politically, there seems little basis for opposing the nation-
> state system per se (see Chapter 2 for further exploration of this), but
> the refugee experience highlights the potential for alternative and
> co-existing forms of belonging to be supported and explored.

1.3 Transnational and translocal development

The territory of the state is not challenged only by the experiences of
forced displacement. The wider flows and networks, or displacements,
which comprise the contemporary experience of globalization and which
stretch across and beyond the borders of states (and localities) also
contribute to changing, even undermining, the role of the state. New
kinds of agents of development emerge in what Castells (1996) has called
the 'space of flows'. In this book we will be exploring transnational
networks (of non-governmental organizations (NGOs) and social
movements) as well as diasporas as potential new deterritorialized
agents of development. It is our view that displacements of all kinds
need to be taken into account if creative alternatives to mainstream and
state-directed developmental agendas are to be encouraged.

For some states, development plans have already incorporated an
explicit concern with various kinds of displacements – development has
effectively already been transnationalized. Singapore, an island city-
state, has encouraged local companies to capitalize on their easy social
and cultural access to the Chinese mainland. With the specific support
of the government, firms and workers have embarked on a process of
diasporic development, stretching their production activities and
employment to include China. More modestly, perhaps, countries such
as Mexico, Bangladesh and the Philippines encourage the migration of
labourers to wealthier countries. Migrant remittances maintain an inflow
of foreign currency and help support broader development goals.

In all these cases, national development planning has become
transnationalized, stretching across state borders and incorporating
specific flows and trajectories of migrants and capital.

But while many flows and networks relevant to development cut across
national borders (and in that sense are transnational), some can perhaps
be better characterized as *translocal*, drawing two different local places
together, or tying a local area closely into national and international
circuits of capital investment and exchange. More generally, we will
argue, alongside a range of other writers, that the character of 'local'
places is profoundly shaped by translocal ties, or what we have been

calling displacements. Massey (1995) has helpfully described this way of thinking about places as a 'global sense of place'. The case of Otavalo, Ecuador, illustrates this. Here a thriving local and ethnically focused industry producing textiles and woven goods has built on indigenous skills and culture, as well as benefiting from external, or translocal, influences such as national legislation, policy interventions, national and international markets, labour migration and tourist visits. Bebbington outlines the successful image of the Otavaleno merchants:

> Known to tourists through its weekend market and 'ethnic' products, and nationally through traveling Otavaleno merchants in market places selling textiles for popular consumption, this weaving center has a special reputation. Otavalenos are seen as proud, well dressed, and successful, and the transformation of Otavalo into a relatively vibrant regional economy was seen early on as a possible model for community development elsewhere.

> (Bebbington, 2000, p.507)

The region had a pre-Hispanic weaving culture, which was drawn into a Spanish production system after conquest in the 1500s, using tied and indebted labour*. But local people found ways to gain access to their own land through the first half of the twentieth century, which opened up the opportunity for labour migration to improve incomes and further consolidate land ownership and improvements. Small indigenous-owned (Quichua) textile enterprises were started up, and with them a semi-proletariat emerged, no longer dependent on migration for an income. By the mid-twentieth century a trading class operating nationally and internationally had been consolidated. These beginnings were followed by a range of state policies, including import-substitution industrialization policies in the 1960s and 1970s, which protected local textile industries. Technical and financial support from the state, as well as the presence of numerous NGOs and religious organizations, all fed positive external influences into supporting a thriving market economy and dynamic local culture (Figure 1.4). Far from undermining indigenous culture and political representation, these external influences have been harnessed to transform the local community and promote indigenous development at the same time.

*Indigenous labour was tied by brute force in many cases. It was also tied in return for access to plots of land. In other cases, especially into the 1700s, some labour was also conscripted under a taxation system in which communities had to provide labour as a tax. (A. Bebbington, personal communication, 2002)

In contrast with this example, where local communities and external forces are seen to interact positively with one another, development studies has more often prioritized the local community above external influences (Chambers, 1998) or explored locally based alternatives to external development agendas (Escobar, 1995). The local area has also become a privileged site for mainstream development initiatives working to promote democratic governance and decentralization, or to build civil society through local networks, which can be understood to represent a form of **social capital*** (Fine, 1999; Mohan and Stokke, 2000). In all these cases, a stark distinction has been made between local and external forces which overlooks the many flows and interactions cutting across

*Chapter 3 explores the concept of social capital in more detail, and Chapter 6 revisits the implications of displacement for how we understand and use this concept.

Figure 1.4 Distinctive textiles on sale in an Otavalo market.

that division and, more importantly, shaping the futures of local places, as in the case of Otavalo. As Bebbington (2000) suggests, the apparent developmental successes of Otavalo are the result of a combination of pre-existing social capital and new dynamics and influences. What is 'local' today is often a result of previous engagements with wider processes – in this case, the Spanish conquest and early twentieth-century international economic trends.

> **Social capital:** Social capital is an aspect of human capital; that is, capital which is embodied less in land, factories and buildings and more in human beings, their knowledge and skills. Part of that human capital is to do with the ability of human beings to associate, which in turn comes from shared values. Out of shared values comes trust, which has 'a large and measurable economic value' (Fukuyama, 1995; cited in Thomas, 2000a, p.37).

Taking this idea of wider resources further, some of the key resources for the local determination of development paths are shaped by wider networks. For example, some writers have argued that 'thickening' or increasing social capital in a local area often depends on interventions from external agents, such as the state, NGOs, religious organizations and international allies. Fox (1996) describes the celebrated Mexican example of the Zapatistas (to be discussed further in Chapter 5), who built on church organizations, state reforms and international allies to thicken social capital and enhance their political campaigns. This can also work the opposite way: creating a strong sense of local community might be a crucial strategy for gaining access to external resources, as in examples of effective community mobilization and protest. It should be remembered, though, that external forces are not always potential resources; there are also many ways in which they might be seen to impact negatively on local communities, such as through rising prices of commodities or decreases in state services.

We see, therefore, through examples such as Otavalo and the Zapatistas that local areas can function to draw together different interests and activities from further afield and offer a platform from which local people can shape and control their own development futures more effectively. Chapter 4 considers the specific case of cities, and how the diverse flows and networks which stretch far beyond the physical extent of urban space can be creatively utilized to promote more equitable and productive cities. We will explore how within the space of global flows cities emerge as key staging grounds for global economic activities. Even as nation-states seem less able to shape a country's economic fortunes, cities have emerged as important focal points, or territorializations, of the global economy. It is our suggestion that development studies needs to bring into view the flows and networks which shape individual and collective futures; but it also needs to be alert to new kinds of territorializations which can provide opportunities for improving livelihoods and well-being. Once again the close entwining of place and displacement is clear. The examples of local communities (like Otavalo) and the city both illustrate how development policy and practice can benefit from keeping both flows and territories (wider economic networks, and local places) in view.

In the face of a globalizing economy, then, cities and local communities offer new foundations for imagining economic futures. But this is just one of many new opportunities for alternative forms of development that are presented by the growing flows of information and interaction across the globe as a result of new information technologies. In this light, Chapter 5 explores the growth of NGO and community networks, which have taken the opportunity to link together and campaign for change on a global stage. Bridging local and global institutions, networking across common interests, lobbying for changes in the intergovernmental agencies which regulate the global economy, and campaigning in novel ways across national borders, the new transnational spaces of alternative development are a prominent feature at the turn of the twenty-first century. But they, too, have their territorializations: local communities still provide an important base for development-related mobilizations, and global campaigns often culminate in protests at key locations, whether it be outside the World Bank offices in Washington, a biotech laboratory in Germany, or in places where key intergovernmental agencies are meeting, like Seattle, Prague or Melbourne. Most importantly, we are reminded that the power relations of globalization are not predetermined, and the challenges which these activities represent to governments, trade organizations, transnational corporations and proponents of neoliberalism are potentially significant. The spaces of globalization, like other territories, flows and movements, are subject to contestation and, like place and displacement, cannot be assumed a priori to be either positive or negative in their consequences.

1.4 Reframing development studies

Overall, we suggest that the explorations of displacement (and place) which follow in this book contribute to a much wider task of reframing development studies. Changes across the world are constantly challenging the rubrics of 'development' – and calling into question not only what it does and who does it, but whether it should be done at all. The decline of the state as the principal agent of development has opened the field for new agents of development, including NGOs, multilateral agencies and local social movements (Thomas, 2000b). This book suggests that we extend our appreciation of the cast of development agents to include also transnational networks, diasporic communities and cities. We suggest that those in search of alternative forms of development, or even alternatives to development, need to stretch their imaginations, this time beyond the local area as the source of alternatives or resistance to dominant development visions. Transnational and translocal networks, as well as the wider flows that shape local areas, are potentially sites where creative development alternatives will emerge.

*It has long been a matter of debate as to which terms should be used to describe the industrialized, or developed, North and the non-industrialized, or developing, South of the globe. The term 'Third World' initially meant a group of countries that was seeking an alternative way to development, distinct from either the capitalist or the socialist path.

The vision of development we would like to contribute to is one which avoids the macro-territorializations which have so profoundly shaped the field: geographical divisions of the world into 'First', 'Second' and 'Third' worlds; or even more broadly 'North' and 'South'*. We hope that this book will help to support the emergence of a field of development (in all its ambiguity and contestation) which traverses diverse contexts, and which is concerned with inequality as well as poverty alleviation at whatever scale and wherever it is found. We hope that these efforts to reframe development will encourage challenges to the power imbalances which sustain poverty and inequality. Favouring neither the global nor the local, we perceive a range of development practices and visions which track across different localities, building on their best creative instincts, but also following the inventive paths of their connections. The conclusion to the book will draw on the four chapters which follow, to explore in more detail how it is that bringing displacements more fully into view might help to reframe the field of development.

2 Forced displacement and the nation-state
by David Turton

Contents

Introduction

The argument that lies behind this chapter can be summarized as follows: *Forced displacement is both a threat to, and a product of, the international system of nation-states. It therefore exposes fundamental inconsistencies in the ideology that underlies the nation-state system.* States are engaged in an effort to overcome these inconsistencies by responding to (and in some cases deliberately creating) forced movements of population, thereby aiming to reproduce themselves as viable and morally legitimate political communities, and preserving the illusion that the 'national order of things' (Malkki, 1992) is also the *natural* order of things. The study of forced displacement should therefore tell us something about the pressures the nation-state is under at the beginning of the twenty-first century and how it is likely to change in response to those pressures.

I shall focus on two categories of forced migrants (I use this term to avoid the less elegant 'forced displacees'):

1   Those who have moved across an international border in order to escape from serious harm in their home state. I shall call members of this first category **refugees**, since most of them would be recognized as falling under the mandate of the Office of the UN High Commissioner for Refugees (UNHCR).

2   Those who have been forcibly resettled by their own governments in order to make way for infrastructural development projects, such as dams and roads. These I shall call **forced resettlers**, a term borrowed from Cernea and McDowell (2000, p.2).

According to the UNHCR, there were between 11 million and 12 million refugees in the world at the end of December 1999. Approximately another 7 million people were in a sufficiently 'refugee-like situation' to be classified as 'of concern' to the agency (UNHCR, 2000, pp.306–309) – this category consists mainly of over 4 million **internally displaced persons** (IDPs), a term most commonly applied to those who have been displaced by war and who may well be, therefore, beyond the de facto protection of their state even though they remain within its borders. Forced resettlers, although usually internally displaced, are specifically *not* included in this category. The most quoted figure for the number of forced resettlers comes from Cernea (1996, p.18) who estimates, on the basis of World Bank data, that around 10 million people annually 'enter the cycle of forced displacement and relocation in two "sectors" alone – namely dam construction and urban/transportation' (that is, the clearance of slums and squatter camps, and improvement of the transport infrastructure).

Refugees and forced resettlers are usually treated separately, both in the literature on displacement and by agencies and bureaucracies concerned with the displaced. There are good practical reasons for this, to do with the protection of individual and group rights under international law, even though, as Cernea (2000, p.17; see also Cernea, 1996) has pointed out, 'both involuntary resettlers (displaced by development projects) and refugees fleeing violence (wars or armed civil conflicts) confront many strikingly similar social and economic problems'. Refugees are defined under international law as falling outside both the protection of their state and its international borders, and as therefore requiring, and being in a position to receive, the protection of the international community. The 138 states which by the end of 1999 had signed the 1951 UN Convention Relating to the Status of Refugees and/or its 1967 Protocol, are legally bound not to return a refugee to a situation in which he or she could be put at further risk. Forced resettlers, by contrast, are neither outside the protection of their state nor outside its territorial boundaries, but have been moved deliberately, with provision made for their resettlement, by, or with the approval of, their government in order to advance regional or national development goals. Not even those calling for the UNHCR's mandate to be formally extended to internally displaced persons would include forced resettlers in this category.

My reason for focusing on the forced resettler as well as the refugee in this chapter is not that they both confront 'similar social and economic problems' – although they certainly do – but that they both expose underlying tensions in the ideology of the nation-state. I shall first expand upon this claim, through a discussion of the coming together of the idea of the nation with that of the territorial state in what Bauman (1998, p.4) has described, ironically, as a 'marriage made in heaven'. This will allow me to introduce some conceptual and definitional points relevant to the rest of the chapter. In the second section, I shall outline the principal changes that have taken place in the international response to refugee flows over the past 50 years, in order to see how these reflect changes in the role of the nation-state as a principle of political organization over the same period. In the third section of this chapter I shall discuss what Cernea (1996, p.23) has called the 'sad reality' of development-induced displacement, and show how resistance to forced resettlement by grass roots organizations and transnational social movements contributes to a critique both of the nation-state model of political organization and of traditional state-centred approaches to development. The chapter will end with the suggestion that refugees and forced resettlers epitomize the situation of the world's poor and marginalized people in general and that they therefore raise fundamental questions about identity and membership, and about our obligations to fellow citizens and fellow human beings.

2.1 Tensions in the nation-state model of political organization

The term 'nation-state' refers to the fusing, in one political community, of the idea of the nation and the idea of the state. This process is generally considered to have begun around 200 years ago, though the term itself did not enter into common use until after the First World War (MacIver, 1999, p.2). *As a nation*, the nation-state is ideally a homogeneous cultural community, with a common language and common values, sentiments and attachments. It is based not just on common interests but also, and more fundamentally, on assumed common historical characteristics: it provides, or aspires to provide, its members with their dominant source of collective identity. *As a state*, the nation-state has a unitary apparatus of government that exercises ultimate control over a given territory, within which it has the monopoly of legitimate violence*. (See Thomas and Allen, 2000, pp.190–192 for a fuller discussion of the 'key features of states'.)

*States claim a monopoly over the legitimate use of violence within their territory, although there are many instances where this aspect of a state's sovereignty is challenged – insurgents, criminals, civil war and weak state capacity can all undermine this claim.

2.1.1 A marriage made in heaven?

The story of nation building and state formation over the past 200 years is the story of the coming together of these two ideas, in a mutually reinforcing union which has become the universal political organizing principle of the modern era. These are mutually reinforcing concepts because each provides for the political community what the other lacks. They were, in a sense, 'made' for each other.

> Nations needed states to forge the 'locals' into nationals, to melt local dialects into a national tongue, to replace the local rhythms of rites and celebrations with unified national calendars of commemorative festivities ... None of this could be done without the state, without legal codes, police, courts, jails ... On the other hand, the state needed a nation – so that it could demand discipline in the name of sentiment, conscience and patriotic duty, prompt its subjects to act in the name of common tradition, and blackmail the lukewarm into compliance through the invocation of the common fate. Indeed, a perfect marriage, one made in heaven.
>
> (Bauman, 1998, p.4)

Two main variants of the union of state and nation can be distinguished. In the first, an already existing nation or people becomes the basis for a claim to independent statehood. Here statehood is seen as necessary to allow an existing nation to achieve its historical 'destiny'. An example would be the aspiration of Scottish nationalists to achieve a fully independent Scotland, rather than devolved government within the nation-state of the United Kingdom. The second variant is represented by the United Kingdom itself, where the idea of the nation has been used to meld together the members of a culturally and linguistically diverse population into a single territorially bounded state. Here, the development of a common national identity is seen as necessary to enable the state to mobilize and control its citizens. In the first variant, then, the nation is the basis, or *raison d'être* of the state, while in the second, the state is the basis or *raison d'être* of the nation.

This distinction corresponds to that which is usually made between, on the one hand, the 'ethnic' or 'cultural' concept of the nation, 'in which the nation is defined as an ethnic community with a distinctive culture' and, on the other, the 'liberal' or 'civic' concept of the nation, 'in which the nation is defined ... through membership in a civil society with distinctive civil institutions, associations, values and interests' (MacIver, 1999, p.3). However, for the purposes of my argument, we need only look at the general characteristics of the nation-state which apply to both variants. Following Connolly (1991; quoted in Soguk, 1999, p.212), these characteristics may be described as

- 'the grounding of an internal politics upon a contiguous territory';
- 'the recognition of a people (or nation) in that territory, bound together by a web of shared understandings, identities, debates and traditions, which ... provides the basis upon which distinctions between citizen/alien and member/stranger are constituted'; and
- 'the recognition, as sovereign, of external entities ... making it possible for the internal politics of legitimate rule to be ratified by recognition of the sovereignty of each state by others'.

In reality, of course, the great majority of nation-states come nowhere near to achieving the congruence of political and cultural boundaries, or the degree of shared understandings, identities and traditions that the fusion of state and nation ideally calls for. Two hundred years after the nation-state project began, there are still many more language groups in the world (over 600) and even more ethnic groups (around 5000) than there are nation-states (184) (Kymlicka, 1995, p.1). Kymlicka also notes that it would be more accurate to call many of today's states, including many Western democracies, '*multi*nation-states' rather than 'nation-states', because of the co-existence within them of more than one nation, where 'nation' means 'a historical community, more or less institutionally complete, occupying a given territory or homeland, sharing a distinct language and culture' (Kymlicka, 1995, p.1; see also Allen and Eade, 2000). And whether in this sense multinational or not, virtually all states today are becoming more, not less, ethnically and culturally diverse, as a result of international migration (Castles and Miller, 1998).

From this point of view then, the nation-state project must be judged a failure. And yet its very failure has been a consequence of its success. As just noted, one of the main sources of cultural diversity in almost every one of today's states has been international migration. But international migration has been enabled and facilitated by the exhaustive division of the world into territorially exclusive, legally defined and supposedly homogeneous units of population, all based on the union of state and nation.

...states in the plural, locked into a system of similarly constituted units, have created an encompassing communicative grid and regularized interchange of information, resources, and people: there are no more white spots on the landmap. Whereas traditional empires were alone in the world, shielded by border zones beyond which communication was haphazard and erratic, the modern state system has made the world one, and with it immigration as a permanent structural option.

(Joppke, 1998, p.5)

And not only an 'option': some migration has been the result of inter-state wars; some has been deliberately orchestrated by the industrialized states of the developed world, as in the guest-worker schemes of post-Second World War Europe, and some has been the result of population exchange, internal wars and ethnic cleansing. Most migratory flows in the modern era, including refugee flows, have been, in various ways and to various degrees, provoked and encouraged by the activities of states and by the process of state formation. The principle of sedentariness on which the nation-state system is based, then, conflicts with the mobility of things and people which the universal spread of that system has encouraged and facilitated.

It is paradoxical that a principle of political organization with such a strong sedentarizing bias should have helped to bring about a situation in which mobility – of things as well as people – has become, as some would argue, not just *a* defining feature, but *the* defining feature of the modern world.

Sedentariness, not mobility is their [modern states'] constitutive principle. Fixed to territory, and segmentarily rather than functionally differentiated, states are an archaic anomaly within the organization of modern society, which is based on the principle of non-territorial, functional differentiation. This functional order integrates individuals only in specific respects (e.g. as workers, consumers or churchgoers), but never in their totality, thus requiring them to be multiply oriented and allied, and in this sense perpetually flexible and mobile. States are an exception to this. They include the individual as a whole and involuntarily by ascription at birth, further expecting her to be attached to just one state among a plurality of similarly conceived states, and not to change this attachment over a lifetime ... Unlike Schumpeter's classes, states cannot afford to be like buses*, always full, but always filled by different people (see Schumpeter 1927, 1953, p.171).

(Joppke, 1998, p.6)

*Joseph Schumpeter, an economist, likened social class to a bus – rather than being a fixed characteristic of individuals, class was a more fluid category and individuals could change which class they belonged to, much as one might get on and off a bus.

There is a conflict or tension, then, between the sedentarizing bias of the individual nation-state and what might be called the 'mobilizing' bias of the nation-state system.

So, on the one hand, we have a situation where the nation-state fixes people to a particular place or territory, but, on the other hand, as an all-encompassing spatial division of the world into like units, the system of nation-states enables the movement of people and things across those divisions to become predictable and routine. To put this in a slightly different way, the universal spread of the nation-state idea as a principle of political organization conflicts with the achievement of cultural homogeneity and exclusivity by individual states. It seems that if a state is to make its political and cultural boundaries congruent, it should not be surrounded, on all sides and as far as the eye can see, by other states with the same ambition, for the consequent movements and flows across state borders undermine these founding ambitions of the nation-state. If such fundamental goals of the nation-state project are in conflict, then the 'marriage' on which it is based was clearly made very much on earth. In order to illustrate and epitomize the inconsistencies at the heart of the nation-state idea, and thereby to demonstrate its 'earthly' origins, we can do no better than turn to the figures of the refugee and the forced resettler.

2.1.2 The refugee and the forced resettler

In a useful phrase, Adelman (1999, p.93) has described the refugee as 'the Achilles heel' of the nation-state system. In a world exhaustively divided into nation-states, the individual's rights cannot be upheld and enforced except through his or her membership of a state – but not any state. For the nation-state exists, by definition, to protect the rights only of its own citizens, who are assumed to be members of a single historically continuous and culturally homogeneous nation, not a collection of people who just happen to be living within the same territory, like co-passengers on one of Schumpeter's buses. So the refugee, as a person who is unable or unwilling to obtain the protection of his or her own state, makes visible a contradiction between citizenship as the universal source of all individual rights, and nationhood as an identity ascribed at birth and based on a sentimental attachment to a specific community and territory.

> Thus the twentieth century became the century of refugees, not because it was extraordinary in forcing people to flee, but because of the division of the globe into nation-states in which states were assigned the role of protectors of rights, but also that of exclusive protectors of their own citizens. When the globe was totally divided into states, those fleeing persecution in one state had nowhere to go but to another state, and required the permission of the other state to enter it.
>
> (Adelman, 1999, p.90)

The figure of the refugee, then, exposes an underlying tension in the idea of the nation-state as both a culturally homogeneous political community and as the universal principle of political organization. The refugee is 'out of place', not just in an empirical or physical sense but also in a logical or definitional sense. He or she is an anomaly produced by the universalization of the nation-state as a principle of political organization. And like any anomaly, the refugee is an affront to the classificatory system of which he or she is a by-product. Things out of place, of course, are frequently associated with danger and pollution (Douglas, 1966), which may help to explain why the members of host communities commonly express feelings of fear and antagonism towards refugees.

The figure of the refugee is also a necessary outcome of the sovereign power of the state to define 'insiders' and 'outsiders', a power which is underwritten by the state's monopoly of legitimate violence. 'By being a self-defined sovereign body, the state is necessarily exclusive and hence violent' (Warner, 1999, p.261). And because the nation-state aspires to be such an all-embracing and all-subsuming source of the individual's collective identity, the figure of the refugee exemplifies not just difference but also 'otherness'. The refugee, as a person excluded from the protection of his or her state, occupies a grey area, which has been created by the system and which, by demonstrating that the system is contingent rather than necessary, is also a threat to it. Looked at in this light, the response of the nation-state system to what is frequently called 'the refugee problem' has been to find ways of normalizing or institutionalizing the figure of the refugee, by which I mean incorporating it into the regular institutional and legal arrangements that govern the affairs of the international community of states. The way this process has developed over the past half-century is the subject of the second part of this chapter.

The figure of the forced resettler, displaced 'in the national interest' to make way for large-scale development projects, highlights a related tension within the idea of the nation-state. This is a tension between the nation-state as the ultimate source of legitimate political control over a given territory and as a community of equal citizens. For, in development-induced displacement and resettlement projects, the state exercises its monopoly of legitimate force to uproot a group of its own citizens, usually, as we shall see, a relatively impoverished and powerless group of citizens and usually with disastrous consequences for their socio-economic well-being. Such projects include the construction of dams for river basin development and hydroelectric power generation, transportation systems, slum clearance and 'urban renewal' schemes, and the creation of nature reserves and national parks. The main objective of development-induced resettlement projects is, of course, to benefit a much wider population than that of the displaced themselves. And the key characteristic of this wider population is that it shares with the displaced population membership of the same nation-state. Co-membership of the nation-state, therefore, makes legally and morally legitimate a situation in which, as Cernea (2000, p.12) has put it, 'some people enjoy the gains of development while others bear its pains'. But who are these 'others' who are also fellow citizens? In what sense are they 'other'? Is it just that they are 'not us' or is it, more fundamentally, that they are 'not *like* us', that they have a different, and systematically inferior, relationship with the sources of state power? If the latter position is correct, the figure of the forced resettler challenges not only policy-makers and planners to come up with better planned and implemented schemes, but also the ideology of the nation-state itself as a community of equal citizens and as the principal 'agency of development' (Thomas and Allen, 2000, pp.195–199). As we shall see, the evidence does suggest that this second answer is indeed the correct one.

But first, we shall focus on the refugee and on the international apparatus of laws, norms and institutions, or 'regime' that has grown up for managing and controlling refugee flows (see Box 2.1 in the next section). As we would expect, the story reflects changes that have taken place in the role of the state over the same period. On the one hand, the regime has become less state-centred as state borders have become less relevant to the international management of refugee flows and as powerful non-state agencies have taken on increasingly important responsibilities in this area. On the other hand, the figure of the refugee has become a focus for concerns about national and regional security, as states attempt to contain refugee flows and assert their right to control entry to their territories, with increasingly restrictive asylum practices.

Summary of Section 2.1

- Although the term 'nation-state' implies a territorial coincidence between sovereign states and ethnic nations, this has not occurred. Instead, over time territorial states have emerged, but with a range of different associations with 'nations' and 'ethnic' groups within and beyond their territories.

- The refugee raises questions about who is included or excluded from the nation, and challenges the idea of a pre-defined membership of the nation-state.

- The forced resettler similarly challenges another claim of the state – to represent equally all citizens. Often marginal populations, resettled people are called upon to sacrifice their well-being for the development of the rest of the nation.

- The contradictions inherent in the concept of the nation-state bring into question the role of the state as the building block of international order.

2.2 The International Refugee Regime: 'normalizing' the refugee

The key point for this section lies in the phrase 'international refugee regime' itself. There is, in theory, no reason why individual states should not be left to respond independently to the arrival at their borders of refugees from other states. No reason, that is, unless or until the world becomes exhaustively divided into states whose legitimacy as sovereign political units is seen to derive from their presumed identification with specific national communities. As was explained above, the refugee phenomenon then becomes not a temporary problem or 'blip', produced by external events impinging on individual states, and which those states can be left to deal with in an ad hoc manner, but a structural anomaly, produced by, and from within, the system itself and therefore requiring a system-level response.

The International Refugee Regime (Box 2.1) is the nation-states' response to the refugee problem, from which it follows that the prime purpose of the regime is not to protect refugees but to protect the international system of nation-states by 'normalizing' the figure of the refugee.

This does not mean that humanitarian motives were not of decisive importance in the setting up of the regime, and still less does it mean that such motives do not drive the work of those who are responsible for its day-to-day operations. It simply means that, from the point of view of the international system of nation-states which set up the regime, these motives are, and must be, subordinate to the need to protect itself from the consequences of its own internal contradictions. This should not surprise us, since it is the first and inescapable task of any system, and indeed of any social institution, to ensure its own survival.

Box 2.1 The International Refugee Regime

The International Refugee Regime is a set of laws, norms and institutional structures, agreed and established by the international community, for the purpose of managing and controlling (or 'regimenting') refugee flows.

The principal *laws* are the 1951 UN Convention Relating to the Status of Refugees and its 1967 Protocol (see Box 2.2 in the next section).

The principal *norms* are the right to claim asylum and the right of voluntary return.

The principal *institutional structure* is that of the Office of the UN High Commissioner for Refugees (UNHCR). Other relevant institutions include the International Committee of the Red Cross (ICRC), the International Organization for Migration (IOM) and the Office of the High Commissioner for Human Rights (OHCHR). Non-governmental organizations (NGOs) have come to play an increasingly important part in the operation of the regime over the past 20 years, and especially during the 1990s, as 'implementing partners' of the UNHCR.

2.2.1 The regime is established

The first formal recognition of the refugee 'problem' as an issue of specifically international and inter-state concern took place in Europe in the years between the two World Wars. It came in response to the turmoil created by the break-up of the Ottoman, Austro-Hungarian and Russian Empires, which led to the displacement of more than 20 million people. In 1921 the International Committee of the Red Cross appealed to the League of Nations, as 'the only supranational authority' to take overall control of efforts to solve the problem of refugees in Europe (League of Nations, 1921, p.227; quoted in Soguk, 1999, p.104).

In the same year, the Norwegian explorer Fridtjof Nansen was appointed 'High Commissioner on behalf of the League in connection with the problem of Russian Refugees in Europe' (quoted in UNHCR, 2000, p.15). Later, the High Commissioner's responsibilities were extended to other national groups of refugees (e.g. Armenian, Greek, Hungarian and German), the refugee being defined as 'a person who, for one reason or another, is not protected by the government of the state of which he has been, or still is, a national' (Hope-Simpson, 1939; quoted in Soguk, 1999, p.170). This established the refugee, for the first time, as a figure of international concern, and was instrumental in justifying the common designation of the twentieth century as 'the century of the refugee'.

(a)   (b)

Figure 2.1 (a) The headquarters of the Office of the UN High Commissioner for Refugees (UNHCR), Geneva. (b) A UNHCR spokesperson being interviewed on a satellite phone by the BBC World Service as Hutu refugees return home across the Tanzania–Rwanda border, 1996.

The International Refugee Regime as we know it today dates from the establishment in 1950 of the Office of the United Nations High Commissioner for Refugees and the promulgation of the UN Convention Relating to the Status of Refugees in 1951 (Box 2.2). Although many of the norms and mechanisms by which refugee flows came to be managed under this 'modern refugee regime' had already been implemented under the pre-war regime of the League of Nations, the approach adopted by the international community to the refugee phenomenon during the second half of the twentieth century differed significantly from the approach it had adopted during the first half in three key ways.

1   The focus of attention shifted from specific national groups of refugees to a universal definition of the refugee as any individual who was outside the protection of his or her state. The task was no longer seen as allocating displaced groups to their appropriate territorial spaces, and adjusting the boundaries of those spaces as necessary, but as providing displaced individuals with the protection that they were unable or unwilling to obtain from their home states.

2   Since the refugee was now defined according to his or her individual rather than national characteristics, the definition was generalizable without restriction to time or place. The figure of the refugee was, as it were, cut adrift from its national moorings, so that one might argue, as does Adelman (1999, p.94–95), that, 'In the post-war regime, the focus became the state rather than the nation. Borders remained sacrosanct, and refugees were recognised as having rights to the protection of *some* state' (my emphasis).

3   By signing the 1951 Convention, states agreed not to return (*refouler*) a refugee to a situation in which he or she would be put at risk, thereby accepting a limitation on their right of control over whom they were able to admit to their territory (see Box 2.2).

The 1951 Convention, then, sought to normalize the figure of the refugee within the international system of nation-states as an individual member of a legally defined category with a specific right to the protection of the international community, rather than as a member of a specific national group in search of its proper location on the nation-state grid. This 'major departure from historical precedent' (Zolberg *et al.*, 1989, p.29) constituted both an admission of responsibility on the part of the system for having created the 'refugee problem' in the first place, and an acceptance of responsibility on the part of states signatory to the Convention for the care and protection of individual refugees. It was also a recognition that, since the international system of states had created the problem, it could only be solved by individual states formally surrendering some part of their statehood; some part, that is, of their sovereign right to control the entry of non-citizens into their territory.

Box 2.2 The 1951 UN Refugee Convention and its 1967 Protocol

Adapted from UNHCR (2000, pp.23, 53)

The 1951 Convention Relating to the Status of Refugees was adopted by the United Nations Conference on the Status of Refugees and Stateless Persons held in Geneva in July of that year. The Convention spells out the obligations and rights of refugees, and the obligations of states towards refugees. It also sets out international standards for the treatment of refugees. It embodies the principles that promote and safeguard refugees' rights in the field of employment, education, residence, freedom of movement, access to courts, naturalization and, above all, the security against return to a country where they may risk persecution. Two of the most important provisions are found in Articles 1 and 33 of the Convention:

Article 1: Definition of the term 'refugee'

A(2) [Any person who] owing to a well-founded fear of being persecuted for reasons of race, religion, nationality, membership of a particular social group or political opinion, is outside the country of his nationality and is unable or, owing to such fear, is unwilling to avail himself of the protection of that country; or who, not having a nationality and being outside the country of his former habitual residence ... is unable or, owing to such fear, is unwilling to return to it...

Article 33: Prohibition of expulsion or return ('*refoulement*')

(1) No Contracting State shall expel or return ('*refouler*') a refugee in any manner whatsoever to the frontiers of territories where his life or freedom would be threatened on account of his race, religion, nationality, membership of a particular social group or political opinion...

The refugee definition contained in the 1951 Convention was limited to persons who became refugees 'as a result of events occurring before 1 January 1951'. Furthermore, when becoming party to the Convention, states had the possibility of making a declaration limiting their obligations to refugees from events occurring in Europe.

By acceding to the 1967 Protocol Relating to the Status of Refugees, states agree to apply Articles 2–34 of the 1951 Convention to all persons covered by the refugee definition, without reference to time or geographical limitations. By 31 December 1999, 131 states had acceded to both the 1951 Convention and its 1967 Protocol, and 138 states had ratified either one or both of these instruments.

But the Convention aimed to keep the number of refugees likely to be involved to a minimum, therefore also reducing the potential loss of state sovereignty. This was done, first, by making persecution targeted at the individual the key criterion for the award of refugee status, it being assumed (though not stated) that the agent of persecution would be the state – that is, the refugee's own government (Zolberg *et al.*, 1989, p.25). This resulted in a much narrower definition than that used by the League of Nations. The League's definition, although always linked in practice to a specific national group, did not specify the reason why the refugee had lost the protection of his or her own government. In universalizing the refugee definition, then, the Convention also narrowed it, this being the trade-off for making it potentially applicable to individuals, irrespective of their nationality. The second way in which the drafters of the Convention sought to limit the number of potential refugees was by making its provisions applicable only to people who had become refugees before the Convention was promulgated and who had been made refugees by events occurring in Europe. However, these temporal and geographical limitations became untenable in the face of subsequent events, notably the exodus from Hungary following the Soviet invasion in 1956 and the mass refugee flows created by wars of independence in Africa during the 1960s. By dropping these limitations, the 1967 Protocol to the Convention (Box 2.2) amounted to a formal recognition that the refugee phenomenon was not a temporary 'blip', confined to one region of the world, but an enduring and universal feature of the nation-state system.

What the 1967 Protocol did not do, however, was tamper with the definition itself and, in particular, with the choice of individual persecution as the key defining characteristic of the refugee. This created something of a paradox. It meant that most of those making up the refugee flows just referred to, and whom the 1967 Protocol had been designed to bring potentially within the ambit of the refugee regime, nevertheless remained outside the formal scope of the Convention, for they had not been singled out as specific targets by their governments but were escaping from a situation of generalized violence. This paradox was addressed in 1969 by the Organization of African Unity (OAU) 'Convention on Refugee Problems in Africa', which broadened the definition to include amongst the reasons for refugee flight 'external aggression, occupation, foreign domination, or events seriously disturbing public order'. But while this was a highly significant and influential step in the development of the post-war refugee regime, it was not binding on the international community – and particularly not in the case of Western governments, which were the main funders of the regime – and it led therefore to a practical rather than a formal expansion in the regime's activities. This gave potential receiving states a good deal of flexibility in deciding whom to admit to their territory on 'humanitarian' grounds – on a voluntary basis, that is, rather than in accordance with their obligations under international law.

The Convention was also a powerful weapon in the Cold War armoury of the Western powers. For this reason, and even after the Convention became manifestly inapplicable to the great majority of people who were accepted as refugees in a de facto sense, retaining its standards did remain attractive to would-be receiving states.

> The recognition of East European emigrants as refugees stigmatized their countries of origin as wilful violators of the human rights of their citizens ... Indeed, Western governments encouraged the flow from East to West in order to weaken their rivals ideologically and to gain political legitimacy in their Cold War struggle. The Federal Republic of Germany, for example, offered automatic asylum, generous resettlement assistance, and citizenship to all East Germans ... These inducements created a 'pull factor' that resulted in the outflow of hundreds of thousands more people than might otherwise have migrated.
>
> (Loescher, 1993, p.59)

Loescher goes on to note that of the 233 436 refugees admitted to the United States between 1956 and 1968 'all but 925 were from communist countries'. It follows that, if we are to understand the way in which the International Refugee Regime has developed over the past half-century, we must recognize that the laws, norms and institutions which continue to constitute its bedrock were a product of the Cold War opposition between East and West. More than this, and as the above quotation from Loescher illustrates, we must recognize that the regime was one of the key mechanisms by which this opposition was sustained and reproduced. It is only to be expected therefore that, once the East–West divide was no longer relevant to the maintenance of the world political order, the repercussions of this would be seen in the attitude of states to the International Refugee Regime and to their role in its operations.

2.2.2 From asylum to containment

It is useful to think of the development of the International Refugee Regime over the past 50 years as having gone through three phases, marked by changes in the dominant approach adopted to the 'solution' of the refugee 'problem' (Crisp, 2000).

In the immediate post-Second World War period until the late 1950s the focus was on East–West flows in Europe. Given the Cold War context in which these flows took place, repatriation was simply not an option. The work of the UNHCR consisted chiefly of arranging for the permanent resettlement of refugees, mainly from Eastern Europe, in countries of immigration, such as the United States, Canada and Australia, as the best way of normalizing the figure of the refugee. Crisp therefore calls this the **resettlement phase** in the history of the post-war regime (Figure 2.2a).

This situation changed in the 1960s, a decade during which most of the world's refugees were located in Africa – about 1 million by the end of the decade (Loescher, 1993, p.77) – and when the focus of the regime shifted away from Europe (UNHCR, 2000, p.37). There now began a huge expansion in the role and activities of the UNHCR. The main source of refugees was the developing countries of the 'Third World', the main cause of their flight being wars associated with independence struggles and decolonization, and the main direction of their flight being South–South. Most refugees moved freely into neighbouring states (particularly in Africa which was noted for the 'open door' refugee policies of its governments) and either settled independently amongst the local population or were collected in camps and settlements where they were given land and encouraged to become self-sufficient. Mainly because of the large numbers involved, resettlement in a third country, i.e. not in the country of first asylum, was not a realistic possibility for the great majority of refugees. During this period, therefore, which lasted roughly until the mid-1980s, there were only two potential 'solutions' for the great majority of refugees: integration in the country of first asylum or voluntary return to the country of origin. Crisp calls this the **asylum phase** in the development of the post-war regime (Figure 2.2b).

By the end of the 1980s the total number of refugees and others 'of concern' to the UNHCR had risen to about 30 million and it had become usual to refer to the 'refugee crisis'. The response of states and the UNHCR to this 'crisis' allows us to discern the beginnings of a third phase in the development of the modern refugee regime, coinciding roughly with the end of the Cold War and lasting into the present. In this phase, not only resettlement in a third country but also integration in the country of first asylum became increasingly problematic. The main cause of refugee movements continued to be internal or intra-state wars and, as the number of refugees continued to rise, the role of the UNHCR and of a growing number of NGOs in providing emergency relief, both for refugees and for the internally displaced, continued to expand. At the same time both Western states and developing countries took increasingly determined steps to prevent or dissuade refugees from settling in their territories. Western European governments, faced with an increase in annual asylum applications from around 200 000 in 1989 to around 700 000 in 1992 (UNHCR, 2000, pp.156–158), set about constructing what came to be known as 'Fortress Europe' (we will discuss this further in Box 2.4 in the next section), while African governments, which had hosted the majority of the world's refugees for the past two decades, began to retreat from their 'open door' policy (Rutinwa, 1999). The focus of the regime over the past ten years, therefore, has been neither on resettlement nor on integration in the country of first asylum, but on **containment**, that is, on preventing refugee flows from occurring in the first place or, when they do occur, confining them to their region of origin and/or taking firm measures to ensure that refugees return to their home states as quickly as possible (Figure 2.2c).

The main assumptions lying behind this **containment phase** in the development of the refugee regime have been usefully listed by Crisp (2000) and are reproduced in Box 2.3. They might also be described as the main 'strategic principles' of the current regime. But it is important to note that they represent an emergent strategy, by which I mean that they impose coherence, retrospectively, on a series of more or less ad hoc policy responses made by the international community and the UNHCR to the main refugee-producing events of the 1990s. One of the most important of these responses, because it set a precedent for what came later, was the 'humanitarian intervention' in Iraq in April 1991, named 'Operation Provide Comfort'. When, following the end of the Gulf War, Turkey refused to admit Kurdish refugees from northern Iraq into its territory, the UN Security Council, in passing Resolution 688, not only demanded that Iraq end its repression of the Kurds but also insisted that 'Iraq allow immediate access by international humanitarian organizations to all those in need of assistance in all parts of Iraq' and

(a)

(b)

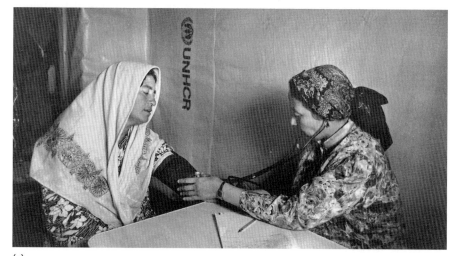

(c)

Figure 2.2
(a) Resettlement of refugees, 1951. Seen here are displaced persons from camps in Germany, Austria and Italy on their way to start a new life in the USA, boarding a ship chartered by the predecessor to the UNHCR, the International Refugee Organization.
(b) Voluntary repatriation to Namibia: a group of returnees board a UNHCR-chartered plane. After more than 15 years of exile in Angola, Zambia and other African countries, some 41 000 refugees went home in 1989.
(c) When civil war erupted in Tajikistan in May 1992, at least 20 000 people lost their lives, half a million were displaced and a further 60 000 fled to Afghanistan, including this medical doctor and patient. Most internally displaced persons and refugees had returned home by mid-1995.

'make available all necessary facilities for their operations'. There followed an agreement between the UN and Iraq, which allowed coalition forces to establish safe havens for Kurds in northern Iraq, reinforced by a no-fly zone which continues in existence to this day (2002) (see Figures 2.3). The provision of emergency relief to these areas was coordinated by the UNHCR until September 1992, when UNICEF took over this role.

Box 2.3 A new approach to normalizing the refugee: 'containment'

Adapted from Crisp (2000)

Over the past ten years, in a series of more or less ad hoc responses to refugee emergencies mainly in Africa and the Balkans, a new set of assumptions has come to dominate the work of the International Refugee Regime. Taken together, these assumptions represent a new phase in the development of the regime, a phase in which the main priority is to prevent or 'contain' the movement of refugees, rather than to provide them with asylum. The main assumptions of this new approach are as follows.

- displaced people do not necessarily have to leave their own country to find protection and, in some instances, it may be legitimate to dissuade or prevent them leaving and seeking asylum elsewhere;
- those who do leave their own country and find asylum in another state should be kept within the same region;
- asylum is strictly temporary and should not be equated with permanent settlement and integration;
- people who leave their home country and find asylum in another state should return to their homeland as quickly as possible;
- to achieve these objectives, it is legitimate to deny refugees freedom of movement, access to land and income-generating opportunities;
- it is legitimate to require or even force refugees to return to their homeland if they prove reluctant to do so; and
- international assistance should be used to 'anchor' people in their country of origin, both to avert new population displacements and to facilitate return and reintegration of those who have already been displaced.

The twin policies of **humanitarian intervention** through the use of military force, and **preventive protection** through the distribution of relief in, or as close as possible to, areas from which people were being displaced, was put into effect on a much larger scale in the former Yugoslavia between 1991 and 1995. Here, a number of UN-designated safe havens were established, under the protection of the United Nations Protection Force in former Yugoslavia (UNPROFOR), and the UNHCR

(a)   (b)

Figure 2.3 The Iraqi/Kurdish 'no-fly' zone: (a) patrolling the zone and (b) a helicopter breaking the restrictions.

was given the role of lead agency for the provision and co-ordination of humanitarian relief. The enormity of this task may be judged from the list of responsibilities which the UNHCR itself saw as included within it, namely 'logistics/transport, food monitoring, domestic needs, shelter, community services, health, emergency transition activities in agriculture and income generation, protection/legal assistance, and assistance to other agencies in sectors under their responsibility' (Martin, 2000, p.22). The UN Secretary General's letter (November 1991; quoted in Goodwin-Gill, 1999, p.237) inviting the UNHCR to take on the role of lead agency, spoke of the need 'to assist in bringing relief to needy internally displaced persons affected by the conflict', which might have a 'welcome preventive impact in helping to avoid the further displacement of population'. By July 1993, however, 3.6 million people had been displaced, both across international borders and internally (Soguk, 1999, p.199).

Here was a situation in which the geographical and cultural proximity of the Balkans, and the scale of the emergency – the largest forced displacement in Europe since the Second World War – left Western European states with little option but to open their doors to the displaced. They did so, however, on the basis of minimum conditions which, although laid down by the UNHCR, fell far short of those which would have been required under the 1951 Convention. These conditions were that there should be respect for human rights and the principle of non-*refoulement* and that repatriation would take place when conditions were suitable in the country of origin. The refugees would be given protection as a group, not as individuals (a condition reminiscent of the way in which the League of Nations had approached the refugee problems of its day), and only for as long as the conflict lasted. The protection being offered was not only temporary then, but it was also oriented towards repatriation rather than resettlement and it existed 'side by side with, and usually as an alternative to, Convention refugee status. In return for group protection [the refugees would be] denied access, either temporarily or permanently, to Convention status even though many would have an individual claim to it' (Gibney, 2000a, p.695).

At least 700 000 Bosnians received asylum in Europe on these terms, of whom more than 310 000 had been repatriated by 1998 (Gibney, 2000a, p.703). A year later, around 900 000 Kosovar Albanians fled into Macedonia, Montenegro and Albania following the NATO bombing campaign in Serbia and Kosovo. By October 1999, over 96 000 Kosovars had been evacuated under a 'Humanitarian Evacuation Programme' from camps on the Macedonian border and given temporary protection in Europe, the United States and Australasia. It was estimated by the UNHCR that approximately 90% of these had returned to Kosovo by May 2001.

Figure 2.4 Bosnian refugees arriving in the UK, December 1995.

Compared with refugee crises in the 'Third World', the crisis in the Balkans received massive allocations of aid: 'On one estimate UNHCR spent $1.23 [per person] on refugees per day in the Balkans, eleven times more than the 11 cents it spends on refugees in Africa ... By August 1999 over sixty nations and dozens of organisations had already pledged some two billion dollars in aid' to assist with return to, and reconstruction in, Kosovo (Gibney, 2000b, p.28). These figures suggest that, alongside the humanitarian objective of preventing and relieving suffering, there were other incentives and motivations at work in the response of the international community to the crisis in the former Yugoslavia.

Gibney (2000b) suggests three reasons for the (relative) 'popularity' in Europe of refugees from Kosovo, two of which apply also to those from Bosnia:

1 the relative proximity to key Western states of the 'refugee-generating situation', which raised with particular clarity for donor states the prospect of huge numbers of refugees arriving at their borders;

2 a feeling of common identity, based on shared cultural characteristics, which made it relatively easy for other Europeans to identify with the suffering of these particular refugees; and

3 (in the case of Kosovars) a feeling of responsibility for the events (i.e. the NATO bombing campaign) that had preceded their flight.

The first of these reasons is most relevant here, because it relates to the prevention and containment of refugee flows and is extendable not only to the case of the Bosnians, but also to that of the Kurds. Security Council Resolution 688 condemned the repression of the Kurds by the Iraqi government, linking the abuse of human rights to the creation of a 'massive flow of refugees' which was seen to threaten 'international peace and security' and therefore justifying the right to intervene with military force, under Chapter VII of its charter. And as Frelick (1993; quoted in Soguk, 1999, p.200) wrote of the 'safety zones' approach adopted by European governments in Bosnia, 'The rhetoric was humanitarian … But there was something else going on: the prevention of a refugee flow.' It is by the prevention and containment of refugee flows, then, rather than by resettlement and asylum, that the International Refugee Regime today attempts to accommodate the figure of the refugee within the international political order of nation-states or, as Soguk puts it, 'deal with' this 'aberrant category of people' (1999, p.194).

2.2.3 Implications for the role of the nation-state

How does this change in the focus of the International Refugee Regime relate to the changing role of the state? It is impossible to give a totally unambiguous answer to this question. On the one hand, one can argue that the changes outlined above have reduced the significance of state borders in the operation of the regime, thereby making it less 'state-centric' (Mertus, 1998). On the other hand, one can argue that these changes have made the control and management of refugee flows a key area for the exercise of what Soguk (1999) calls 'statecraft' and for the assertion of the right, and ability, of states to determine who shall be allowed to enter their territories. Three interconnected developments need to be considered here:

- the end of bipolar confrontation as the basis of the world political order;

- the impact of economic and technological globalization on the territorial exclusiveness of state power;

- and the growing role of non-state actors, especially NGOs, in the operation of the International Refugee Regime.

The end of the Cold War: borders lose their meaning

The end of the Cold War helped to reduce the significance of state borders in the operation of the regime in at least three ways.

1   There were no longer political gains to be made by Western states in admitting refugees from Eastern block countries. As a result, the particular state border that had been crossed by the refugee could no longer be used as the basis of the regime's decision-making about the channelling of aid and the granting of asylum. As Mertus (1998, p.326) puts it, 'Would-be receiving states and donors can no longer tell whom they are supposed to help based on clear-cut ideological grounds.'

2   The end of the Cold War can be linked to a huge increase in the number of internally displaced persons, the total number of whom was estimated to have reached between 20 million and 25 million by 1999, or around double the number of people displaced across international borders (UNHCR, 2000, p.214). In the 1980s, refugee-generating conflicts in the developing world had been shaped and fuelled by the overarching superpower confrontation (Loescher, 1993, pp.88–90). What distinguished the 1990s was the disengagement of the superpowers from such local wars and the withdrawal of economic and military support from ailing states which were no longer of strategic foreign policy importance. The result – as for example in Somalia, Rwanda and the former Yugoslavia – was a proliferation of internal, identity-based conflicts, in which civilian populations and civic infrastructures were deliberately targeted and huge numbers of people were displaced, the majority of whom did not cross state borders and did not, therefore, come within the de jure mandate of the UNHCR.

3   As a consequence of this, humanitarian intervention within refugee-generating states became more feasible, both because of the weakening of the central governments of these states and because military intervention was less likely to trigger superpower confrontation.

Globalization: the nation-state strikes back

The reduced significance of state borders, which is reflected in the change from an asylum-oriented to a containment-oriented regime, was not, of course, a simple product of the revolutions that occurred in Central and Eastern Europe in 1989 and the dramatic and unanticipated collapse of the Soviet Union in 1991. These events were themselves a product of far-reaching changes in the organization of industrial production, in transport and communication technologies and in the mobility of capital and finance which rapidly gathered pace in the 1990s, and which are generally referred to by the blanket term

globalization. The cumulative effect of these changes has been to
deterritorialize, or free from the constraints imposed by territorial
distance and territorial boundaries, some of the main activities and
processes – most of them economic – that affect the lives of citizens in
all of today's states.

> Deterritorialisation, indeed, is what sets globalisation processes
> apart crucially from the parallel (but state-centred) processes of
> 'internationalisation' or 'interdependence' (denoting increased
> exchanges between countries), or 'liberalisation' (denoting the opening
> of borders between countries). 'Global' phenomena do not cross or open
> borders so much as transcend them, extending across widely dispersed
> locations simultaneously and moving between places anywhere more or
> less instantaneously: territorial distance and territorial borders 'hold
> limited significance in these circumstances: the globe becomes a single
> "place" in its own right' (Scholte, 1997, p.431).
>
> (Collinson, 1999, p.4)

The relationship between globalization and the state has been the subject
of much debate over the past few years (see for example, Harriss, 2000;
McGrew, 2000; Scholte, 1997; Strange, 1996a) and there is no need to
enter into the details of this debate here. For our purposes, the important
thing to note about globalization is the contrast it has highlighted
between, on the one hand, the international movement of goods,
information, finance and capital which has been both enabled and
encouraged by the international system of nation-states; and, on the
other hand, the redoubled efforts of states, over the past decade, to
control and limit the international movement of people. This is another
symptom of the tension, described earlier, between the 'sedentarizing'
and 'mobilizing' tendencies of the nation-state system.

A good case in point is the 'harmonization' of asylum policies within the
European Union, a process which has been taking shape over the past
decade. The aim of this has been to reinforce the external border controls
of the EU, at the same time as barriers to the free movement of people
between member states were being dismantled (see Box 2.4). This
Fortress Europe policy was implemented in the context of an increase in
asylum applications to Western European countries, from less than
100 000 in 1984 to a peak of nearly 700 000 (over half of which were to
Germany) in 1992. There has been a significant decline in applications
since then, which no doubt reflects these restrictive asylum practices
introduced by European governments in the 1990s. But numbers have
remained high by comparison with the early 1980s. In 1997 there were
around 280 000 applications and this increased to 350 000 in 1998.
Applications to the United Kingdom increased from 26 200 in 1990 to
71 100 in 1999 (Crisp, 1999; UNHCR, 2000, pp.322–324). The reasons for
the increase included a growth in the number of people fleeing war and
human rights violations in various parts of the world and the global

spread of new transportation, communication and media technologies. But another important reason was the introduction by European states of stricter controls on low- and semi-skilled labour migration, following the economic recession of the early 1970s. This encouraged the growth of a highly organized international industry in human trafficking as people attempted to enter states illegally and also led more and more would-be labour migrants to use instead the asylum process as a route to permanent migration.

In order to deal with these 'mixed flows' of refugees and others who were using the asylum route to circumvent restrictions on labour migration, European governments introduced various measures which were designed to combat illegal migration and the abuse of asylum systems. These included:

- measures aimed at preventing would-be asylum seekers from arriving at the state's border in the first place, such as fines against airlines for transporting passengers without proper documentation ('carrier sanctions');

- measures designed to send asylum seekers back to countries through which they had passed and in which they could have applied for asylum ('safe third countries');

- measures which encouraged member states of the EU to apply the refugee definition more narrowly, notably by restricting 'Convention refugee status' to those who had been persecuted by their governments rather than by 'non-state agents';

- finally, there were measures aimed at deterrence, such as the increasing use of detention, and restrictions on the right to work and on access to social welfare.

Box 2.4 Building Fortress Europe

Based on UNHCR (2000, p.159) and Telekon (1999)

Attempts by member states of the European Union to create an 'ever closer union' have included steps to 'harmonize' their policies on immigration and asylum. These steps, which are summarized below, have taken an overwhelmingly restrictive direction.

1990 Dublin Convention

This established common criteria for EU member states to determine the state responsible for examining an asylum claim. The aim was to ensure that one member state would take responsibility for examining a claim, thus preventing asylum-seekers from 'shopping around' for the most favourable country in which to ask for asylum. Anyone arriving in the EU without a visa would now have to file an application in the first country signatory to the Convention which he or she reached. It became binding for all EU member states in 1997.

1990 Schengen Convention

This aimed to reinforce external border controls whilst allowing free movement within participating states. It included provisions to strengthen police and judicial co-operation and to introduce common visa policies and carrier sanctions. All EU member states except Denmark, Ireland and the United Kingdom are signatories.

1992 Maastricht Treaty on European Union

This empowered Justice and Home Affairs Ministers to establish a framework for a European-wide asylum policy and introduced the concept of EU citizenship. It came into force in 1993.

1992 London Resolutions

A meeting in London of ministers responsible for immigration approved three non-binding resolutions and conclusions. The first embodied a safe third country concept, allowing states to refuse individuals access to their asylum procedures if the applicant had already entered and could have sought protection in another 'safe' country through which they had passed. The second defined 'manifestly unfounded' asylum claims and gave member states wide scope for rejecting asylum claims on formal grounds and for limiting appeal procedures. The third resolution allowed for an accelerated procedure in the case of applicants coming from countries in which there is generally considered to be no serious risk of persecution (everyone has the right to claim asylum under international law, even if their state is considered generally safe).

Other resolutions and recommendations during the 1990s

During the 1990s the EU Council of Ministers approved a number of non-binding resolutions which represented 'harmonization' on the basis of the lowest common denominator; that is, the standard was set by those member states with the most restrictive asylum policies. Among these were recommendations (1994 and 1995) establishing a model agreement for returning asylum seekers to countries through which they had passed; a Resolution on Minimum Guarantees for Asylum Procedures (1995); and a 'Joint Position' on the definition of the term 'refugee' (1996), which allowed member states to limit recognition to persons persecuted by a government and its agents.

1997 Treaty of Amsterdam

This includes a commitment by member states to develop a common immigration and asylum policy within five years. Once this policy is established, the further development of common asylum policies will then come under the Council of Ministers, where unanimity is not always required. The Treaty came into effect in 1999.

Bauman (1998) has suggested that these efforts to strengthen the external borders of the EU represent an attempt by member governments to divert public attention from their impotence in the face of those invisible external forces that ultimately determine the security and well-being of their citizens.

> ...governments cannot honestly promise [their] citizens secure existence and a certain future; but they may for the time being unload at least part of the accumulated anxiety (and even profit from it electorally) by demonstrating their energy and determination in the war against foreign job-seekers and other alien gate-crashers, the intruders into once clean and quiet, orderly and familiar, native backyards.
>
> (Bauman, 1998, pp.10–11)

We may not wish to accept this as a complete explanation of the increasingly restrictive asylum practices of European states (I shall return to this issue at the end of the chapter), although there has undoubtedly been a large element of populism in the approach of European politicians to the asylum issue. What we can be sure of is that:

- the development of a global market economy could not have occurred without the 'encompassing communicative grid' (Joppke, 1998, p.5) provided by the exhaustive division of the world into nation-states;

- this has nevertheless reduced the ability of states to control the growing transnational movements of finance and capital which directly affect the lives of their citizens; and

- states have 'struck back', with tighter controls on the movement of people.

In the language of Soguk (1999, p.211), these controls are 'practices of statecraft', in the sense that they 'afford the state its "reasons for being" in a world where its practical relevance to the lives of people is being attenuated day in and day out'.

The growth of non-governmental organizations: bypassing the state

One notable consequence, or at least concomitant feature, of economic and technological globalization has been the emergence of a 'transnational civil society', consisting of 'citizen groups, corporations, trade unions, employers organizations, industrial organizations, social movements, NGOs and international pressure groups of all kinds' (McGrew, 2000, p.357). These non-state agents of social change have become important players in an international political arena that was previously dominated by governments and by organizations set up by governments to further inter-state cooperation ('intergovernmental organizations'). No better example of the accommodation between governmental and non-governmental agents of social change can be found than the trend for official development assistance (ODA) to be channelled, by donor governments and by intergovernmental organizations, through NGOs rather than through 'Southern' governments in an attempt to ensure more effective development interventions (Thomas and Allen, 2000, pp.212–213). This trend began in earnest in the 1980s and, by the mid-1990s, 'approximately 30 per cent of NGO income came from official sources, compared with an estimated 1.5 per cent in the early 1970s' (Hulme and Edwards, 1997, pp.6–7). (These trends and their consequences are explored in more detail in Chapter 5.)

It was inevitable, therefore, that, as the UNHCR developed its policy of preventive protection by taking on the role of lead agency in humanitarian emergencies, the involvement of both national and international NGOs in the refugee regime would grow dramatically. The number of NGOs working in the refugee camps in Goma, just inside the Zairean border, during the Rwandan emergency, is said to have 'peaked at between 90 and 100, all of which had ready access to the camps' and 21 of which were directly funded by UNHCR (Borton, 1996, p.312). During the Bosnian conflict, more than 90% of the UNHCR's humanitarian assistance was channelled through local NGOs (UNHCR, 2000, p.194) and, at the height of the crisis, 'more than 250 international humanitarian organisations operated under UNHCR co-ordination, with the ICRC [International Committee of the Red Cross] the only major agency operating independently' (Martin, 2000, p.22). Like the League of Nations refugee agency before it, the UNHCR had always been expected to collaborate with private as well as public organizations. What was new about the 1990s was not the fact of collaboration between the UNHCR and NGOs, but its scale.

> ...in 1999 UNHCR channelled US$295 million through 544 NGO implementing partners. Some 50 per cent of all UNHCR programmes are now implemented by international NGOs, 34 of these NGOs receiving more than US$2 million each in 1999.
>
> (UNHCR, 2000, p.194)

What do these figures allow us to conclude about the changing role of the state in the International Refugee Regime? As in the case of globalization, the answer is not clear-cut. On the one hand, the channelling of UNHCR assistance through NGOs means that state structures (where they exist) are effectively bypassed. On the other hand, the 'proliferation' of national and international NGO activities that took place in the 1990s was itself a product of the policies of powerful donor states, whose political and aid agenda it served.

> The growth of [NGO] activities since the 1980s has in fact largely been a consequence of the way in which ODA [Official Development Assistance] has been allocated. Many multilateral and bilateral agencies have been less willing to transfer resources to Southern governments, both because they are viewed as inefficient and possibly oppressive, and because of the neoliberal view that states should be cut back as much as possible. In the 1990s the extreme neoliberalism of the 1980s may have eased, but there was also less need to prop up 'friendly' regimes.
>
> (Thomas and Allen, 2000, p.213)

The channelling of official aid through NGOs also enables governments and intergovernmental organizations to show that they are concerned with 'bottom–up' and 'participatory' forms of development, notwithstanding the fact that 'NGOs are in practice more accountable to their donors than they are to their beneficiaries (however much they would like the situation to be otherwise)' (Thomas and Allen, 2000, p.213). The phrase in brackets, however, is crucial here because it refers to an ideological commitment which unites all organizations commonly referred to as NGOs, and which makes it reasonable to conclude, despite the points just made, that the increased involvement of NGOs in the International Refugee Regime is indeed an indication that the regime has become less 'state-centric'.

Here we need to remind ourselves that the term NGO is used to refer to an enormously wide range of organizations, differing amongst themselves in size, purpose and function. We can distinguish between three broad categories of NGO (Thomas and Allen, 2000, pp.211– 213):

1   national and international service-providing organizations, such as Oxfam and Save the Children;

2   campaigning organizations, such as Greenpeace and Amnesty International; and

3   'grass roots' organizations, which exist at the local level to further the interests of their own members.

It is NGOs of the first type which have been used by donor states to advance their political and aid agendas and which have come to play an increasingly important part in the operation of the International Refugee Regime. Those of the campaigning and grass roots types have a less 'cosy' and more obviously antagonistic relationship with governments and intergovernmental organizations. They have become prominent, for example, in the organization of resistance to state-sponsored resettlement projects, as we shall see in the next part of this chapter.

All three categories of NGO, however, merge into each other and have overlapping functions and objectives. Thus, international service-providing NGOs may engage in significant campaigning activity, while grass roots organizations may become (or become linked to) international campaigning organizations. The overriding ideological commitment that unites all development NGOs is the alleviation of poverty, suffering and injustice, as an end in itself and irrespective of the interests of a particular state and/or of the international system of states. This includes a commitment to helping local people identify their needs and preferences so that they may become active participants in the development process. It is true that 'participation' is a notoriously ambiguous concept and that many, if not most, NGOs, especially those which are heavily dependent on official funds, fail to be accountable to those whom they are attempting to help. But the legitimacy of all NGOs nevertheless depends on how far they are seen to be putting the needs, preferences and interests of those people first, while avoiding the inefficiencies inherent in the bureaucratic systems of governmental and intergovernmental agencies. The heavy involvement of NGOs in the operation of the International Refugee Regime makes it necessary, therefore, to reassess my earlier statement that the purpose of the regime is to 'protect' the international system of nation-states, rather than protect refugees, and can be taken as evidence that, over time, the regime has become less 'state-centric'.

Summary of Section 2.2

- The International Refugee Regime, established after the Second World War, has changed its focus over time from offering asylum to refugees meeting internationally defined criteria, to an emphasis on containing refugees in their regions of origin.

- Both versions of the International Refugee Regime have shored up the nation-state system and have been implemented in ways which advance the interests of states, e.g. through the Cold War, or preventing large flows of refugees.

- Refugee flows may highlight some of the processes which appear to deterritorialize nation-states, but the refugee regime and its growing emphasis on restricting refugee entry to European states is an example of 'statecraft' and emphasizes the re-territorialization of certain elements of states in a context of globalization.

- The growing role of NGOs in managing refugee flows and associated humanitarian crises highlights that the refugee regime is becoming less state-centric and is not entirely concerned with defending the nation-state system but must also respond to refugee and NGO demands.

2.3 Forced resettlement, development and the state

Consideration of the role of NGOs in the International Refugee Regime provides us with a useful bridge to our discussion of forced resettlement and the tensions it reveals within the nation-state model of political organization. As NGOs have grown in number and become increasingly significant 'players' in the international political arena over the past few years, they have also become increasingly involved in development-induced displacement and resettlement. However, whereas the involvement of NGOs in the International Refugee Regime has been mainly as 'implementing partners' of bilateral (i.e. government development agencies such as the UK Department for International Development) and multilateral agencies (i.e. intergovernmental organizations such as the World Bank), their involvement in resettlement has been mainly as campaigning and grass roots organizations, representing the interests of local people in opposition to state bureaucracies and 'official' development agencies, such as the World Bank. This has made resistance to resettlement one of the catalysts of so-called 'globalization from below', an 'alternative vision of development which starts from the assumption that "all economics is local" and which seeks above all the empowerment of people, human security and environmental sustainability' (McGrew, 2000, p.362).

2.3.1 Dams and development

The literature on forced resettlement shows a distinct bias towards (a) dam-displacement and (b) publicly planned and implemented projects. The two biases are obviously interconnected, since dam construction involves such a major investment of financial and other resources and such long-term planning that the public sector has to be a major player, while private sector involvement is likely to be confined to the provision of financial and contractual services. In fact, smaller-scale projects, such as mining, road construction and urban development, probably account for more human displacement overall and are increasingly likely to be undertaken by private sector interests, with or without the participation of the state. However, I shall focus on dam-induced displacement, because it enables the tension between the state as the ultimate source of sovereign political power and as a community of equal citizens to be highlighted with particular clarity. There are four main reasons for this:

1 Dam construction not only typically involves huge capital investments, often financed internationally, but dams also have a monumental character which makes them ideally suited to be treated as symbols of national unity and state power, especially in relatively newly formed states. For Nehru, one-time Prime Minister of India, dams were 'the temples of modern India' (Roy, 1999, p.15), while for former President Nkrumah of Ghana the Akosombo Dam on the Volta River was 'a scheme which transcends any political consideration, and which is, in the truest sense, an expression of our national unity and aspirations' (Lumsden, 1973, p.117; quoted in de Wet, 2001, p.11).

2 Following on from the first point, dams have become virtually synonymous with 'intentional development' (Thomas, 2000a, p.25) in the post-colonial state, and have thereby provided a physical representation of one of the main legitimizing ideologies of such a state – its role as the principal agent of development (see Box 2.5).

3 Dams have displaced huge numbers of people, especially in the world's most populous countries, China and India, which have built, between them, 57% of the world's large dams (World Commission on Dams, 2000, p.17).

> The overall level of physical displacement [by large dams] could range from 40 to 80 million. According to official statistics, dams

have displaced 10.2 million people in China between 1950 and 1990 (34% of all development-related displacement including that due to urban construction). Independent sources estimate that the actual number of dam-displaced people in China is much higher than the official figure, with 10 million displaced in the Yangtze Valley alone. Large dams in India displaced an estimated 16–38 million people … The level of displacement has increased substantially after 1990 with the construction of projects such as Three Gorges in China. Among the projects involving displacement funded by the World Bank, large dams account for 63% of displacement.

(World Commission on Dams, 2000, p.104)

4   Finally, dam construction, possibly more than any other form of development-induced displacement, has provoked highly organized and successful resistance movements, focusing on both the environmental and social costs of large dams. Many such movements have owed their success to their ability to link up with a global network of grass roots organizations, NGOs and transnational social movements.

Box 2.5 Large dams as instruments of development – some figures

Adapted from World Commission on Dams (2000)

A 'large dam' is defined here as having a height of at least 5 m and a reservoir volume of more than 3 million cubic metres or being 15 m or more in height. By the end of the twentieth century there were over 45 000 such dams in the world and an average of between 160 and 320 new dams were being built annually. During the 1990s an estimated $32–46 billion was spent every year on large dams, roughly four-fifths of it in developing countries. Of the $22–31 billion invested in dams each year in developing countries, about four-fifths was financed directly by the public sector. The main contribution of dams to development comes through irrigation, water supply and electricity generation.

Irrigation
The majority of large dams in Africa (52%) and Asia (65%) are for irrigation, which accounts for the single largest use of fresh water in the world today. Irrigated agriculture accounts for about 40% of world agricultural production, and 30–40% of such irrigated lands world-wide rely on dams. In the two countries with the largest irrigated areas – India and China – large dams supply approximately 30–35% of irrigation water.

Water supply
On average, about 12% of large dams world-wide were built to supply water for industrial use and urban centres, and about 60% of these are in North America and Europe. In Africa, about 20% of dams supply water to urban areas.

*The OECD or
Organization for
Economic Co-operation
and Development:
member states of the
OECD come mainly from
Western Europe and
North America, but they
also include Australia,
Japan and New Zealand;
see Hewitt (2000, p.291).

Electricity generation

Nearly 20% of the world's electricity supply is generated by dams
and about a third of the countries in the world rely on dams for more
than half their electricity needs. Between 1973 and 1996, dam-
generated electricity in non-OECD* (less-developed) countries grew
from 29% to 50% of world production, with South America increasing
its share by the greatest amount. In Africa, 6% of large dams are for
electricity generation, while for North America, South America and
Europe the percentages are 24, 26 and 31%, respectively.

In case after case of development-induced displacement, we see the
state exercising its right to appropriate private property for public use
(i.e. exercising its right of **eminent domain** within its sovereign
territory) against a relatively impoverished and powerless group of its
own citizens, with typically disastrous consequences for their
economic, physical, psychological and socio-cultural well-being. In
many cases, especially those of dam-induced displacement, the
displaced population are members of an indigenous minority and are
displaced from, or from part of, their 'home' territory. They are
marginal to the nation-state within which they were incorporated in the
process of state formation, not merely economically but also
geographically (they often live in peripheral border areas), politically
and culturally. The situation is well described by Colson (1971) in a
classic study of the impact of resettlement on the Gwembe Tonga of
Zambia, following the construction of the Kariba Dam on the Zambezi
River in 1957–58 (see the case study in the next section). The Gwembe
Tonga were, Colson (1971, p.3) writes, 'asked to make enormous
sacrifices for which the only human justification lay in the long-term
good of a larger national community which would benefit from the
dam, and this community was not one with which they identified
themselves'.

So persistent, so widespread and so obviously interconnected are these
negative features of development-induced displacement that they must
be judged, at least in an empirical sense, as amongst its defining
characteristics – things could be otherwise, but they almost never are.
As we shall see, some would argue that even this is too optimistic a
view, and that forced resettlement projects are so inherently
complicated that they are bound to make at least some people worse
off. The price of development-induced displacement, then, is 'a price
worth paying', provided it is paid by 'them' rather than by 'us', where
'them' refers not just to other fellow citizens, but to fellow citizens
whose relationship with the nation-state is different from our own.
They are insiders who are also outsiders. They are excluded, in a de
facto sense, from the benefits of full and equal membership in the
political community, even as they are included, in a de jure sense, in

order to justify the 'pain' they are expected to bear for the 'gain' their displacement brings about for their fellow members. Before coming to the issue of resistance to resettlement, I shall enlarge on the claim that it typically affects an already impoverished and relatively powerless group of citizens, with disastrous consequences for their socio-economic well-being.

2.3.2 The 'sad reality' of forced resettlement

All observers agree that forced resettlement usually has 'overwhelmingly negative consequences' for those displaced, 'resulting in social and psychological disruption, and often long-term economic impoverishment' (de Wet, 2001, p.2). There is also no disagreement that 'the people most vulnerable in the face of powerful state and capital interests are those who occupy the lands (for example, in highland, forest, riverine or other isolated areas) most commonly targeted for development projects' (McDowell, 1996, p.4). One consequence of this is that forced resettlers are often members of indigenous minorities, with limited access to the centres of state power. All this is extensively and comprehensively borne out by the World Bank's 1994 review of the projects involving involuntary displacement that it financed between 1986 and 1993, a review which Fox (2000, p.303) describes as 'a still unmatched precedent in terms of rigor, comprehensiveness, transparency and self-criticism'. Its most relevant finding for our present purpose is that:

> The majority of the displaced are rural and poor because new projects are brought to the most under-developed, poorest areas, where infrastructure is lacking and land and political costs are lowest ... The remote locations of many dam sites are often inhabited by indigenous peoples, ethnic minorities and pastoral peoples, which explains why ... cultural differences are so prominent in resettlement...
> (World Bank, 1994, p.93; quoted in Fox, 2000, p.314)

It follows that there is 'a direct association between large projects involving displacement and the lack of political representation of displaced peoples' (Fox, 2000, p.314). Further confirmation of these points, relating specifically to dam-induced displacement, is provided by the recent report of the World Commission on Dams, which includes seven detailed case studies of large dams, five of them in developing countries, and country studies of India and China.

> Examination of the case study dams confirms that those who receive the benefits, usually urban dwellers, commercial farmers and industries, are typically not the same groups that bear the social costs. Immigrants generally provide most of the labour force in construction works ... they develop and operate tourism facilities and manage commercial fishing companies. While many small-to-medium farmers participate in irrigation schemes such schemes also benefit large

landowners and those from privileged groups. Electricity generation has mostly benefited the industrial and mining sector ... and urban areas ... Fresh water supplied by dams is mainly directed to the industrial sector and urban areas.

(World Commission on Dams, 2000, p.125)

One of the case studies in the World Commission on Dams survey was of the Kariba Dam, on the Zambia–Zimbabwe border, which I mentioned earlier. This is one of the largest dams in the world, and has been the subject of probably the most intensive long-term study of the social consequences of resettlement ever undertaken (see the case study below). Based on this study, and a familiarity with many other cases in, amongst other countries, India, China, Sri Lanka, Kenya and Ghana, Scudder (1993, p.148) comes to the carefully considered conclusion that 'dam-induced displacement more often than not leaves the majority [of local people] worse off'. This raises the question: could things be otherwise, or is there something about such large-scale infrastructural development projects that makes it practically impossible to avoid the negative impacts on resettlers and other affected people which have been so extensively documented?

A huge amount of evidence now exists, much of it collected by the World Bank itself, which allows us to be fairly clear about the process of impoverishment that invariably results from forced resettlement, including dam-induced resettlement. Michael Cernea, who was for many years the Bank's Senior Adviser on Sociology and Social Policy, has identified eight main 'sub-processes' or 'components' which interact with each other to produce impoverishment for those physically displaced, as well as for those otherwise adversely affected by resettlement (Cernea, 1996, pp.21–22; 2000). The result is a checklist of items, most of which can be ticked off for virtually any historical case of forced resettlement: loss of land, employment and housing; economic and social marginalization; food insecurity and undernourishment; increased morbidity and mortality; loss of access to common property resources; and the dismantling of social networks and communities. Cernea's main interest, however, is not in understanding and documenting past resettlement failures, but in using knowledge of these failures to improve the chances of future success. He sees the items on his list as 'a set of potential risks ... that will undoubtedly become real if unheeded, or can be avoided if anticipated and purposively counteracted' and which therefore constitutes a 'risk prediction model' that can be used to 'destroy it's own prophecy' (Cernea, 1996, p.22).

> ...a risk prediction model becomes maximally useful not when it is confirmed by adverse events, but, rather, when, as a result of its warnings being taken seriously and acted upon, the risks are prevented from becoming reality, or are minimized, and the consequences predicted by the model do not occur ... This is how the ... model contributes to destroying its own prophecy.
>
> (Cernea, 2000, p.33)

| Case study: The social consequences of resettlement – the Kariba Dam |

Based on Colson (1971), Scudder (1993) and the World Commission on Dams (2000)

The dam

The construction of the Kariba Dam, on the Zambezi river, where it forms the border between Zambia and Zimbabwe, was responsible for the first major dam-induced displacement in sub-Saharan Africa. Its construction was announced in 1955 by the newly formed (but short-lived) Federation of the Rhodesias and Nyasaland, consisting of what are now Zambia, Zimbabwe and Malawi. Partly financed by the World Bank, its purpose was to generate power for the Zambian Copperbelt and the growing industries of Zimbabwe. It would also create the world's largest artificial lake, which, along with the dam itself, 'would be permanent symbols of the power of the new State and its dedication to economic progress' (Colson, 1971, p.4).

Figure 2.5 The Kariba Dam, Zimbabwe.

The resettlers

Construction of the dam began in 1956 and by the time it was sealed in December 1958, 57 000 people had been resettled. Before construction, both banks of the middle Zambezi were inhabited by the Gwembe Tonga, who took advantage of the annual flooding of the Zambezi and its tributaries to plant two crops a year. Typical crops were maize, millet, sorghum and sweet potatoes, as well as tobacco and cotton. They also raised livestock, mainly sheep and goats. It was originally estimated that only 29 000 people would need to be resettled, for which the budget allocated was £4 million. The number actually resettled was nearly double this number, but the resettlement budget remained unchanged. The cost of Stage 1 of the project, which included resettlement, nevertheless rose from an estimated £72.2 million to an actual £77.61 million. In Zambia resettlers were given cash compensation for the loss of customary rights and for loss of earnings while building new houses. In Zimbabwe, there was no cash compensation but food was provided during the resettlement period and adult males were exempted from the annual £2 poll tax for two years.

The people to be resettled were not involved in the decision-making and planning process, and so had no opportunity to explore alternative options or state their views and preferences. The resettlement itself was carried out hurriedly. Most people were resettled about 50 km from the dam. Many moved on foot but many were also transported in lorries and left at their new homes. There was very little open resistance, although one group of villagers scheduled to move to an area below the dam charged police who were attempting to get them to board lorries. The police opened fire, killing eight people and wounding at least 32.

The local costs

Most of the land to which people were moved was of relatively poor quality, required periodic fallowing and could only be cultivated during the rains, making only one crop possible per year. Population densities increased as a result of resettlement and many people were moved to areas where the resource base was inadequate to support them with their existing technology. Thirty years later, Scudder (1993, p.146) reported that 'several areas have become so seriously degraded that they remind one of the West African Sahel which has perhaps half the annual rainfall'. There were significant increases in mortality and morbidity (human sleeping sickness, dysentery, measles and chickenpox) in the years immediately following resettlement. Over the years, relatives and friends living in the south (Zimbabwe) and the north (Zambia) lost contact with each other because of the distances that now separated them.

The local benefits?

Since the Tonga were not seen as 'stakeholders' in the dam, no attempt was made by the planners to explore ways in which they could derive benefit from it. Despite the fact that the main purpose of the dam was power generation, no Tonga areas were connected to the national grid until 25 years after the first generator went into operation, and then only below the dam, where less than 20% of the people had been relocated. Apart from power generation, the dam gave rise to two other opportunities for economic development which had not been foreseen and investigated in the original project plan: irrigation agriculture and fishing. Although local people have gained some advantage from these activities, they have not been the main beneficiaries. The best land for irrigation was handed over to an international company for development, which led to further forced resettlement. For about ten years after the original resettlement, fishery was an important source of employment and capital for local people, but productivity dropped substantially after the lake stabilized. A large and more lucrative fishing industry arose in the 1970s, based on an introduced species of sardine, but local people have found it difficult to participate in the industry, because of its intensive nature and high capital development costs.

In Cernea's view, all forced resettlement projects 'are prone to major socio-economic risks, *but not fatally condemned to succumb to them*' (Cernea, 2000, p.19). In other words, things can be otherwise, provided the risks are 'taken seriously and acted upon'. For this to happen, those responsible for planning and implementing forced resettlement projects must do more than merely provide compensation for expropriated property, as required by the letter of their national law. They must ensure that the institutions responsible for resettlement have sufficient administrative and organizational capacity. And they must involve the displaced, and their hosts, in the planning and implementation of resettlement projects. These and other conditions of successful resettlement have been set out by the World Bank in a series of resettlement guidelines for borrower states receiving development loans (see Box 2.6), making it 'the first multilateral organization to enact a policy framework for displacement and to provide a benchmark for standards on resettlement' (Feeney, 1998, p.90).

Box 2.6 The World Bank's policy on involuntary resettlement

Extracts from Feeney (1998, pp.89–90)

Based on ... the lessons it learnt from large-scale development projects in the 1970s, in 1980 the World Bank adopted a resettlement policy. Over the years the policy was strengthened and incorporated the findings of social science research on resettlement. By issuing resettlement policy guidelines and procedures, the Bank became the first multinational institution to enact a policy framework for displacement and to provide a benchmark for standards on resettlement, which were slowly incorporated into the policies of other donors.

- Involuntary displacement should be avoided or minimized whenever possible, because of its disruptive and impoverishing effects.

- Where displacement is unavoidable, the objective of Bank policy is to assist displaced persons in their efforts to improve, or at least restore, former living standards and earning capacity. The means to achieve this objective consist of the preparation and execution of resettlement plans, which should be integral parts of project design.

> ■ Displaced persons should be compensated for their losses at displacement cost, given opportunities to share in project benefits and assisted in the transfer and in the transition period at the relocation site.
>
> ■ Resettlers and the community already living at the relocation site (the 'hosts') should participate in planning the resettlement.

Unfortunately, however, during the 20 years since this policy was first initiated, and even though the guidelines have been internationally recognized and adopted by other international organizations (such as the Organization for Economic Co-operation and Development) and national governments, their implementation by borrower nations has remained 'consistently problematical' (Oliver-Smith, 2001, p.98).

A case in point is that of the Kedung Ombo Dam in Java, Indonesia, which displaced about 32 000 people (World Commission on Dams, 2000, p.108) and was the first World Bank-funded project in Indonesia to provoke significant grass roots opposition (Ramansara, 2000). The focus of the opposition, which did not begin until 1987, two years before the dam gates were closed, was an (ultimately unsuccessful) attempt to obtain fair compensation for loss of land. The resettlers were excluded from participation in decision-making about resettlement and eventually obtained compensation at a rate equivalent to less than 15 US cents per square metre, or a tenth of the then market price (Ramansara, 2000, p.126). A more recent example of failure to observe internationally agreed guidelines, though one in which World Bank funding is not involved, is the Turkish government's plan to build a dam on the Tigris River, 65 km from the Syrian and Iraqi borders, with the help of a construction consortium formerly led by the British company Balfour Beatty*. Known as the Ilisu Dam, it is expected to displace, or otherwise affect, around 36 000 people, mainly belonging to the ethnic minority Kurdish population. According to a report commissioned by the British government, which was asked to supply £200 million of export credit guarantees to Balfour Beatty, 'Local stakeholders have been waiting for more than 20 years to be informed directly about resettlement' and 'believe that they have no forum to express their concerns over adequate compensation for expropriated assets, decisions over new settlement locations and loss of cultural and social capital' (see the Ilisu Dam Campaign website, http://www.ilisu.org.uk/).

*Balfour Beatty withdrew from this project in 2001.

One obvious reason why adherence to the World Bank's guidelines remains 'consistently problematical' is that they can be seen as a potential infringement of national sovereignty. As Oliver-Smith points out, there is no more striking demonstration of the state's monopoly of the management of violence than its right 'to exert ultimate control over the location of people and things *within* its territory' (Oliver-Smith, 1996, p.78; my emphasis). As an expression of state sovereignty, this right is surely on a par with (and likely to be as jealously guarded as) the right of the state to exclude outsiders from its territory. But another reason has to do with the failure of the Bank itself to live up to the demands of its own policy, the Kedung Ombo Dam being, again, a good case in point. It was acknowledged in the Bank's completion report on this project that it was an especially blatant case of non-compliance with its policy on involuntary resettlement (Fox and Brown, 2000). The reasons for non-compliance presumably have to do with institutional logic; primarily, I suggest, the pressures experienced by staff members of the Bank, as in any organization, to avoid behaviour that could have a negative impact on career advancement. Fox (2000, p.320) quotes the following comment from an internal Bank review of 'project supervision': 'The feeling that greater attention and firmer actions on resettlement will affect their relationship with the borrower country is not uncommon among them [project managers within the Bank].' Additionally, compliance with its own policy reforms may conflict with the Bank's first obligation which is, as for any social institution, to ensure its own survival.

> While the World Bank has in a few cases withdrawn from the funding of projects already in progress, it is in the first instance a bank, that is concerned to fund development. For development banks as a matter of course, and on a regular basis, not to fund development projects, mainly because their resettlement components are not in order, would be to pull the plug on the kind of infrastructural project which is integral to a capitalist-oriented bank's vision of development in the first place.
>
> (de Wet, 2001, p.12)

By contrast, however, it should be noted that the question of compliance with policy reforms would not arise if there were no policy framework against which to measure performance, and, as highlighted previously, the Bank has been unusually rigorous and self-critical in setting out its resettlement policy (Fox, 2000). In addition, the existence of this policy has become a powerful weapon in the armoury of external critics of particular projects, notably advocacy and campaigning NGOs. This in turn has given added leverage to internal advocates of reform within the Bank, such as Cernea himself.

Nevertheless, it seems fair to conclude that to place one's faith in the ability of international financial institutions to adhere to their own guidelines and policy reforms is as unwise as to place one's faith in the political will and good intentions of states to see that resettlement projects are implemented in accordance with internationally agreed standards.

What improvements there have been in the design and implementation of resettlement projects over the past 20 years have been mainly confined to those risks in Cernea's list which are highly visible and relatively easy to deal with over the short term – those of homelessness, food insecurity and health. As Koenig (2000, p.14) points out, 'The problem is ... that ... many resettlement projects stop after addressing these social welfare [issues] and do not go on to development initiatives that will deal with these and other risks over a longer term'. When forced resettlement does have positive outcomes, furthermore, at least for some resettlers, these are often unintended 'spin-offs' from the project – the result of serendipity rather than of planning (de Wet, 2001, pp.19–21). One example of such an unintended spin-off is the fishing enterprise which, during the first five years after the completion of the Kariba Dam, made a significant contribution to the incomes and savings of many local people (Scudder, 1993, p.144).

The wide gap that exists between good policy (i.e. the World Bank's guidelines) and poor outcomes has led some observers to conclude that the problem lies in the very nature of large-scale forced resettlement projects themselves. According to de Wet (2001, p.18), it is virtually impossible to plan and implement forced resettlement projects in the rational, 'top–down', state-centric way beloved of national and international bureaucracies, without leaving most resettlers worse off, 'because of the inherent complexity of what is involved when we try to combine moving people with improving their condition'. In order to minimize the number of those who end up worse off, what is required is an 'open-ended, adapt-as-you-go approach' which genuinely involves the affected population in decision-making and which is flexible and adaptable enough to enable objectives and methods to be changed in the light of the inevitable unforeseen obstacles and problems. But for this to work, both the funders and the borrower government would have to give up control of the project 'to a considerable degree' (de Wet, 2001, p.25).

This brings into view the key issue of **state power** – the right of the state, as a self-defined sovereign body, to administer and control a particular territory – which underlies the discussion of both the refugee and the forced resettler. In the case of the refugee, the state's sovereignty is constrained by the statutes of international law relating to the treatment of refugees. In the case of the forced resettler, the World Bank's guidelines are the nearest equivalent to an internationally agreed framework for the protection of their rights. But since these guidelines are not legally binding, the rights of the forced resettler can ultimately only be secured by the government that forced him or her to move in the first place.

> Development-induced displaced persons (DIDP) generally remain in their country of origin and their legal protection should theoretically be guaranteed by the government. In terms of the international state system, the government is responsible for ensuring that the rights of people under its jurisdiction are respected ... The complexities of DIDR [development-induced displacement and resettlement] result specifically because the government that is responsible for the displacement is also responsible for ensuring the protection of DIDPs.
>
> (Barutciski, 2000, p.6)

In forced resettlement, therefore, the state is both the problem and the solution, the key player as well as the referee.

This is why resistance to resettlement, to which we must now turn, is normally carried on outside the formal constitutional and political structures of the state.

2.3.3 Resistance: 'Who owns this land?'

The forced resettler, as I wrote earlier, is an 'insider' who is also an 'outsider'. By resisting resettlement, the forced resettler challenges not just a particular project, and the development policy of a particular state, but the idea that underpins the state's claim to sovereign power over its territory: that it is a national community of equal citizens. Resistance to resettlement challenges the legitimacy of state power.

It is no wonder, therefore, that resistance is rarely articulated through the institutions of the state itself but typically takes the form of a grass roots movement, which becomes more effective the more it is able to link its own protest to those of other similar movements, at both the national and transnational levels. By linking the local to the global, such campaigns help to strengthen and define a sense of local identity, while transforming the way the affected community interacts with the state's political and administrative structures. A development project, financed by transnational financial institutions and initiated in the name of the nation-state, can be resisted, with the help of national and international NGOs, by a local interest group which is politically and often geographically remote from the centre of state power. Paradoxically, then, although resistance may be cast as a battle to defend the cultural identity and autonomy of a local population, it may profoundly and permanently alter that population's view of itself, by connecting it in new ways to wider structures, regionally, nationally and internationally. The continuing campaign against the Sardar Sarovar Dam on the Narmada River in the Indian province of Gujarat, described by Wirth (2000, p.62) as a paradigm case of 'project specific partnership advocacy', illustrates these general points.

Case study: The Sardar Sarovar Dam

Based on Fox (2000), Gray (2000), Roy (1999), Udall (2000) and Wirth (2000)

The dam

The Sardar Sarovar Dam is the centrepiece of one of the world's most ambitious river valley development schemes, involving the construction of 30 major dams and many more smaller ones on the Narmada River and its tributaries in the states of Madhya Pradesh, Maharashtra and Gujarat, north-western India. The foundations of the Sardar Sarovar

Dam, in Gujarat, were laid in 1961 but construction did not get seriously underway until 1988, three years after the World Bank approved a loan of $450 million towards its estimated overall cost of $6 billion. The dam is planned to reach a height of 155 metres and is intended to provide irrigation, drinking water and hydroelectric power. Estimates of the number of people to be displaced by the reservoir vary between 100 000 and 200 000. Work on the dam was stopped until further notice in 1995 by a ruling of the Supreme Court, on the grounds that the rehabilitation of displaced people had not been adequate. The dam was then 80 metres high and its reservoir had submerged a quarter of the area eventually to be flooded. In October 2000 the Supreme Court allowed construction to go ahead up to a height of 90 m.

(a)

(b)   (c)

Figure 2.6 (a) The Sardar Sarovar Dam on the Narmada River, Gujarat, India. (b) and (c) Protestors campaign against the dam.

The movement

The Narmada Bachao Andolan (NBA) or 'Save the Narmada Movement' was founded in 1988 through the coming together of various grass roots movements which had been putting pressure on the Indian government and the World Bank to improve the implementation of the project for the benefit of local people. The movements had individually been campaigning for comprehensive land surveys to ensure just compensation, the inclusion of people who would be affected by subsidiary projects, such as canal construction, in resettlement and rehabilitation plans, and the provision of full information on all aspects of the dam. As a result, it was discovered that a comprehensive plan for resettlement and rehabilitation had not been completed, even though this was a formal condition for the approval of World Bank funding. The failure of the Indian government (which claimed that the issues were simply too complex for local people to understand) and the World Bank to respond to these demands led to the hardening of attitudes amongst the activists and their coming together, under the umbrella of the NBA, to declare total opposition to the Sardar Sarovar project.

In December 1990/January 1991 the NBA organized a 'long march' on the dam by people from all three affected states, which ended in a 30-day stand-off at the Gujarat border between the marchers and the police and military. As well as mobilizing local people, the NBA established co-operative links with NGOs and social movements all over India and internationally. Its activists, including the charismatic Medha Patkar (a social scientist and former member of the Tata Institute of Social Sciences in Bombay), travelled to international meetings in the United States, Europe and Japan to lobby governments and financial institutions. The campaign was documented on film, the support of celebrities, such as the Booker Prize winning novelist Arundhati Roy, was obtained and a website was established by the 'Friends of River Narmada' (Friends of River Narmada website, http://www.narmada.org). As it evolved, the campaign broadened into an international movement to oppose state-centred and corporate models of development in general. In an appended comment to the report of the World Commission on Dams (2000, pp.321, 322), of which she was a member, Patkar wrote that 'The problems of dams are a symptom of the larger failure of the unjust and destructive dominant development model' and warned of the 'massive gulf between a statement of good intent and a change in practice by entrenched vested interests'.

The Bank

Although the consequences of the Sardar Sarovar project for local residents and potential forced resettlers remains uncertain, the campaign against it has had an important impact, both directly and indirectly, on the resettlement policy of the World Bank. One direct result was the commissioning by the Bank, in 1991, of an independent review of the project under Bradford Morse, former director of the United Nations Development Programme (UNDP). The report of the 'Morse Commission' bore out the NBA's criticisms. It concluded that the Bank should 'step back' from the project, which it eventually did, although the Indian government announced that it would continue without Bank funding. The report provided support for NGO activists attempting to make the Bank more accountable and responsive to local people, and leverage for those who were arguing for reform from within the Bank itself. It was in the wake of the Morse Commission's report that the Bank undertook its review of all projects involving involuntary resettlement between 1986 and 1993 (World Bank, 1994). This review found that the Bank's compliance with its own resettlement guidelines increased in projects approved after 1992, when the conflict over the Sardar Sarovar Dam was at its height. As Fox (2000, p.305) remarks, 'the timing of the increased compliance strongly suggests that external political pressure was a critical factor'.

Infrastructural development projects, especially those which displace large numbers of people and have drastic impacts on the environment, are quintessentially expressive of the 'modernization', or 'economic growth', view of development and of the view that the state has the ultimate right to claim trusteeship over the development of its citizens (Thomas, 2000a). Resistance to large dams, therefore, provides an ideal space within which campaigning organizations of all kinds, but especially those concerned with human rights and the environment, can pursue an alternative, 'people-centred' or (to put it more strongly) 'people-managed' view of development, according to which development 'starts with and is controlled by civil society', thereby reducing 'the importance of the corporate capitalist economy and the state' (Martinussen, 1999, p.332). As the case of the Sardar Sarovar Dam illustrates, resistance movements can create alliances across a vast range of 'people's organizations', from small 'membership associations', with highly specific local objectives, to powerful international NGOs with global objectives, seeking to change the policy agendas of donor governments and multilateral financial institutions. The research and advocacy literature of forced resettlement is consequently packed with some of the most resonant key words of the contemporary development debate, such as 'participation', 'accountability', 'empowerment', 'rights-based development' and 'sustainable development'. I shall comment briefly on the two issues which cut across virtually every case of resistance to dam-induced displacement and bring into question the role of the state: human rights and the environment.

Human rights and state sovereignty

The development of international human rights law since the end of the Second World War represents a challenge to the doctrine of the sovereign equality of states and has been responsible for some erosion in the concept of state sovereignty (Chinkin, 1998). Reisman (1990) considers that, in modern international law, sovereignty resides in the citizens of a state, not, as formerly understood, in its government. Violation of this 'people's sovereignty' by the state itself (i.e. by its governing élite) raises the possibility, therefore, of one state legally intervening in the affairs of another in order to protect the rights of the offending state's citizens.

> International law still protects sovereignty, but ... it is the people's sovereignty rather than the sovereign's sovereignty. Under the old concept, even scrutiny of international human rights without the permission of the sovereign could arguably constitute a violation of sovereignty ... but no serious scholar still supports the contention that internal human rights are 'essentially within the domestic jurisdiction of any state' and hence insulated from international law...

> ...In modern international law, sovereignty can be violated as effectively and ruthlessly by an indigenous as by an outside force, in much the same way that the wealth and natural resources of a country can be spoliated as thoroughly and efficiently by a native as by a foreigner.
> (Reisman, 1990; quoted in Chimni, 2000, pp.408–410)

A slightly different approach is to see the rights of citizens as a counterweight to the rights of the state. If the *raison d'être* of the state is to uphold and protect the rights of its citizens, by failing to do so it loses its claim to legitimacy, thus making intervention by other states justifiable (Chinkin, 1998, p.111; referring to Teson, 1988). Both arguments have been advanced in the context of justifying the use of military force for humanitarian purposes, although, as noted earlier, where the UN Security Council has sanctioned such action, as in the case of its Resolution 688 on Iraq, it has done so under Chapter VII of its charter, which charges it with securing 'international peace and security' rather than with preventing the abuse of human rights.

Nevertheless, these changing interpretations of the concept of sovereignty are clearly relevant to the state's use of the principle of eminent domain (see p.50 above) to expropriate the property of its own citizens 'in the national interest'. This is especially evident when, as is so often the case in dam-induced displacement, the citizens in question belong to an indigenous group – that is, to a 'nation' of their own, whose attachment to their land is based on a tradition of continuous occupation which pre-dates the formation of the nation-state of which they are a part. However, the rights of citizens have yet to be formally invoked in the international arena as a basis for intervention in the territory of a sovereign state.

There are at least two considerations that raise doubts about the legitimacy of the use of the principle of eminent domain in these circumstances, given the 'new' interpretations of sovereignty that make it the duty of the state to protect the human rights of its citizens.

1   First, one has to ask whether the principle of eminent domain, based as it is on the idea that the political community making up the state consists of a single nation, may be legally extended to cover the territory of what is in fact another nation existing within the same state (Colchester, 1999). Indeed, the expropriation of the territory of indigenous groups to build large dams may be interpreted as part of the process, often deliberately intended, though not necessarily so, of nation-building: thus dams and resettlement come to be part of a 'power struggle between the nation-state as a homogeneous all-embracing oppressive entity consisting of government and economic élites, and the peoples whose ties to the land pre-date the formation of the national society' (Gray, 1996, p.108).

2   Second, one has to ask: who decides in practice, what 'the national interest' is? The answer, of course, is those same 'government and economic élites', whose goals are political as well as economic and who tend systematically to underestimate the long-term environmental and social costs of projects involving forced resettlement, including, most fundamentally, the number of people likely to be affected. Arundhati Roy, in her stinging polemical attack on the Narmada Valley dams, 'The greater common good' (1999), has some harsh words for these 'élites', whom she identifies as members of 'the international dam industry'.

> The international dam industry is worth 20 billion dollars a year. If you follow the trails of big dams the world over, wherever you go ... you'll rub up against the same story, encounter the same actors: the Iron Triangle (dam-jargon for the nexus between politicians, bureaucrats and dam construction companies), the racketeers who call themselves International Environmental Consultants (who are usually directly employed by or subsidiaries of dam-builders), and, more often than not, the friendly, neighbourhood World Bank...
>
> ...It's a skilful circus and the acrobats know each other well. Occasionally they'll swap parts – a bureaucrat will join the Bank, a Banker will surface as a project consultant. At the end of the play, a huge percentage of what's called 'Development Aid' is re-channelled back to the countries it came from, masquerading as equipment costs or consultants' fees or salaries to the agencies' own staff.
>
> (Roy, 1999, pp.29–31)

The environmental costs of large dams

During the relatively short time that large dams have been operational –
the average age of large dams today is 35 years (World Commission on
Dams, 2000, p.9) – it has become obvious that their technical
efficiency can be much less, and their environmental costs much
greater, than anticipated. The World Commission on Dams report,
Dams and Development: A New Framework for Decision-Making
(2000), revealed that 'Large irrigation dams ... have typically fallen
short of physical targets, failed to recover their costs and been less
profitable in economic terms than expected' (p.42). As for hydro-
power dams, 'over half the projects in the sample fell short of their
power production targets' (p.50), while water supply dams 'have
generally fallen short of intended timing and targets for bulk delivery
and have exhibited poor financial cost recovery and economic
performance' (p.56).

The negative environmental impacts of large dams have also become
increasingly evident over the past 20 years. They may be divided into
those which affect the global environment, such as reductions in
biodiversity due to the flooding of valley bottoms, the physical
transformation of river systems and the emission of greenhouse gases
from reservoirs; and *those which directly affect the livelihoods of
people living in the vicinity of, or downstream from, the dam*, such as
alterations in the flood regime, loss of soil fertility due to silt reduction
(both of which have a negative impact on 'recessional' or 'flood retreat'
agriculture), and reductions in fish stocks. For obvious reasons,
adverse effects on local livelihoods are of most relevance to the
present discussion, but the problem of greenhouse gas emissions is
worth noting in passing, because it is an example of an 'ecosystem
impact' which has only recently been identified and the existence of
which suggests that some qualification is needed to the 'conventional
wisdom' that hydro-power is necessarily 'environmentally friendly'
when compared with power generation through the burning of fossil
fuels (World Commission on Dams, 2000, p.75; Woodhouse, 2000,
pp.145–146).

> The emission of greenhouse gases (GHG) from reservoirs due to rotting
> vegetation and carbon inflows from the catchment is a recently
> identified ecosystem impact (on climate) of storage dams.
> (World Commission on Dams, 2000, p.75)

The environmental costs of large dams, then, like the exploitation of
the world's tropical forests by commercial interests (Woodhouse, 2000,
pp.156–157), brings into view two issues that have helped to shape the
debate about international development in the 1990s: the global
environmental consequences of economic growth and the problem of
'environmental degradation' in less developed countries. The key
concept here is 'sustainable development', defined by the World

*The World Commission
on Environment and
Development (WCED)
is also known as the
'Brundtland' Commission.

Commission on Environment and Development* as 'development that meets the needs of the present without compromising the ability of future generations to meet their own needs' (Woodhouse, 2000, p.158).

As with other key concepts of the debate, which I mentioned earlier (e.g. 'participation', 'empowerment' and 'accountability'), everyone can agree that sustainable development is a good thing, but there is disagreement about the ways and means of achieving it. These disagreements largely boil down to the conflicting economic interests of states – especially those of industrialized versus less industrialized states. Thus the 'neoliberal' view, which treats the environment as 'natural capital', enables schemes to be worked out whereby industrialized states are able to commit themselves to reducing their emissions of greenhouse gases, but only on paper, by buying 'emission rights' from less industrialized (and therefore less polluting) states. As Woodhouse (2000, p.159) points out, such arrangements may be tantamount to less industrialized states selling their options for industrial development to the more industrialized.

The forced resettler, of course, plays no part in such high-level inter-state wrangling, whether over global carbon emissions, or the preservation of the planet's biodiversity, except perhaps through the agency of an international NGO. But he or she hangs like a gaunt and ghostly presence over the debate about sustainable development, representing a 'community based' or 'people-centred' view which is not so much an alternative to the neoliberal view as a radical critique of its state- and market-centric assumptions.

Herein lies one of the striking paradoxes of campaigns of resistance against forced resettlement: they begin as highly localized grass roots movements with a highly specific objective limited to the immediate interests of their members, but the stronger and more successful they become, so their horizons are broadened to encompass, and ask radical questions about, issues of political and economic control of the most fundamental kind. They come to question, in effect, the legitimacy of the political order itself.

Unfortunately, and as Arundhati Roy explains for the Narmada campaign, this widening of the resistance agenda, although in one sense a sign of success, may not be so helpful in enabling the campaign to achieve its original, and more limited, objectives.

> In India over the last ten years the fight over the Sardar Sarovar Dam has come to represent far more than the fight for one river. This has been its strength as well as its weakness. Some years ago, it became a debate that captured the popular imagination. That's what raised the stakes and changed the complexion of the battle. From being a fight over the fate of a river valley it began to raise doubts about an entire political system. What is at issue now is the very nature of our democracy. Who owns this land? Who owns its rivers? Its forests? Its fish? These are huge questions…

...For the people of the valley, the fact that the stakes were raised to this degree has meant that their most effective weapon – specific facts about specific issues in this specific valley – has been blunted by the debate on the big issues. The basic premise of the argument has been inflated until it has burst into bits that have, over time, bobbed away.

(Roy, 1999, pp.9–10)

As I noted earlier, resistance to forced resettlement is, at base, nothing less than a challenge to the legitimacy of state power. It is easy to understand, therefore, why it should develop into what amounts to a no-holds-barred questioning of the moral legitimacy and political viability of the nation-state system itself.

Summary of Section 2.3

- Development-induced resettlement highlights a contradiction inherent in claims to state sovereignty: modernizing developments which proclaim the achievements of the state on behalf of the population as a whole impose hardships on marginal and impoverished groups.

- International attempts to regulate resettlement processes also call into question state sovereignty by intervening in internal decisions and undermining states' independence.

- Opposition to development-induced resettlement has drawn on transnational networking to campaign against state policies, pointing to further challenges to territorial state sovereignty and the state-based international political order.

2.4 Conclusion: who are we?

I have argued in this chapter that the refugee and the forced resettler epitomize tensions within the nation-state model of political organization. I have shown that states have attempted to 'normalize' or accommodate the figure of the refugee within the international system of nation-states by means of an international regime, based on a legally binding international convention. This regime has, over the past ten years, moved away from a policy of asylum in host countries towards one of prevention and containment in countries and regions of origin. This move has been accompanied by the introduction of increasingly restrictive asylum practices by industrialized states, practices which are designed to exclude from their territories those 'asylum seekers' (assumed to be the great majority) who are using the 'asylum route' not to escape from genuinely life-threatening situations but to gain access to better life chances for themselves and their families.

In the case of the forced resettler, 'normalization' has been attempted through the formulation of internationally agreed policy guidelines which are not legally binding and which have so far failed to reverse the 'sad reality' that forced resettlement typically leads to the increased impoverishment of an already impoverished and politically marginalized population.

I now want to suggest, by way of conclusion to this chapter, that forced resettlers, and the increasingly blurred category of refugees, asylum seekers and economic migrants, may be taken to represent the world's 'impoverished and politically marginalized population' as a whole.

This is not because of their absolute levels of poverty, but because their situation, and the way states respond to it, raises fundamental questions about identity and membership, questions such as 'Who counts as one of us?', 'Who counts as a fellow citizen?', 'Who counts as a fellow human being?' and even, 'Who are we?'

2.4.1 The increasing gap between rich and poor

It is incontrovertible that, over the past 20 years, increasing numbers of people have been 'marginalized and disenfranchised by the forces of economic globalization' (McGrew, 2000, p.355), with the result that the gap between rich and poor has increased markedly. While this process has occurred both within and between states, it is also clear that the greatest inequality has opened up between the populations of 'developed Northern' states and 'developing Southern' states.

> Since 1980, there has been a dramatic surge in economic growth in some 15 countries, bringing rapidly rising incomes to many of their 1.5 billion people, more than a quarter of the world's population. Over much of this period, however, economic decline or stagnation has affected 100 countries, reducing the incomes of 1.6 billion people, again more than a quarter of the world's population. In 70 of these countries average incomes are less than they were in 1980 – and in 43 countries less than they were in 1970 ... While 200 million people saw their per capita incomes fall during 1965–80, more than one billion people did in 1980–93.
>
> (UNDP, 1996; quoted in Castells, 1998, p.81)

This increasing economic polarization of the world's rich and poor countries must be considered one of the factors – along with cheaper international travel and globalized information media – responsible for fuelling the increased 'migration pressure' that rich states have seen themselves facing in the 1990s. We should note, however, that the link between poverty and migration is unlikely to be a simple causal one, of the kind 'more poverty equals more migration'. One obvious reason for this is that there are significant costs involved for migrants from poor countries in 'negotiating entry' (Koser, 1997) to rich ones, including payments made to smugglers, whose services are becoming more sought after as border enforcement policies are strengthened. It has been estimated for the European Union, for example, that 'a large majority of asylum seekers now enter in an irregular fashion' and that the majority of these make use of smugglers (Morrison and Crosland, 2001, p.17).

In the early 1990s, the average fee paid to smugglers by asylum seekers and 'irregular' migrants to the EU was said to be between $2000 and $5000, and this amount has presumably increased since then. For the same period, figures four and five times higher than this have been quoted for Chinese and Sri Lankans entering the United States and Canada, respectively (Morrison and Crosland, 2001, p.3). This suggests that, at very low levels of income, poverty will be an obstacle to migration and that the propensity to migrate will increase as income levels rise, thus making it unlikely that the very poorest countries will have the highest levels of emigration. What empirical evidence there is supports this hypothesis (Stark and Taylor, 1991; Rowlands, 1998), while at the same time confirming the intuitive expectation that 'the urge to escape from economic distress and the search for better opportunities' are important determinants of migration flows (Ghosh, 1998; quoted in Rowlands, 1998, p.4). As Rowlands (p.5) points out, 'one would not expect to observe substantial migration from rich to poor countries'.

We saw earlier that the imposition of stricter controls on labour migration by European governments since the economic recession of the early 1970s had led increasing numbers of migrants, who would otherwise have sought entrance under the provisions of immigration law, to apply for political asylum. This in turn has led European governments to impose stricter controls on the 'asylum route', the expressed purpose of which has been to maintain the integrity of the asylum system by blocking entrance to labour migrants masquerading as refugees. The same need has been felt even by governments of countries which see themselves, historically, as countries of immigration. In introducing a new Immigration and Refugee Protection Bill in May 2000, Canada's Minister of Citizenship and Immigration, Elinor Caplan, stated that:

> …closing the back door to those who would abuse the system will allow us to open the front door wider – both to genuine refugees, and to the immigrants Canada will need to grow and prosper in the future.
>
> (Elinor Caplan; quoted in Van Kessel, 2001, p.13)

This sounds entirely reasonable until one recognizes that, by focusing attention on their 'back doors', as a condition for opening their 'front doors', rich Northern (developed) countries have made asylum policy virtually a function of immigration policy. Their obligations under international law to provide protection for refugees has been subsumed under their overriding domestic priority, which is to control the movement of people.

> The importance of the control rationale among governments … goes a long way to explain why the governance of refugee protection in the North has all but entirely been taken over by the strengthening of the immigration control regime.
>
> (Collinson, 1999, p.16)

As we also saw earlier, it is possible to interpret this concern – perhaps even 'obsession' – with immigration control as the nation-state 'striking back' against the forces of economic globalization in an area where it continues to have some power to influence events. Thus, Bauman's comments on the strengthening of border controls, which I quoted earlier in Section 2.2.3, almost amount to the proposition that they are a kind of con-trick, or public relations exercise, designed to convince the citizenry that the state remains the ultimate guarantor of their physical, social and economic security and well-being. Warner comes close to the same position, writing:

> Migration and citizenship are really the last bastions of state authority. If the state cannot protect its territory from outsiders, then it no longer has a *raison d'être*. Gatekeeping has become the primary state function ... the state must protect its borders because that is what states do...
>
> (Warner, 1997, p.60)

While these comments are valid, they do not consider the possibility that, given the huge and increasing disparities in living standards and economic opportunities between developed and developing countries (or 'North' and 'South'), coupled with new technologies of transport and communications, immigration to developed Northern countries could, in the absence of border controls, reach very high levels indeed. The question then becomes whether there is a level at which immigration would threaten, not just the material conditions of at least some of a country's citizens but also the democratic rights and institutions which all of its citizens have come to take for granted. The argument that there is such a level assumes that the maintenance of democratic political institutions, and the commitment of people to redistributive forms of social justice, depend upon a degree of solidarity, shared understanding and mutual trust that could be weakened by a large and sudden influx of new members (Gibney, 2002).

Of course, we do not know, in practice, whether an 'open borders' policy would result in a substantial increase in immigration to developed Northern states, nor what level immigration would have to reach, in a particular state, for it to have the effects just described – we are considering merely a theoretical possibility. We can certainly be confident that the rich countries of the North could accept far higher numbers of immigrants than they do now, without adverse consequences for their citizens. In the end, however, 'migration capacity' is determined, in a democracy, by the ballot box, and if public opinion is opposed to further migration we know that any political party that proposed dismantling all border controls would be unelectable.

2.4.2 Nation-states: territorial limits to redistribution

If the theoretical possibility is accepted that uncontrolled immigration could undermine or weaken the democratic institutions of a state, and if it is also accepted that governments are obliged to give priority to the interests of their own citizens, then it follows that they also have an obligation to control immigration into their territories. Liberal democratic states can protect the lifestyles and democratic rights which their own citizens have come to expect, and which they would, in principle, like to see extended to all human beings, only if they are prepared, in principle as well as in practice, to deny these benefits to outsiders. As Hirst (2001, p.9) puts it, 'Borders function now not to exclude invading armies, but to keep economic migrants out of welfare states.'

Here we are faced with yet another tension, or inconsistency deriving from the nation-state idea, between obligations to fellow members ('us') and obligations to fellow human beings ('them'), and it follows from the nature of the nation-state as a 'particularistic moral agent'* (Gibney, 2002).

*The state draws its authority to act not from the human community in its entirety, but only that particular portion of humanity over which it claims to rule, i.e. the citizens of that state. Its moral claims and interventions are thus not universal, but particularistic.

Gibney traces the particularism of the modern state to three developments which have progressively strengthened the bond between the state and its citizens:

1   the linking of the ideas of state and nation which occurred in the late eighteenth century;

2   the spread of the idea of representative democracy; and

3   the expansion of the state's responsibilities to include the provision of economic goods and services to its citizens.

These developments have bolstered the authority of the state, thereby helping it to survive and flourish over the past three centuries and to become the world's overwhelmingly dominant principle of political organization. But they have also made it a condition of the state's success that it should put the claims and interests of its own citizens first, with the result that 'modern states are highly resistant to the moral claims of outsiders'.

> Criticising the state for putting the needs and interests of insiders first is like criticising a public company for seeking to make a profit for its shareholders – in neither case is one's criticism likely to offend the institution in question. To expect it to do so is fundamentally to misunderstand the nature of the agent in question...

> For while most states are responsive to the needs of outsiders *in extremis*, they do not equate the needs of outsiders with the needs of citizens. When states accept refugees they are responding to extremity, not equality. The extreme need of outsiders never dislodges the fundamental relationship between citizen and state; it never challenges

the state's claim to be the state of a particular human community. If this special relationship were to be transcended – if people or governments were in a position to charge the state to act impartially between their own interests and those of outsiders – we would have transcended the need for the modern state. We would be ready for world government … For the time being, however, the practical agenda of immigration and refugee debates within Western states will be set principally by the (perceived) consequence of entry on the interests of citizens, rather than by the benefits of entry for strangers.

(Gibney, 2002, in press)

Various developments over the past half-century give grounds for believing that 'transcending the special relationship' between the territorial state and a particular national community has already begun. These developments include the increasing political and economic interdependence of states, which has made inter-state war virtually a thing of the past; the growth of intergovernmental and non-governmental organizations which now share the global political arena with nation-states; the 'pooling' of sovereignty' in such supra-national institutions as the European Union; and the signing by individual states of human rights instruments which makes them accountable to the United Nations for the protection of human rights within their borders.

But, as Gibney suggests, this process will be completed only when governments routinely treat the interests of outsiders as on a par with those of insiders, which would be the equivalent of extending the boundary of the state to include the whole human species. One only has to consider the way states respond to refugees, economic migrants and forced resettlers, to realize how far short of this goal we are. Indeed, we could be forgiven for concluding from such a consideration that the living standards of the rich minority of the world's population continue to rise, not despite the increasing immiseration of the poor, but *because* of it. And we might also conclude that this is not simply a matter of the greed and rapaciousness of the rich, but also of the 'particularism' which has enabled the nation-state to become, over the past 200 years, the world's dominant political organizing principle.

It is easy to see that there is a direct relationship between the costs borne by forced resettlers and the benefits which accrue to the wider community, and also that those who suffer are often culturally distinct from this wider community and geographically remote from the 'native backyards' of the decision-makers. Writing about the contribution of forced resettlers to the 'greater common good' in India, Roy notes that well over half of those due to be displaced by the Sardar Sarovar Dam belong to ethnic minorities which make up only 8% of the Indian population as a whole. She comments:

This opens up a whole new dimension to the story. The ethnic 'otherness' of their victims takes some of the pressure off the Nation

Builders. It's like having an expense account. Someone else pays the bills. People from another country. Another world. India's poorest people are subsidising the lifestyles of her richest…

(Roy, 1999, pp.18–19)

Nehru summed up the justification for this situation, speaking to villagers who were to be displaced by the Hirakud Dam in 1948, in the words 'If you are to suffer you should suffer in the interests of the country' (quoted in Roy, 1999, p.7). This is similar to the justification that has sometimes been openly advanced by political leaders in Western democracies for accepting relatively high levels of unemployment amongst a minority of the national population as 'a price worth paying' in order to keep inflation and interest rates down for the benefit of the majority. It is a price worth paying, one cannot help feeling, provided someone else pays it, and yet the justification put forward is that those who 'gain' and those who 'bear the pain' are all members of the same national community. It is almost as though the politicians were claiming that the nation itself, as a sentient being, was bearing the pain, not a particular group of its members. Roy exposes the hollowness of such a claim by asking this pointed question of her well-off fellow citizens:

Would you like to trade your beach house in Goa for a hovel in Paharganj? No? Not even for the nation?

(Roy, 1999, p.55)

The American philosopher Richard Rorty offers a philosophical analysis of what is involved here, based upon the concept of a 'moral community', meaning a 'community of reciprocal trust', the members of which are prepared to help each other when they are in need: 'To answer the question "Who are we?" in a way that is relevant to moral questions is to pick out [those] for whom one is willing to do something to help' (Rorty, 1996, online edition). The question Rorty invites us to consider is whether, given the growing gap between rich and poor, both within and between countries, it is anything more than empty posturing to speak of the citizens of a country, let alone of all human beings, as members of a single 'moral community'?

The existence of a moral community which can plausibly and without qualification identify itself as 'we, the people of the United States', is still a project rather than an actuality … In most respects, however, it is losing ground. For the gap between … rich and poor Americans is widening steadily, and the latter are increasingly bereft of hope for their children.

A recent article by Richard Posner … contains a sentence that underlines this lack of hope. Judge Posner wrote that 'The very high crime rate of black (American) males is an aspect of the pathological situation of the black underclass, but there do not appear to be any remedies for this situation which are at once politically feasible and likely to work' (Posner, 1995, p.3). In the context in which Posner writes, 'politically feasible' means 'compatible with the fact that the American middle class will not let itself be taxed to save the children of the underclass'. This unwillingness creates a situation in which those children cannot hope for a decent chance in life … [They] are no longer, if Posner's judgement of political feasibility is right … among 'we, the people of the United States', any more than their slave ancestors were when the US Constitution was written.

(Rorty, 1996, online edition)

Extrapolating to the global level, Rorty (1996) suggests that making 'decent life chances available to the poorer five billion citizens of the member states of the United Nations while still keeping intact the democratic socio-political institutions cherished by the richer one billion' is practically impossible, given that

> …nobody has written a scenario which shows how the people in the lucky industrialized democracies might redistribute their wealth in ways which create bright prospects for the children of the undeveloped countries without destroying the prospects of their own children and their own societies. The institutions of the rich democracies are now so intertwined with advanced methods of transportation and communication, and more generally with expensive technology, that it is hardly possible to imagine their survival if the rich countries had to reduce their share of the world's resources to a fraction of what they now consume. Democratic institutions in these countries depend on the existence of things like universal literacy, meritocratic social mobility, bureaucratic rationality, and the existence of many competing sources of information about public affairs. Free universities, a free press, incorruptible judges and unbribable police officers do not come cheap.
>
> (Rorty, 1996, online edition)

In the absence of such a scenario, it is either hypocritical or self-deceptive, according to Rorty, for the rich to claim membership of the same moral community as the poor, whether they are their fellow citizens or their fellow human beings, because 'to believe that someone is "one of us", a member of our moral community, is to exhibit readiness to come to their assistance when they are in need … Moral identification is empty when it is no longer tied to habits of action.' So long as the rich have no practical means of helping the poor which will leave the rich 'still able to recognize themselves', they are in a position equivalent to those fortunate survivors of a catastrophic accident or natural disaster whom the over-stretched and under-resourced medical staff have had to separate out from other survivors as 'appropriate recipients of the limited medical resources available'. Those who have to make these life and death decisions are

> …answering the question 'Who are we?' by excluding certain human beings from membership in 'We, the ones who can hope to survive'. When we realise that it is unfeasible to rescue a person or a group, it is as if they had already gone before us into death … For the sake of their

own sanity ... the doctors and nurses must simply blank out on all those moaning victims who are left outside in the street. They must cease to think about them, pretend they are already dead.

(Rorty, 1996, online edition)

This analogy from medical triage would not, of course, apply to the distribution of economic and social goods if there were a politically feasible scenario (that is, one which left the rich 'still able to recognize themselves') for narrowing the gap between the rich and the poor and, ultimately, for closing it. If there is such a scenario, it will certainly involve drastic changes to the role of the state as a 'particularistic moral agent' whose current territorial form provides the basis for defending privilege within its borders. If there is not, we must face the possibility that the governments of the industrialized states, their 'upper-class "clubs" (Galtung, 1998, p.212) such as the Organization for Economic Co-operation and Development and G8, the intergovernmental financial institutions they control and the inter-governmental and non-governmental organizations they fund, are engaged in an exercise of 'economic triage', the purpose of which is to maintain and improve the life chances of 'We who are rich'. We return to consider these troubling questions in the final chapter of this book, after exploring three more examples of displacement and development in the chapters which follow.

3 Diaspora and development
by Giles Mohan

Contents

Introduction to diaspora and development

The processes that relate to development have, generally, been linked to specific, quite fixed, notions regarding territories, boundaries, spaces and places. For example, we can identify forces which operate on a national scale, such as state-directed development or political action for social change. Then there are more local processes, which relate to individuals' responses to these effects and place a great deal of emphasis on participatory development, focusing on 'the community'. Finally, and directly linked to the others, is a sense in which those in the 'Western world' see 'development' as taking place 'out there' in a complex and indistinct region which has been called the 'Third World'.

None of these approaches to development is inaccurate or wrong, but they fail to capture a very important set of processes which I would argue is crucial to understanding contemporary development. This revolves around the simple fact that not all people who experience economic and political hardship are 'fixed' in their home communities. As Lavie and Swedenburg (1996, p.14), comment, 'the phenomenon of diasporas calls for re-imagining the "areas" of area studies and *developing units of analysis that enable us to understand the dynamics of transnational cultural and economic processes, as well as to challenge the conceptual limits imposed by national and ethnic/racial boundaries*' (my emphasis). A focus on diaspora and development challenges many of those geographical and historical preconceptions we have about development: that it is nationally or locally centred and, above all, that it occurs only in the 'Third World'.

For numerous reasons, people have been *displaced*, either voluntarily or involuntarily, as part of the process of development and/or as a response to underdevelopment. There are different motivations for moving and some individuals or groups, such as the better educated or more affluent, tend to be more mobile and to have more choice in any decision to move. The linkages between development and displacement are as diverse as they are numerous. Think about the millions of West Africans who were taken against their will to work as slaves on the plantations which enabled European industrial development. Or consider the thousands of colonial officials from Europe who travelled to far-flung parts of their respective empires to develop the interests of their homeland and (in their view) to 'advance' the 'natives'. Finally, consider the hypothetical case of an Indian migrant recently arrived in Britain, seeking advancement through higher education and intending to use these enhanced skills and increased earning power to support family back home. Although the motivations and impacts of these activities are obviously different, they all link displacement to development, as well as breaking down the assumption that the lives of people in the developed and developing worlds are unconnected.

This chapter develops these important issues. The displacements I am concerned with are not random groupings of people following random pathways across the globe, but they relate to those people who in some way identify themselves as sharing common cultural characteristics with co-members of a group and some sort of common heritage, which may be nothing more than their shared experience of displacement. The chapter examines how such transnational groupings, or **diasporas**, relate to processes of development. It seeks to examine *both the developmental forces generating diasporas and, perhaps more importantly, the ways in which diasporas play a role in development.* Diasporas are fragile transnational communities which often have to negotiate harsh new environments and frequently choose to connect with, and seek security from, people identified, in some way, as 'the same'. Such connections are cultural in the sense that 'sameness' is a perception rooted in practices and traditions as well as, more problematically, in race and skin colour. Questions of identity are important here, because they help us understand both the positive and negative experiences of diaspora and development. On the negative side, for example, one group may undertake ethnic cleansing based on perceived cultural differences and force another group to flee. On a more positive note, a shared identity might open up developmental opportunities, such as a New York-based construction company hiring workers from the owner's same ethnic group or homeland.

This chapter addresses three related questions:

1   What are diasporas, and what developmental factors generate them? Diasporas form for very different reasons and it is vital to understand these motivations, because they have implications for the social composition of diasporas and the type of developmental activity that they engage in.

2   Given the diverse origins of diasporas, how do we differentiate them from other transnational movements of people, such as tourists, and yet still be able to capture their unique features? Much of this differentiation revolves around questions of identity and the processes by which people determine who is and who is not part of a group, and the effects of this 'belonging' on the actual developmental activities of diasporas.

3   Once formed, how do diasporas contribute to the development of people in the diaspora as well as those back 'home'?

To examine these questions, the chapter has two main elements. The first, comprising Sections 3.1 and 3.2, is broadly conceptual and examines the theories of diaspora and the relationship between diaspora and identity. The second element, comprising Sections 3.3–3.6, concerns the emergence and impacts of diasporic developmental activities.

Section 3.1 examines differing theories and definitions of diaspora because, like most concepts in social science, diaspora is a contested and ever-changing term. It will become clear that the forces which generate diasporas create complex social, political and economic flows and connections. Diasporic communities simultaneously connect to their original 'homes', and make connections with members of the same diaspora within their new locality, as well as linking to diasporic members in other localities besides their home. Underpinning these connections are certain group affinities which we need to understand, and these issues are addressed in Section 3.2. Section 3.3 examines the complex inter-connections between diaspora and development. In order to do this I have devised a threefold categorization of development *in*, *through* and *by* the diaspora. However, in the lived experiences of people in diaspora, such 'academic' categories make little sense so it is vital that we also examine, through case studies, the ways in which these different aspects come together in the real lives of diasporic communities. The remaining sections focus on this: Sections 3.4–3.6 examine different aspects of diasporic development, looking at different networks and flows within diasporic groups. The final section is the conclusion, where I assess the future of diasporic development.

There are two main case studies running through these discussions, both of which relate to Africa and the African diaspora. The first of these considers the case of Freetown, the capital of Sierra Leone. Freetown was created for, and derives its name from, the freed slaves who were settled there in a philanthropic experiment which accompanied the abolition of slavery. From these utopian beginnings we will look at how the city, the country and various diasporas have evolved and how these ebbs and flows have supported or undermined development. The second example we pick up on relates to relatively recent African migrants seeking a living in France and the United States. We will see that the class background of migrants, in particular, makes a great difference to the opportunities open to them.

3.1 Conceptualizing diaspora and development

This section draws out the meanings associated with diaspora, especially those which distinguish diasporas from other sorts of international movements of people such as tourism or those resulting from warfare. Like any analytical definition, the key is to develop an understanding which can encompass the diversity of diasporic experiences without the term becoming so elastic that it is rendered meaningless.

3.1.1 Defining diaspora

The derivation of the word diaspora is a good starting point, because we can then see how its meaning has shifted in line with the changing political usage of the term. Diaspora is made up of the Greek verb *speiro* (to sow) and the preposition *dia* (over) (Cohen, 1997). From the point of view of the Ancient Greeks, diaspora had positive, if imperialist, connotations because it signified migration and the productive colonization of Asia Minor. However, diaspora gained more negative meanings in the subsequent millennia. Firstly, the enslavement and exile of the Jews from their Promised Land to Babylon around 586 BCE* saw diaspora associated with oppression, forced displacement and the endless search for a true homeland. Other 'victim' diasporas followed. The most notable have been those of East and West Africans through slavery, Palestinians through Israeli expansionism in the late 1940s and Armenians through persecution by the Ottomans from the late nineteenth century. These examples are united by the experience of being forced to leave a place either to avoid persecution and death or by being physically expelled by another group. We will look at such experiences in more detail a little later.

*BCE: before the Common Era

Figure 3.1 The expulsion of the Jews from their Promised Land to Babylon. This is an example of one of the earliest 'victim' diasporas.

From these conceptual beginnings we can identify a set of criteria for defining diasporas. Here I borrow Cohen's (1997) classification, which is presented in Box 3.1. Cohen's classification is particularly useful, because it extends beyond the rather narrow use of the word diaspora as referring to an essentially victim-based experience.

Box 3.1 Defining features of diaspora

Robin Cohen's (1997, p.26) nine-point typology captures both the positive and the negative associations of diaspora as well as the host of complex processes which link diasporic groups to their 'homes'.

1 Dispersal from an original homeland, often traumatically, to two or more foreign regions.

2 The expansion from a homeland in search of work, in pursuit of trade or to further colonial ambitions.

3 A collective memory and myth about the homeland, including its location, history and achievements.

4 An idealization of the putative ancestral home and a collective commitment to its maintenance, restoration, safety, prosperity, even to its creation.

5 The development of a return movement that gains collective support.

6 A strong ethnic group consciousness sustained over a long time and based on a sense of distinctiveness, a common history and the belief in a common fate.

7 A possibly troubled relationship with host societies, suggesting a lack of acceptance and/or the possibility that another calamity might befall the group.

8 A sense of empathy and solidarity with co-ethnic members in other countries of settlement.

9 The possibility of a distinctive creative, enriching life in host countries with a tolerance for pluralism.

Cohen's classification avoids the limitations of the more narrow definitions of diaspora in a number of ways:

First, it is noted that *not all diasporas are involuntary*, something which strongly affects their composition, outlook and developmental potential. Cohen (1997, p.27) observes that 'Being dragged off … being expelled, or being coerced to leave by force of arms appear qualitatively different phenomena from the general pressures of overpopulation, land hunger, poverty or an unsympathetic political regime'. In fact, as we shall see, some individuals actively use diasporic connections in order to exploit the interstices of a global economy which many would believe is simply the preserve of huge corporations. That said, and following Mitchell (1997, p.535), we must analyse all diasporic experiences empirically so that we do not romanticize or abstract these concepts 'away from the situated practices of everyday life'. For some, diaspora may be liberating, while for others their displacement is an ever-present trauma. It is for this reason that I give space in Sections 3.4–3.6 to examining the lived experiences of different diasporas.

Second, Cohen includes characteristics which see both 'a collective memory of home' (point 3 in Box 3.1) and a 'commitment to its physical well-being and rejuvenation' (points 4 and 5) as crucial to defining diasporas. This borrows from Safran's (1991, p.83–84) six-point 'ideal type' of diaspora. In terms of the origins and developmental activities of diaspora, Safran argues that a diaspora exists once people 'have been dispersed from a specific original "center" to two or more "peripheral", or foreign, regions [and] they regard their ancestral homeland as their true, ideal home and as the place to which they or their descendants would (or should) eventually return'. However, Clifford (1994) has argued that Safran builds his model too exclusively upon the Jewish experience, and also misunderstands the complexities of the Jewish diaspora. For example, the Jewish diaspora is much less homogeneous than Safran believes. As Cohen observes, it is actually only certain factions of this heterogeneous diaspora that have called for the restoration of an exclusive homeland, with many others reasonably content to put expulsion behind them and live in permanent 'exile'. More generally, though, it is true that members of a diasporic community with strong affinities with a homeland are more likely to support, either financially or politically, development efforts which seek to recreate or strengthen it.

Third, Cohen mentions that a 'sense of identification ties diasporas together' (points 6 and 8 in Box 3.1). In terms of the geographies of diaspora, point 8 adds a degree of complexity which will help us to understand how diffuse connections around the globe can be a developmental benefit for some diasporic communities. Safran stresses a binary pattern where all connections ultimately (aspire to) return 'home'. For Clifford (1994, p.306), and for our analysis of diasporic development, 'lateral connections may be as important as those formed around a teleology of origin/return'. This means that rather than viewing diasporas as comprising two points – home and exile – where exiles simply want to return home, we need to think about multiple sites of exile and, crucially, the connections between them. As diasporas evolve over time, the members (or their subsequent generations) may move again, yet retain links to their home, their original site of exile and those places in which other diasporic members have relocated. This greatly complicates the spatiality of diasporas and produces a geography of diaspora which is built around multiple localities connected by ever-changing networked relationships and flows.

The understanding of diaspora has altered since the word first came into being. It now denotes the spreading around the globe of people who share a number of common cultural traits. To differing degrees these people are connected through networks, although a relationship with 'home', either tangible or imagined, still exists. Diasporas differ in their origins and in the motivations of their members. Some are negative and others more positive, so it is important not to generalize about them. This means that we need a definition of diaspora which allows us to examine different types of diaspora as well as to examine in more detail the lived experiences of people in diaspora, especially in relation to development. It is to the first of these tasks that we now turn.

3.1.2 Development and the origins of diaspora

Having outlined Cohen's general definition of diasporas, I want to begin to examine its implications for our more specific focus on diaspora and development. The first task is to appreciate the origins of diasporas, and some of the different developmental factors which have led to their emergence.

Types of diaspora

Cohen (1997) identifies types of diaspora, all of which are tied to different origins, different motivations and different effects (see Box 3.2).

Box 3.2 Types of diaspora

In his book Robin Cohen (1997) discusses, chapter by chapter, different types of diaspora. He begins with the foundational 'victim' diasporas which, as we have seen, have tended to dominate the imagining of diasporas. However, other diasporas – both positive and negative – do exist and they all link to development in various ways:

- **Victim diasporas** involve concerted persecution of one group by another and the forcible eviction of the persecuted from their homeland. It most often refers to the Jewish experience, but Africans, Armenians, Irish and Palestinians, amongst others, can also be considered to be victim diasporas.

- **Trade diasporas** involve a group proactively dispersing to serve one or more markets in places other than their homeland. They circulate between home and these distant places and tend to congregate with fellow traders in their host societies. Hence, they are always identifiably different from their local communities and never really settle, remaining sojourners. Examples of trade diasporas include the Phoenicians, Venetians, Lebanese and Chinese.

- **Labour diasporas** involve groups either travelling voluntarily in search of a range of employment opportunities or under semi-forced conditions, in the case of indentured labour, to work in menial labouring jobs. Examples of these diasporas include Indians, Chinese, Sikhs, Turks and Italians.

- **Imperial diasporas** involve the proactive colonization of foreign lands to be used as resource bases to service the imperial home. These diasporas include the Ancient Greeks, British, French, Dutch and Russians.

- **Cultural diasporas** have created shared cultural codes and styles which unite communities in their exiled status and lead to new de-territorialized identities. These include the Caribbean and Indian diasporas.

Cohen's typology shows that people have been displaced by various mechanisms and for various reasons. In some cases it is the forced displacement of one group by another in the name of nationalism, or as a result of civil strife. These are essentially *negative* motivations for entering diaspora. However, other reasons are more proactive, with groups seeking to improve the opportunities for their country in the case of imperial diasporas, or individuals aiming to make money for their family through trading. These are more *positive* motivations for entering diaspora. On top of this, many diasporas evolve over time in a piecemeal and circular fashion, with different motivations operating at different time periods and for different social groups. There may have been an original *negative* event which forced people into exile, but successive generations may follow family and kin members for more *positive* reasons and, therefore, have different experiences of the diaspora. So, diasporas are spatially and temporally dynamic with previous flows generating new flows and, on occasion, return flows. We will look at these issues for the case of Freetown, Sierra Leone.

Case study: Out of Africa

Here I want to use Cohen's definition and typology of diasporas to examine the case of one set of African people who were forced to leave their homelands and became part of a slave diaspora, subsequently going on to settle again in the capital city of Freetown, Sierra Leone. It may seem strange to begin our elaboration of development and *displacement* with a case study of a *settlement*, but as Massey (1994, p.154) comments, places 'can be imagined as articulated moments in networks of social relations and understandings, but where a large proportion of those relations, experiences and understandings are constructed *on a far larger scale* than what we happen to define for that moment as the place itself' (my emphasis); in short, Massey describes the idea of 'a global sense of place'.

From its inception Freetown has been the product of both place-specific and larger-scale development processes, with three distinct phases in the *outward* movement of people from Sierra Leone and from West Africa more generally. The first phase is associated with slavery, the second with commonwealth citizens seeking livelihoods in the colonial 'motherland', and the third with a response to the post-colonial crisis of development.

The first phase
It was the Portuguese who, in the sixteenth century, 'discovered' the hilly peninsula on the west coast of Africa and named it Sierra Leone. ('Sierra Leone' translates as 'Lion Mountains' – from the sea the mountains resembled a lion's head. Paradoxically, no lions have ever been seen in the territory that encompasses modern Sierra Leone.) For the next two centuries, the west coast of Africa became notorious as

the source of slaves for the plantations in the Americas and the Caribbean. The slave trade displaced an estimated 10 million Africans, many of whom died before they reached the other side of the Atlantic (Segal, 1998). This absolute exploitation of labour fuelled the industrial development of Western Europe while simultaneously siphoning off the labour and skills that could have aided Africa's own development (not to mention the psychological and social disruption, or underdevelopment, it caused). This period marked the first, and undeniably negative, phase in the creation of an African diaspora. Throughout the rest of the chapter we will see how the movement and settlement of people of African origin as part of the slave trade, be they in the United States, the Caribbean or Europe, have shaped the fortunes of this diaspora.

Figure 3.2 Slaves below deck on a slave ship. The slave trade displaced an estimated 10 million people, with many dying during the journey.

The second phase

With increasing criticism of slavery and its ultimate abolition at the start of the nineteenth century, as we will discuss in more detail in the next section, Freetown became a settlement for released slaves and later a British colony supplying agricultural produce to Britain's booming manufacturing sector. Although Sierra Leone had an acknowledged mineral wealth, it was not fully exploited until the 1950s, when production increased greatly, bringing new corporate arrivals and generating much internal and regional migration (Riddell, 1970). The primary minerals were diamonds, rutile and bauxite. This created massive economic gains at a time when the colony was heading for independence as the 'winds of change' blew across the continent.

During the period around the Second World War, 'some of the more ambitious young men' (Banton, 1957, p.35) migrated to London, which many Sierra Leoneans referred to as 'home', in search of their fortunes. Indeed, Banton goes on, the 'number of these migrants was sufficient to cause the United Kingdom authorities considerable concern in the years following the war so that more effective controls were later imposed.' As I said in the introduction to this chapter, such movements are never random, but follow a certain logic, which in this case was movement to the colonial metropole. This marked the second phase in the outward movement of Africans into diaspora.

The third phase

With independence in 1961 came the arrival of 'kleptocratic rule' where a foreign-dominated minerals sector and crises of governance allowed the political authorities, quite literally, to rule by thieving. This downward development spiral reached its nadir in the mid-1990s (Reno, 1995; 1996; Zack-Williams, 1990). This period saw marked outward migration as mainly middle class professionals travelled to Europe and the United States in search of work and to escape violence. This stripped the country of its human capital base, with, for example, 'a mass exodus of highly experienced (university) staff to other institutions outside Sierra Leone' (Zack-Williams, 1990, p.28). Hence, the third phase in this complex diasporic journey began with Sierra Leoneans travelling to join family and/or diasporic communities in places already settled by previous waves of their kinfolk.

Study of the Sierra Leone case shows that at different times people left because of slavery, to improve themselves in the colonial metropolis or to escape the ravages of maldevelopment and poor governance. The motivations for entering diaspora clearly varied over time, and these varying motivations produced different types and experiences of diaspora. These differences also had different implications for the developmental potential of diasporic communities.

Summary of Section 3.1

In this section we have looked at the theoretical debates surrounding diasporas and their linkages with processes of development.

- Using Robin Cohen's typologies of diaspora we have seen how the term has been expanded beyond its usual associations with victimization.

- In particular, diasporas can form for positive reasons in which individuals and groups seek a better quality of life outside their home.

- The Freetown and Sierra Leone case study demonstrates how different developmental forces have propelled people to leave the area over the past 400 years.

3.2 Identities and diaspora

Having dealt with the developmental forces which generate diasporas we need to turn to the second key issue identified in the introduction to this chapter, concerning cultural identity within diasporic communities. The primary factor which distinguishes a diaspora from other transnational movements is the *shared cultural values that members hold*. Understanding this complex issue is a necessary step before we can look at how these affiliations and sense of belonging affect concrete developmental activities.

Cohen's definition of diaspora (Box 3.1) includes the existence of 'a collective memory and myth about the homeland', 'a strong ethnic group consciousness', 'a troubled relationship with host societies', and 'a sense of empathy and solidarity with co-ethnic members'. These cultural factors relating to 'group belonging' and 'home' are central to the developmental potential of diasporas in two ways:

1   They affect the level of internal cohesion of a diaspora, which influences the degree of solidarity and trust. In turn, this solidarity and trust determines the desire and ability of members of a diasporic community to work with each other, either in a single 'host' locality or through networked relationships to other places where the diaspora is spread.

2   The cultural identity of diasporic communities is in part a product of their affinity with 'home' which in turn affects the degree to which they wish to support, either politically or financially, the development of this home.

An obvious, but paradoxical, dimension of displacement is that it necessarily involves (re)placement, because we all have to exist somewhere in space and time. As Brah (1996, p.182) observes, 'diasporic journeys are essentially about settling down, about putting roots "elsewhere"'. The social, political and economic conditions of the locality where a person is (re)settled, or re-rooted, shape their identity and affect their life choices in that place. For diasporic communities the reception in these new places often ranges from wariness to suspicion to outright hostility. It is this sense of being different from the hosts that, in part, shapes the solidarity and identification with fellow members of the diaspora. However, this identification with fellow members is not built out of nothing, but includes some traces of shared cultural identity associated with 'home' or place of origin. Such a 'double consciousness', of being in a 'new' place but connected to an 'old' place, is central to the experience of diasporic communities and affects their economic, social, political and cultural existence. We will look at these processes at work in the (re)settlement of Freetown, before examining more generally the complex processes of identity formation in place and their potential impacts on development.

Case study: (Re)settling Freetown and making a home in Africa

While the West Coast of Africa was a source of slaves and other commodities, the colonies and states of this region were also (re)settled by waves of different, incoming, diasporas. Just as there were three waves of displacement out of West Africa, there have been three waves of (re)settlement into Freetown.

The first phase

The first phase of settlement occurred towards the end of the eighteenth century and at the beginning of the nineteenth century. In the latter half of the eighteenth century, criticism of slavery grew amongst political reformers, primarily in Britain and the United States. In February 1787, by the arrangement of Granville Sharp and funded by a group of London philanthropists, *The Nautilus* and three smaller ships left Portsmouth bound for West Africa in order to found 'The Province of Freedom'. They carried around 300 former slaves, many of whom had been living in poverty in London after their release from slavery in other countries. On arrival Captain Thompson bought 20 square miles of the peninsula, which he named 'Granville Town'. In 1792, 1000 more former slaves were brought back from Nova Scotia where they had been given land by the British as a goodwill gesture for their efforts in the American Revolution. It was with the Nova Scotians that the settlement of Granville Town grew and became Freetown. This was followed in 1800 by 300 Maroons who had fought in Jamaica and were also returned to Africa by the British. So, Freetown was a diasporic city from the start with its original inhabitants, known as **settlers**, drawn from different points of the Atlantic trade. In addition to these settlers was a European diaspora who sought to create a utopian society which would reflect

Figure 3.3
Granville Sharp
protecting a slave.

all that was noble in Africans. This period in Freetown's development can be seen as a positive attempt to fashion a better society for people of the African diaspora, even though the realities never quite matched the good intentions.

It was hoped that some local form of governance would prevail in Freetown, but the British administration was relatively incompetent and the degree of social solidarity within the incipient colony was lacking. With British support for the experiment floundering, the governance of Freetown was handed over to the Sierra Leone Company (a commercial company sponsored by English opponents of the slave trade) between 1792 and 1807 under the governorship of Lieutenant Clarkson, something which 'guaranteed a degree of order not unlike that of an Enlightened Despotism' (Peterson, 1968, p.15). In 1807 the British Parliament passed an act which abolished slavery. This saw the British Navy patrolling the Atlantic and capturing slaves from the ships of rival powers who persisted in the trade. Without a clear plan of what to do with these slaves, the British decided to settle them also in Sierra Leone. These slaves were known as **recaptives** and marked a major expansion in Freetown's diasporic community. Between 1808 and 1877, approximately 74 000 recaptives settled in and around Freetown in specially designated villages.

The second and third phases

The second phase of settlement (by Europeans and local Africans) coincided with colonial exploitation, which lasted for about 70 years, from the 1890s until independence in 1961. Freetown's subsequent development was fuelled by the massive port facilities, at one time the third largest in the world, and export crops such as palm oil which saw the interior opened up by the railways. In 1896, following the 1884 Berlin Conference which partitioned Africa between the European powers, the hinterland of Freetown became the Sierra Leone Protectorate.

The third phase began around the turn of the twentieth century, when Freetown experienced a small, but significant, influx of another diaspora – the Lebanese. From the late nineteenth century, Lebanese began leaving their country to escape grinding poverty and persecution by the Ottomans. They arrived in small numbers and worked hard in the trading sector, soon establishing themselves as a powerful economic and political force in Freetown. For the Lebanese a negative experience of persecution created a strong desire to succeed, so that being in diaspora became a more positive and enriching experience. Such paradoxes recur within diasporas, because they usually arise from a desire for a better life, so that escaping a negative experience can open up more positive opportunities.

In the sections which follow we will see examples of how some groups manage to use the diasporic condition to build an enriching life.

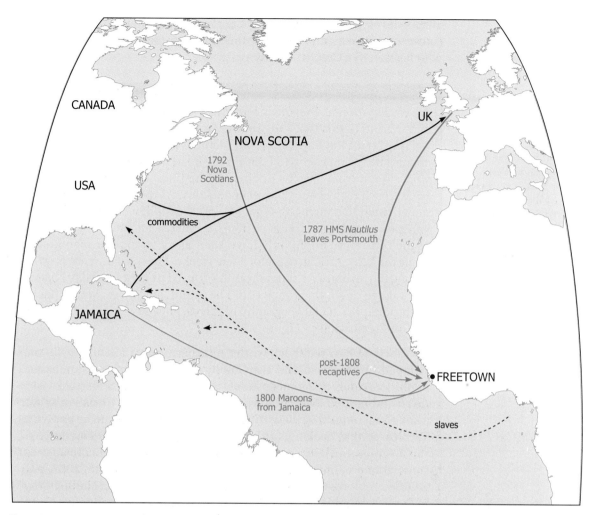

Figure 3.4 The triangular trade and the founding of Freetown: settlers came to Sierra Leone from different points of the Atlantic trade and Europe.

3.2.1 Contested identities in place

As a diasporic community (re)settles it inevitably has to confront and work through the sense of 'difference' that it experiences with respect to already established communities in the same place. This need not be outright hostility, but the relationships between different groups determine the degree to which diasporic community members identify with each other and the practical outcomes of this in terms of livelihood activities. For example, an ethnic group arriving in a new country may be greeted with extreme prejudice, which will force them to seek security and support from fellow group members, thereby reinforcing their sense of commonality and strengthening the tendency to create 'enclave' economies such as Chinatowns. This section untangles these complex cultural relationships 'in place' in order for us to understand, in subsequent sections, the practical means by which this underpins and affects developmental activity. We begin by returning to nineteenth-century Freetown and the fate of the returnees (settlers or freed slaves) who fashioned a Creole identity.

Case study: Identity and development in nineteenth-century Freetown

*A more general definition of the term 'Creole' is given in Box 3.5 in Section 3.2.2 below. Briefly, it refers to the racial and cultural intermixing which occurs in colonial contexts, and which often results in the emergence of distinctive Creole dialects and cultures.

As we have seen, Freetown has always been a diasporic settlement and it is out of this that a distinctive Creole* identity emerged. What is striking about the population of Freetown is that despite the desire to create a utopian beacon to light up the heart of Africa, the freed slaves were drawn from various origins and had no natural affinity besides having been lucky enough to escape slavery. As they settled in Freetown they tended to congregate together with kinsfolk who spoke the same language and shared similar customs. It must be remembered that many of the recaptives might only have been away from their real 'homes' along the West African coast for a few weeks. The most numerous group among the recaptive diaspora was the Yoruba from present day Nigeria, but a range of ethnic groups could be found, and these were reflected in the complex social geography of the various 'towns' which grew up within Freetown (see Figure 3.5).

As Lewis (1954, p.32) notes, the returnees 'were all *mixed up* and *mingled* in Freetown and the Colony villages in the mountains and foothills. Widely different customs, traditions, ideas, racial stocks were *fused* and *melted* together' (my emphasis). However, Christianity was a key element uniting these different groups, who came to be known as Creoles, so that 'lacking any common factor in their African heritage, the Creoles built up their churches, chapels and ecclesiastical associations as important integrative institutions' (Banton, 1957, p.6). Another important integrative factor was education, especially literacy in English, but this sat alongside the development of a distinctive Creole language. As Banton goes on, 'The Creoles wore European clothes and adopted many of the values of Victorian society in their public life. They developed a distinctive dialect version of the English language, known as *Krio*, which incorporates Portuguese, African, and other loan words, has an African rather than a European syntax, and is incomprehensible to the untrained English ear.'

An important aspect of understanding identity is the distinction between what we might call 'relationality' and 'hybridity'. On the one hand, one group's identity can be defined by what another group's is not (i.e. in relation to one another) and at the same time the two groups can influence one another and evolve new cultural mixtures (hybridity). As a result we see the emergence of complex social hierarchies based on perceived and subtle characteristics of difference. This is clearly demonstrated in the changing nature of Creole identity throughout the nineteenth century and its relationship to both the British and 'Africans'. Some Creoles lived amongst the Europeans, but most tended to reside in designated areas or in the purposively established villages across the peninsula. Beyond the Creole villages were the 'native' or indigenous Africans who for the settlers (Creole and European) represented all that was untamed about Africa. The Creoles, quite literally, acted as a bulwark between the Europeans and the natives. Given their position encircling the hinterland of Freetown, they could fend off any attacks from the disenchanted 'tribes'.

This intermediary position enabled the Creoles to secure relatively high status occupations within the colonial civil service, with ancillary interests in trade and property. The Creoles, with one foot in each culture, were ideally suited to the colonial project of exploiting Africans and maintaining law and order. However, by the latter half of the nineteenth century and through the early twentieth century, the Creole oligarchy was under threat, caught between local African resistance and British colonial dominance. The paradoxical identity of the Creoles, fashioned in opposition to both British and African values, has led some to argue that they sowed the seeds of their own demise. The following passages demonstrate this downside of hybridity.

> In a society where Western education and cultural values determined one's position, the original settlers, the returnees, were naturally a favoured group; they were Westernized, educated and, above all, Christians ... [However] neither European nor 'civilized', the liberated Africans [nonetheless] found integration into their new home quite problematic. In employment, they were discriminated against: employers preferred labourers from among those already resident in the area. Others were fortunate to be hired as policemen and teachers; but the majority were resettled in villages on the periphery of central Freetown, to till the land or be apprenticed to tradesman to acquire skills with which they could become useful members of society...
>
> (Abdullah, 1998, p.85)

> [In 1898] a widespread native rising was precipitated by the imposition of a hut tax intended in part to defray the costs of constructing a railway. Nine whites and more than two hundred Creoles were murdered. In these attacks the tribes of the immediate hinterland showed that they regarded the Creoles as black Europeans...
>
> (Banton, 1957, p.10)

The extracts show that the Creoles were caught in a pincer between the British on the one hand and the Africans on the other, despite sharing many cultural values with the former and a superficial similarity of skin colour with the latter. By the turn of the twentieth century the Lebanese diaspora spread to Sierra Leone and took over much of the trade carried out by Creoles; a case study in Section 3.5.1 considers the changing fortunes of the Lebanese trade diaspora. The Creoles consolidated a 'hybrid' identity, drawing on both African and English features, but did so in a tense relational context, caught between indigenous opposition and British domination.

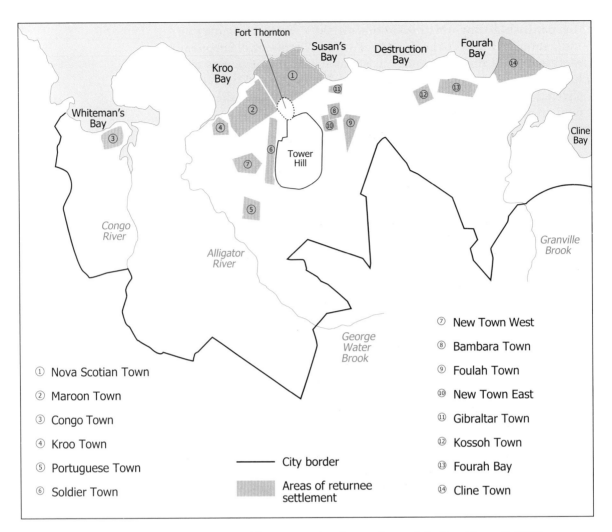

Figure 3.5 'Ethnic' map of Freetown, showing the different areas of settlement. Source: Fyfe, C. and Jones, E. (1968) 'The foundings of Freetown', *Freetown: A Symposium*, Sierre Leone University Press.

The following section draws out some lessons from this case study for understanding diasporic identities in general.

3.2.2 Identity formation

Brah (1996, p.182) suggests that 'if the circumstances of leaving are important, so, too are those of arrival and settling down'. In this section I trace out the cultural relationships between 'host' and 'exile' communities and the ways in which these shape diasporic identity. As the case of the Creoles indicates, identities are formed in relation to other people or groups (Rose, 1995). The Creoles, for example, saw themselves as neither British nor 'African', but as a unique and identifiable group. But the forging of new identities also involves the creation of shared meanings about how a society or group functions –

shared understandings which in this case reflected the emergence of hybrid cultural forms drawing on both African and British influences. The sources of these shared meanings are numerous and include such things as language, religion and place (Hall, 1995). The Creoles, drawing on a range of cultural influences in Sierra Leone and beyond, were united by their Christianity, their use of the English language and their privileged location within the cosmopolitan urban peninsula of Freetown, which was spatially and socially distinct from the rest of Sierra Leone.

Let us discuss in more detail firstly the ways in which diasporic identities are formed in relation to other groups. Rose (1995) argues that identity formation is at least partly about contrasting the self in relation to another, thereby constructing a sense of difference. This encourages a focus on the distinctive features of different groups and the tensions between them.

Hall has written extensively about this, specifically in relation to questions of English identity. The excerpt in Box 3.3 shows that a sense of Englishness, a positive or 'centred' sense of who one is, has partly been fashioned out of negatively defining 'others'. As Hall states 'you are what they are not'. In the Creole example, we saw similar processes at work in the forging of a diasporic group identity. On the one hand, the Creoles saw the 'Africans' as inferior and in need of discipline, while on the other hand they were proud of being black and of their difference from the Europeans. Throughout most of the nineteenth century the Creoles used this relative confidence about their identity to push for decent jobs, housing and the other privileges of 'development'.

Box 3.3 Relational identities and Englishness

This extract from Hall (1991, p.20–21) captures the nature of relational identity as its pertains to a sense of Englishness. The process of identifying differences that Hall talks about can apply to smaller group identifications than a nation, such as a middle class suburb, or even right down to the individual level.

> The 'English eye' sees everything else but is no good at recognizing that it is itself actually looking at something ... That is to say, it is strongly centred; knowing where it is, what it is, it places everything else. And the thing which is wonderful about English identity is that it didn't only place the colonized Other, it placed *everybody* else.

> To be English is to know yourself in relation to the French, and the hot-blooded Mediterraneans, and the passionate, traumatized Russian soul. You go round the entire globe: when you know what everybody else is, then you are what they are not. Identity is always, in that sense, a structured representation which only achieves its positive through the narrow eye of the negative. It has to go through the eye of the needle before it can construct itself.

In this way group identities form relationally, although they are never static, but are continually being renegotiated as relations between groups change. For diasporic groups, such dynamism can be what gives them a relative advantage over the 'host' groups. For example, the Creoles took advantage of their intermediary position between the English and the Africans by assuming the position of the administrative class who could 'understand' the cultures of both groups. However, as the second aspect of identity formation (cultural hybridity) demonstrates, boundaries between and in relation to other groups are never watertight or fixed.

The second process in diasporic identity formation relates to the creation of shared meanings held by the respective group. For communities who have been displaced into new surroundings these shared meanings are rarely 'fixed', but are instead constituted from multiple influences which, in turn, produce many localized and contextual forms. These hybrid identities encompass a variety of what Hall (1995) has termed 'systems of meaning'. He notes that 'cultures consist of different systems which produce meaning, which classify the world *meaningfully*' (p.179). These systems include language, religion, customs and representations such as art. We have seen that for the Creoles their Christianity was perhaps the prime means by which they achieved some sense of meaning and shared cultural identity. Additionally, despite gaining advantage from and being proud of their ability to speak English, we saw that the Creoles also developed their own language – Krio – which marked them out as distinct and different. Language was not only a means of communicating but a way of signifying their uniqueness and providing a means to socialize successive generations into knowing what it meant to 'be Creole'.

The excerpts in Box 3.4 capture the evidence of hybridity in a description of how the shared meanings of black-British identity are drawn from diverse sources and are continually being added to and reshaped. Box 3.5 defines the family of related academic terms used to capture these complex processes of cultural formation.

Box 3.4 Diaspora identity in Britain

These extracts come from Gilroy's (1987) *There Ain't No Black in the Union Jack* which examines the 'cultural politics of race and nation'. The excerpts capture the tensions between group identity forged both in relation to other cultures and through 'syncretism' (see Box 3.5) or multiple cultural influences. Gilroy argues that 'national units are not the most appropriate basis for studying this history for the African diaspora's consciousness of itself has been defined in and against constricting national boundaries' (1987, p.158). There is an interaction between a deterritorialized diasporic consciousness and local urban territorialized experiences, generating a multitude of different 'hybrid' cultural practices and political responses.

Black Britain defines itself crucially as part of a diaspora. Its unique cultures draw inspiration from those developed by black populations elsewhere. In particular, the culture and politics of black America and the Caribbean have become raw materials for creative processes which redefine what it means to be black, adapting it to distinctively British experiences and meanings. Black culture is actively made and re-made... (p.154)

Black expressive cultures affirm while they protest. The assimilation of blacks is not a process of acculturation but of cultural syncretism (Bastide, 1978). Accordingly, their self-definitions and cultural expressions draw on a plurality of black histories and politics. In the context of modern Britain this has produced a diaspora dimension to black life. Here, non-European traditional elements, mediated by the histories of Afro-America and the Caribbean, have contributed to the formation of new and distinct black cultures amidst the decadent peculiarities of the Welsh, Irish, Scots and English. These non-European elements must be noted and their distinctive resonance accounted for... (p.155–156)

Bob Marley's reggae was, like all reggae, a hybrid marked as much by its ties to American rhythm and blues as by its roots in Mento and calypso... (p.172)

...the hip-hop scene formed as the Jamaican sound system culture was adapted to the experiences of urban New York. This expressive sub-culture has in turn been imported into Britain as a style in its own right. Hip-hop revels in the reduction of music to its essential African components of rhythm and voice... (p.211)

Box 3.5 Cultural hybridity

Based on Ashcroft et al. *(1998), Hannerz (1997) and Loomba (1998)*

The language associated with diaspora culture and identity can be confusing. Many writers have adopted metaphors to try to capture the fluidity of diasporic identities which are neither here nor there, but somehow 'in between'. The definitions which follow should help you in negotiating the complexities involved in thinking about diasporic cultures, although it must be stressed that these are a 'family' of linked terms rather than being synonymous and interchangeable.

Hybridity: This is perhaps the most commonly used of these words relating to fluid and changing identities. It is a biological metaphor relating to the cross-pollination of two distinct species to produce a new and unique hybrid species. Recently, cultural theorist Homi Bhabha (1994) has championed hybridity as a productive outcome of colonizer–colonized contact. Rather than seeing this as a process whereby two cultures meet and one is dominant, Bhabha looks at the mutual (or relational) construction of subjectivities that this contact entails. This means that both colonzier and colonized shape each other's sense of identity, suggesting that claims to a hierarchy of bounded and pure cultures (colonizer over colonized) are untenable.

Creole: Originating in the plantation societies of the New World (i.e. North and South America) this referred to a white person born and raised in the Colonies. Later it was extended to all non-Europeans and specifically the languages they spoke, although its meaning varies according to who is using it. For example, in Peru it refers to people of Spanish origin, whereas in Sierra Leone it is those people who are descended from slaves. Creolization refers to the intermixing and cultural change that produces a Creole society, especially in the Caribbean and South American regions. As such it is a process producing an hybridity which is productive and enriching rather than antagonistic and destabilizing.

Liminality: This word derives from *limen* meaning 'threshold'. It refers to an in-between space where cultural change may occur. Again, Bhabha (1994) has popularized the term and uses the image of a stairwell 'between' floors to evoke liminality. It is in the interaction between cultures, then, that new cultural forms emerge.

Mestizo: A Spanish word relating to racial and/or cultural mixing. It was originally used to refer to the contact between the Spanish and the native Indians in South America and the offspring of their inter-racial unions. The rather negative implied meaning has been transformed and now mestizo is played up as a positive 'national' identity in Latin America.

Syncretism: Refers to the combining of two or more distinct traditions into a new cultural form that is different from its 'parents'. A common usage is in the study of religions where 'formal' religions such as Christianity merge with localized belief systems. As such, it is clearly an in-between word, but some prefer it to 'hybridity' because it avoids the racial and genetic inflections of the latter.

In summary, the issue of cultural identity is central to the definition, delimitation and cohesion of diasporic communities. Cultural identity is fashioned along two key axes. The first is in relation to other groups, where one group defines itself in opposition to another. We saw this quite clearly in the example of the Creoles of Freetown defining themselves in relation to both British and African cultures. Second, identities are shaped around shared cultural meanings which are solidified in the practices of a particular group. Such things include customs, religion, language and a sense of place. However, such processes of identity formation are not static, but are dynamic and fluid. This produces multiple hybrid identities which change over time. Just as places are not bounded and fixed but are shaped by external forces, group identities are shaped and reshaped by the ebb and flow of local and non-local influences, as we saw in the case of black-British identity. Such a process of mingling or hybridizing is context-specific so we cannot easily generalize and must, instead, focus on specific cases. However, for diasporic communities the symbolic and actual existence of a home(land) is one crucial and often distinctive element of both their identity and their developmental potential. The following section explores the role of the idea of 'home' in the formation of diasporic identity.

3.2.3 Imagining and developing home(land)s

Diasporic identities often draw heavily on a set of cultural factors relating to the construction of home in the diasporic imagination. This section will consider the effects of this on experiences of exile as well as on desires for the reconstruction or development of home. In Cohen's words, diasporas are defined by a 'collective memory' and often by an 'idealization of a putative ancestral home'. Given that people living in a diaspora are separated from their home, this certainly involves an 'imagined' homeland but, as we shall see, these imaginings can also be linked to important material effects. First, the case study below considers how Sierra Leone has been imagined and constructed as a homeland for various individuals and groups.

Case study: Developing the 'African' homeland

Sierra Leone in the eighteenth and nineteenth centuries presents an interesting example of the imagining of a homeland and the ways in which this fed into discussions of and practices for development. (We will consider such issues further in Section 3.6.3, on pan-Africanism.) The eighteenth- and nineteenth-century abolitionists who organized the resettlement of Sierra Leone were humanitarians who believed in the ideals of the Enlightenment*. For them Freetown was an 'experiment' in humanism and Christian salvation. They felt they could return Africans back to their 'home', where a natural order would then prevail. Hence, they could construct 'a perfect society ... [Granville] Sharp and his supporters sought to create in the West African colony a living memorial to their enlightened values' (Peterson, 1968, p.11). As Lewis (1954, p.32) exclaims, with some irony, 'the new colony was to be a beacon on the coast of savage Africa: a light to lighten the Gentiles still sunk in superstition'. These efforts, while clearly philanthropic, were based upon the idea of Africa as a raw canvas upon which to create an honourable society for a new generation of Africans freed from the degradations of slavery. In Freetown, as we saw, the process of restoring Africa to its 'natural order' was handed over to the enlightened Christian Creoles, but other influential diasporic activists were also part of this endeavour.

*The Enlightenment refers to a period in the latter half of the eighteenth century which is associated with a fundamental change in how people felt society should be organized. In particular, Enlightenment scholars and opinion leaders believed in a rational and ordered society where institutions ensured that citizens were treated fairly and equally.

The work of the African diasporic scholar and activist Edward Wilmot Blyden offers one example of such efforts among the early African diaspora, including its prescriptions for Africa's development. Blyden was born in 1832 on St Thomas, a Danish-held island in the Caribbean, but from 1851 he settled in West Africa, with periods acting as a government official in both Liberia and Sierra Leone. He was a 'proto' pan-Africanist who believed in a unique 'African personality', which is a belief that has informed African nationalists right up to present day 'Afrocentric' historians. Like the European theorists, Blyden saw African and European cultures as quite different, but unlike the Europeans he did not see Africans as irredeemably beyond civilization. Instead, he felt that to nurture and develop the African personality, specific types of learning and action were needed. In his book, *Christianity, Islam and the Negro Race*, Blyden argued:

> The native African, like all Oriental or tropical people, can see no reason or property in extra work, as long as he has enough to supply his wants. But he is imitative. And as the English language is diffused in his country, vivified by its domiciliation on the American continent ... the native will be raised unconsciously; and, in spite of hereditary tendencies and surroundings, will work, not, then, in order to enjoy repose ... but to be able to do more work, and to carry out higher objects...

> (Blyden, 1967; quoted in Mudimbe, 1988, p.103)

For Blyden the only people capable of bringing about African development were 'enlightened' fellow Africans, by which he meant those educated members of the diaspora such as Creoles. His prescriptions presage many of the ideas we find later in Garveyism*, pan-Africanism and Afrocentricity (see Section 3.6.3). These are that Africans are inherently different from Europeans, that African society is communal and 'naïve', and that only enlightened outsiders of African origin can really understand and speak of the African situation and, hence, only they can really 'save' the continent.

*Marcus Garvey was a pan-African nationalist and founder of the Universal Negro Improvement Association. We will return to discuss his ideas further in Section 3.6.3.

Thus, we see that while it is true that members of a diaspora often have an idealistic and unreal view of home, sometimes these images can be informed by the ignorant (and often racist) assumptions of those not of the diaspora. In the example above, Africa was seen by Europeans as a blank canvas peopled by noble, but ill-educated, tribes. There was no real sense of the diversity of African societies, their massive technical capabilities, the structural problems they faced or even the very different geographical conditions they experienced. The African 'home' to which the diaspora might return was imagined by diasporic scholars of the time in these borrowed static and simplistic terms.

Contrasting understandings of home

When thinking about the importance of home in diasporic identities more generally we can approach it in two ways which echo very strongly our earlier discussions of relational identity and cultural mixing. One interpretation suggests that home is a peaceful haven which is unchanging and homogeneous. This invokes a singular essence of home and is termed **essentialist**. An alternative view, like the idea of hybridity, is more complex and suggests that the concept of home is not only dynamic, but that it is defined differently depending on who does the defining and where they are. This view is termed **anti-essentialist** or **pluralist** (Allen, 2000).

Hall (1990) and Gilroy (1993a) have explored the political and cultural effects of conflicting understandings of home in shaping diasporic identity. They both focus on the Caribbean, but despite their focus on a particular, and in Cohen's (1997) eyes peculiarly cultural, diaspora, their discussions can apply more generally. The key is the way in which *a sense of home is constructed in the imagination*.

The essentialist version sees the 'homeland' as utopian and unchanging with exile marking the beginnings of an existence in the wilderness. It is this idealization of 'home' that generates the desire to 'return' or at least to support the development of that 'home'. Cohen (1997, p.106) discusses the examples of the Sikh and Israeli diasporas, and their quest for a homeland. These cases are quite extreme examples of the kinds of development which stem from essentialist imaginings of an 'ideal' homeland and a strong myth of 'return'. In the case of the Israelis, this included the (re)creation of a homeland that the diaspora believed had been taken away from them.

The clear alternative to this is a pluralist sense of home which is related to the ideas about cultural hybridity discussed above. To capture this more complex idea of 'home', Gilroy followed the renowned African-American scholar Du Bois[*] who, in discussing African-Americans at the turn of the twentieth century, described their sense of identity as a form of 'double consciousness'. This meant that being part of the African diaspora means being simultaneously part of the 'West', yet radically different from it because of both racial and cultural difference. Underlying this sense of difference is a distant and complex understanding of home, origins and roots associated with the memory of enslavement and forced displacement. This creates an understanding of cultural identity and belonging that 'is not a fixed essence at all, lying unchanged outside history and culture' (Hall, 1994, p.395). African-Americans, for example, find resources for a hybrid cultural identity in both African and American histories. But equally, it is the movement between places, across the Atlantic and perhaps back again, or between Western and African cultural elements, which shapes their identity. It is

[*]See Du Bois, W.E.B. (1989) *The Souls of Black Folk*, Bantam, New York [first published in 1903].

for this reason that Gilroy (1993b) uses the term 'black Atlantic' rather than African or Caribbean diaspora, because he believes it is impossible and unwise to delimit origins and destinations in what is a continually swirling current of cultural and economic interchange.

From this approach we get a sense of home which is pluralist, because there is no singular and essential home, but a diversity of places and journeys which are drawn on to construct a sense of common identity. This approach also acknowledges the importance of historical change. In talking about the relationship between Caribbean identity and the African home, Hall comments: 'the original "Africa" is no longer there. It too has been transformed. History is, in that sense, irreversible' (Hall, 1994, p.399). In contrast with the Enlightenment imagination of a unified African homeland to which freed slaves could return (as in Sierra Leone), a pluralist understanding leads Appiah (1993, p.26) to argue quite emphatically that 'whatever Africans share, we do not have a common traditional culture, common language, common religious or conceptual vocabulary'. In both these comments we can see home and exile as two dynamic and diverse ends of a complex process of cultural and material connections.

The imagination of home in diasporic identity and consciousness is nonetheless vital for the unity of diasporas and also influences the level of developmental support for home(land)s. The essentialist and anti-essentialist, or pluralist, views see home in very different ways. The former tends to romanticize home and treat it as spatially and historically static. The anti-essentialist view sees the interpretation of home, as well as its actual development, as diverse and dynamic. Any diasporic community is likely to encompass many different ways of imagining home and their understanding of their home country's economic and political evolution is likely to be equally complex and variegated.

The essentialist view can lead to support for grandiose, and often nationalistic, support for the regeneration or restoration of a homeland. By contrast, the anti-essentialist view leads to more interpersonal support for developmental initiatives based on personal knowledge of needs back at home and/or a pragmatic use of home, both physically or culturally, as a base for developmental activity. In Section 3.6 we will look in more detail at the implications of this for developmental efforts. And 'home' here need not be a nation-state, but could be a village, region or even a kinship network. For example, we will see in Section 3.5 how the Chinese trade diaspora around the globe utilizes flexible kinship links which sometimes take advantage of quite specific home-based connections or, when expedient, can choose to play up the perceived 'positive' aspects of a much broader essentialized Chinese identity.

Summary of Section 3.2

- As transnational communities, diasporas are dynamic entities which have some sense of common identity but are also different from both their host communities and those of their homelands. This 'in-between' status has produced complex hybrid identities.

- Identity is important for understanding diaspora and development, because it affects, first, the degree of group cohesion and the ability to trust co-members and, second, the level of support for the well-being of home.

- Identity formulation is complex, involving two entwined processes. The first is that groups identify themselves in relation to other groups, which can lead to antagonism between them. Second, group identity is made up of shared meanings, which for the displaced members of diasporic groups often involves multiple and dynamic cultural influences, resulting in new hybrid cultural forms.

- The creation of identities in relation to other groups and the emergence of new hybrid cultural forms are dynamic processes, shaped simultaneously by happenings in place and beyond place.

- Cultural identification with home is an important component of diasporic identities and can become a material reality when the diaspora seeks to protect and/or develop their homeland and their family within it. This identification with home can be problematic if it relies on an essentialist vision of home.

3.3 Development in, through and by the diaspora

Diasporas are complex social groupings, and our understanding of them has changed over time. However, they share certain characteristics based on common cultural traits, experience of exile, possible hostility from other groups and a connection, both symbolic and physical, with 'home'. It is these shared features which give diasporic communities their cohesion and stability, although we must continually be aware that such cohesion and stability are delicate and dynamic. Groups are never as homogeneous as they may appear and their motivations and organization vary over time. We saw in the Sierra Leone case how successive generations had different motivations for leaving and entering into diaspora, and how once in diaspora their relationship to home and other members of the diaspora changed.

The rest of the chapter examines the material, political and cultural flows within diasporic communities and the ways in which these contribute to development. To structure this I propose a threefold classification which brings out the linkages between diasporas and the different types of network and flow which enable their development potential. I begin by outlining and elaborating upon this classification, whilst stressing the importance of appreciating the diverse, lived experience of diasporic communities so as to avoid unhelpful generalizations. To guard against such generalizations I then introduce two case studies which I will refer to throughout.

3.3.1 Diasporic development

Al-Ali *et al.* (1999) have developed a scheme for examining the developmental activities of refugee groups. They split these into those activities which support the 'home' from where the refugees came and those which benefit the diasporic community in the 'host' country in which they currently dwell. In the context of recently arrived refugees such a home–host division makes sense, but for the purposes of examining diasporas in general this overlooks the linkages, built up over longer periods, which exist between multiple 'host' locations. For this reason I have added a category which looks at the developmental activities enabled through links to other members of the diaspora. Hence, I propose a threefold classification for examining the positive linkages between diaspora and development.

- Development *in* the diaspora: how people within diasporic communities use their localized diasporic connections within the 'host' country to secure economic and social well-being and, as a by-product, contribute to the development of their locality. This is diasporic development 'in place'.

- Development *through* the diaspora: how diasporic communities utilize their diffuse global connections beyond the locality to facilitate economic and social well-being. This is diasporic development 'through space'.

- Development *by* the diaspora: how diasporic flows and continued connections 'back home' facilitate the development – and, sometimes, creation – of these 'homelands'. This is diasporic development 'across space'.

These categories, and the relationships between them, are fuzzy and dynamic, reflecting the inherent tensions between fixity and movement that characterize diasporas. For example, an African trader in Paris, living with diasporic contacts, selling T-shirts sourced from a family member in Hong Kong, and sending part of the profits back to his/her extended family, straddles all three categories. An empirical approach will enable us to examine the specificities of different diasporic experiences, which inevitably cut across these categories. The following section introduces two case studies, both of them of African diasporic communities, which will help us in this.

3.3.2 The lived experience of diaspora and development

Two contrasting examples concerning the recent experiences of the African diaspora in the United States and France run through Sections 3.4–3.6. Additionally, I have supplemented these with other discussions and cases where appropriate. The two main studies are usefully different; one is conducted by a sociologist (Arthur, 2000) and the other by an anthropologist and a sociologist (MacGaffey and Bazenguissa-Ganga, 2000). In terms of methodology, the former study tends to look at aggregate trends and group experiences, whereas the latter study traces the intimate unfolding of personal journeys and their cultural underpinnings. Another difference is that Arthur's study is of 'documented' or legal African immigrants in the United States, who tend to be from a 'higher' social class than those in MacGaffey and Bazenguissa-Ganga's study of 'undocumented' traders in Paris, operating, as the subtitle to their book suggests, 'on the margins of the law'. While this latter group is well educated by the standards of their home countries, they lack the money and status to gain legitimate entry into France. As a result, the emphasis of the studies is somewhat different. The Africans in the United States can engage in a range of professional activities and are not confined to illicit trading, which means they are more open about their ultimate motivations and views for the future, whereas the Africans in France are far more vulnerable and their future is less certain. In Arthur's study of documented Africans in the United States, he gives no indication of (or chooses not to study) any illegal community – assuming that one exists. In the remainder of this section I trace out the motives for these Africans entering diaspora and give a brief introduction to each study.

The origins and motivations of the recent African diaspora

Earlier I argued that to assess the developmental potential of diasporas we need to understand the origins of diaspora and the motivations for people leaving home. In the Sierra Leone case study we saw that as political and economic crises have deepened over the past 30 years, those people able to migrate did so as a means of economic survival and to avoid political persecution. Likewise, the African diasporas in France and the United States are relatively recent and conform to the pattern shown by the Sierra Leone case – while the details and the social composition of the diasporas vary, movements have generally been in response to economic and political hardship in Africa.

Case study: Contrasting the African diasporas in the United States and France

For the Congolese diaspora in Paris, their countries have 'been beset by civil violence and economic crisis ... to which second-economy trade and migration have been a defiant response' (MacGaffey and Bazenguissa-Ganga, 2000, pp.3, 29). In the case of those migrating to the United States from all over Africa, similar pressures lead them to leave, although many have also migrated for educational reasons or to join a spouse already there. This second group is more professionally oriented (although some do become traders), whereas the Congolese, in entering France illegally, have had to be more opportunistic, with many becoming transnational traders after having cut their teeth as traders in Africa. Clearly, the class background of the migrants is crucial in determining their motivations and ease of movement. However, as MacGaffey and Bazenguissa-Ganga note, 'what is new is that making use of kin overseas is becoming an essential strategy for survival and improving life for some populations' (p.134).

These two cases of people deciding to leave Africa and seek securer livelihoods abroad show quite divergent experiences of diaspora. For the Congolese traders, securing a living is extremely difficult and requires many creative solutions to the problems of poverty and illegality. They either came to Paris legally, often on a student visa, but drifted into illegal trade if and when their studies were completed, or they came illegally from the beginning, simply failing to return after coming in as 'tourists'. Given that their existence abroad is both a test of their credibility and a vital source of finance back home these people are under extreme pressure to succeed. The twin forces of illegality and the need to succeed throw them into a complex and creative use of the opportunities offered by globalization. Some people trade locally within Paris and offer services such as hairdressing to fellow members of the Congolese and African diasporas. Others trade internationally by buying goods in one country and selling them in one or more other countries. This may be buying designer clothes in Italy, selling some in Paris and the rest in Congo; other times it might be buying foodstuffs from relatives in Congo and selling them back in Paris. Either way, the links with kin and fellow members of the diaspora who act as both suppliers and consumers, as well as enabling transactions through 'contacts', are crucial. However, the marginal nature of these activities means that the traders are wary of trusting people too much, so that the ties that bind this community are not as strong as the theory of diasporic identity would suggest.

In terms of identity and diaspora, the American case is interesting, because African people settling there could be seen as part of a longer and larger diaspora originating in the slave trade. However, the motivations for entering diaspora are clearly diverse and we should be wary of identifying a single 'African' diaspora on the basis of skin colour or place of origin. Indeed, the African diaspora in Arthur's survey often held extremely negative views of African-Americans (descendants of the former slaves who worked the plantations of America and the Caribbean), despite acknowledging the racism that exists in American society. By and large, these people came to the United States for purposes of education and did so with full legal recognition. Given this class background and the greater, but not substantial, levels of wealth compared with the Congolese traders, such groups have been very successful. They tend to operate in professional occupations and have brought their immediate family to the United States. This means that they are much more secure than the Paris-based traders and are able to save and send significant amounts of money back to relatives in Africa. They also intend to return to their various home countries when they retire, though this is often dependent on the improvement of the political and economic circumstances that precipitated their need to migrate in the first place.

We will see in more detail how the experiences of the different diasporic communities work out in practice and the effects of this on development. However, it is already clear that while the motivations for migration may be similar across different communities, individuals' experiences as part of a diaspora differ according to class background, legal status and the occupations practised. As we have stressed from the outset, it is often inaccurate to generalize about diasporic groups, and we must appreciate the diversity of experiences.

Summary of Section 3.3

- So far, much of the chapter has dealt with the theorization of diaspora and borrowed from existing literature on the topic. Given their predominantly culturalist focus, most studies often ignore the tangible developmental effects which diasporas can generate.

- Diaspora and development can be linked in three ways. First, development in the diaspora involves members of the diasporic community utilizing their affiliations in place to secure well-being. Second, development through the diaspora involves people using the networks of co-members across the globe to exploit economic opportunities. Finally, development by the diaspora involves the conscious development of home by diasporic communities in exile. These three types of diasporic development can overlap and co-exist.

- Given that such complex processes are unique and contextual we need to look at each case separately. To this end we introduced two cases of recent African migrants and the different opportunities they face as a result of class, gender and citizenship status.

3.4 Development in the diaspora

Development *in* the diaspora refers to how people within diasporic communities use their localized diasporic connections to secure economic and social well-being and, as a by-product, contribute to the development of their locality. This is diasporic development in place and it applies to such phenomena as the classic 'Chinatowns' involving spatial clustering of co-ethnic members and where high levels of socio-economic interaction occur between them. We saw in Figure 3.5 that even in nineteenth-century Freetown distinctive 'towns' had grown up around members of different African ethnic groups. According to Cohen's (1997) typology in Box 3.1 diasporas tend to have 'a troubled relationship with host societies, suggesting a lack of acceptance' and, by contrast, 'a sense of empathy and solidarity with co-ethnic members'. These twin processes of identity formation can lead to dense networks of intra-ethnic co-operation and trust. Besides economic transactions, close ethnic ties can lead to the formation of civil, political and social associations which protect and support the diasporic community within the host society. (Table 3.1 in Section 3.6.4 below, summarizes some of these points in the 'Host country focus' section.)

3.4.1 Embeddedness and ethnic business

In Section 3.2 we discussed the importance of cultural identity within diasporic communities and the way in which communities are formed in relation to other groups and around shared meanings within a group. In displaced diasporic communities these processes can be both a problem and a disguised blessing. Some communities can experience hostility from their 'hosts', based on absolute beliefs in difference, which can be demoralizing and dangerous. On the other hand, this hostility may force group members to draw on each other and take advantage of shared meanings, which then become a source of mutual support, and possibly also of competitive advantage. Fellow members of diasporic communities can be trusted more readily and may work more flexibly and cheaply for someone who is facing similar problems. In turn this can strengthen the sense of group identity as networks of ethnically-based businesses develop.

Such processes have been termed **embeddedness** (see the definition below) and they relate to the social and cultural underpinnings of economic activity. Closely related to, and for some synonymous with, embeddedness is the concept of **social capital**, which refers to 'those expectations for action within a collectivity that affect the economic goals and goal-seeking behavior of its members, even if these expectations are not oriented toward the economic sphere' (Portes and Sensenbrenner, 1993, p.1323). Social capital, then, is a form of human capital, which is built out of human associations, social interactions and shared values and which can have substantial positive economic value – see the discussion in Chapter 1 and the definition below. In practice, this can refer to predetermined cultural values which shape the nature of economic transactions, as examined in Weber's (1989; first published in 1922) classic study of the Protestant work ethic, or it can refer to intra-group trust which facilitates reciprocity rather than arm's length exchange. Social capital can also be generated through economic activity which actively creates a shared group consciousness and behaviour. A classic case in Marxist literature would be the example of a working-class consciousness which emerges out of and in relation to shared work-place experiences and the actions of a hostile capitalist class.

Embeddedness: The role of social relationships within economies, as opposed to the more inclusive concept of social capital, which covers political, economic and social relations. 'Embeddedness' was first used to critique the 'optimizing' assumptions of neoclassical economics, which tends to ignore the effects of society and cultural values on people's decision-making in the market place (Crang, 1997). Instead, it was argued that economic practices are *embedded* in social institutions involving 'the role of shared collective understandings in shaping economic strategies and goals' (Zukin and DiMaggio, 1990, p.17). Embeddedness has been used to analyse ethnic businesses which often secure labour, contracts and inputs from members of the same ethnic or racial group.

Social capital: Popularized by Putnam in his work on Italy and, latterly, the United States, the term social capital refers to 'features of social organization, such as networks, norms, and trust, that facilitate co-ordination and co-operation for mutual benefit' (Putnam, 1993, p.36). For Putnam social capital fosters reciprocity, facilitates information flows and generates trust, and once it exists tends to be self-perpetuating as successive generations are socialized into the localized norms which create success. Social capital is a very general term which has been criticized as being vague and amorphous. However, its primary uses have been to explain political participation, institutional effectiveness and aggregate economic development. For example, Putnam (1993) uses social capital to explain why some regions in Italy were more democratic and economically developed than others.

For ethnic business networks embeddedness and social capital are central to their success. For newly arrived immigrants, 'participation in a pre-existing ethnic economy can have positive economic consequences, including a greater opportunity for self-employment' (Portes and Jensen, 1987, p.768). Eventually, the 'solidary ethnic community represents simultaneously, a market for culturally defined goods, a pool of reliable low-wage labor, and a potential source of start-up capital' (Portes and Sensenbrenner, 1993, p.1329). However, while intra-ethnic business can be a source of advantage in the face of hostile political, economic and social forces in a host country, it can also be a disadvantage, because ethnic loyalty may prevent actors from maximizing their economic opportunities. In reality, economic actors, especially the more astute and powerful, have to switch ethnic affiliation on and off depending upon the relative advantages to be gained by either strategy.

What is interesting is that ethnic identity tends to be re-fashioned, if not fully created, in diaspora. Portes and Sensenbrenner (1993, p.1328) discuss the fortunes of Italian immigrants to the United States 'whose original loyalties did not extend much beyond their local villages. These immigrants learned to think of themselves as Italian and to band together on that basis after the native population began to treat them in the same manner and to apply the same derogatory labels.' This is a case where social capital and group identity were formed in relation and opposition to hostile treatment by the host. Hence, the very existence and density of ethnic networks is affected by the hostility of the host society, which can create 'uncertainty'. Portes (1997, pp.7–8) argues that immigrant business networks 'tend to generate solidarity by virtue of generalized uncertainty. Exchange under conditions of uncertainty creates stronger bonds among participants than that which takes place with full information and impartially enforced rules.' In the process of creating diasporic identities and making a living, an ethnic economic network can form and deepen, and once created has a dynamic of its own.

Spatially, such close connections between ethnic group members may generate and strengthen the tendency to cluster in enclaves, such as ghettoes and Chinatowns, although there is not necessarily a link between an ethnic business network and its spatial concentration (Portes and Jensen, 1987). However, such processes of agglomeration are not solely the result of cultural affinity, but are usually influenced by other factors, such as racist real estate markets, the cost of property, the wealth of the ethnic community and the legal status of individuals. For small firms serving local markets, which constitute the majority of diaspora business, the importance of proximity for information exchange is often vital to establishing reputation and respect. Word gets around about who can be relied upon, so it is in this context that one of Waldinger's (1995, p.565) respondents claims 'New York is a small town [where] good and bad news travel fast.'

3.4.2 Settling in and making a living

In the two studies of the African diasporas in the United States and France that run through these sections, new diasporic members make use of existing diasporic contacts, either in order to migrate or upon arrival. Again, this varies from case to case, depending upon the legality or illegality of the migrant. In the case of Africans' migration to the United States, new immigrants need to have letters of sponsorship, from an educational institution or a family member already in residence, for example. On arrival, new immigrants use contacts from within their diasporic communities to help them settle in. However, it is here that we need to be specific about how we define and delimit a diasporic community. Obviously, in cases where a migrant is joining a relation, it is this relative who helps socialize the new arrival. In addition, there are formal organizations set up around particular ethnic, national or interest groupings. For example, in Atlanta there are the Ashanti and Ewe mutual aid associations, both of which relate to ethnic groups in contemporary Ghana. There are also Ghanaian associations, alumni organizations of those educated in Ghana, as well as more general immigrant support organizations. Hence, there is no single 'African' diaspora although most immigrants recognize the 'necessity of pursuing a pan-African identity' (Arthur, 2000, p.71), which I will discuss in more detail in Section 3.6.3.

These formal organizations mentioned above

> ...have become a vital part of the network of associative relationships. Immigrants have always established such associations in host countries to *forge closer ties among themselves, with the members of the host society, and with their places of birth.* The African immigrant associations are the building blocks for the creation of African cultural communities in the United States...
>
> (Arthur, 2000, p.71; my emphasis)

This forging of ties is both 'in place' and 'across space' and clearly links the developmental fortunes of Africans living at home and abroad. In contrast, given the illegal status of the Congolese traders in Paris, such organizations are impossible, and they are forced to rely on more informal contacts. In their study MacGaffey and Bazenguissa-Ganga also refer to the concept of social capital, which for them relates to individual and family connections, kinship relations, ethnic affiliation, religious grouping or political contacts. All these may be drawn upon to enable the trader to pursue his or her commercial activities.

In both cases, whether legal immigrants with access to support organizations, or illegal immigrants dependent upon more informal contacts, the African diasporas tend to stay relatively separate from their white 'hosts'. And in the United States, the African middle classes tend to 'form much closer relationships with [other] black immigrants of the African diaspora ... than they do with the native-born black American population' (Arthur, 2000, p.80). Arthur goes on to detail the mutual suspicion that exists between the African immigrants and the African-Americans. Many of the African immigrants, particularly if they are parents with children in the United States, perceive of African-Americans in much the same way as racist whites do. That is, they believe that African-Americans are lazy, unintelligent and have squandered their chances. These prejudices are heaped onto their children, as these statements by Arthur's respondents make clear.

> [My daughter] was a stellar student in Africa before coming to America. [Now] she spends her allowance on *Vibe* magazine and gangsta CDs. Those gangsta rap musicians have stolen the mind and innocence of my child...
>
> (Arthur, 2000, pp.116–117)

> My son now tells me that college is not for everyone ... Today he is on the verge of dropping out because he hangs out with the wrong crowd, always talking about Tupac Shakur, Ice Cube ... and the latest musical video on Black Entertainment Television.
>
> (Arthur, 2000, p.116)

Clearly, the implication is that the bad 'urban' attitudes of African-Americans have corrupted their children. Indeed, some parents send their children back to relatives in Africa so that they receive a disciplined education. Interestingly, the African-Americans see the African immigrants as aloof and arrogant and even accuse them of having 'come to their country and taken their jobs' (Arthur, 2000, p.83). On both sides, then, there are deep-seated ethnocentric prejudices about the 'other' which work against a united anti-racist stance.

The Congolese in Paris show similar cultural affinities, although the details are, of course, different. They too tend to mingle with fellow immigrants who are mainly, though not exclusively, of African origin. MacGaffey and Bazenguissa-Ganga's study suggests that the traders 'were not part of any structured trade diaspora but operated as individuals ... personal networks ... are not structured and permanent but are activated when they are needed by individuals trading on their own behalf, and not as part of ethnic trading communities' (MacGaffey and Bazenguissa-Ganga, 2000, p.12). MacGaffey and Bazenguissa-Ganga felt the traders were too individualistic and opportunistic to be considered a true diaspora. However, their trade is organized, as we shall see in Section 3.5.3, through various co-operative cultural ties while their shared 'pariah' status forces new bonds to develop. This cultural identity was formed around the ideas of *la débrouillardise* (meaning to fend for yourself in order to survive) and *la Sape* (a stylistic movement which values European designer labels and conspicuous consumption, members of which are called *sapeurs*). The following account by a young *sapeur* about *la débrouillardise* captures the common identity that emerges out of this precarious existence, whilst at the same time a strong individual streak is retained.

> Most compatriots have this spirit before leaving the country. If in France you're often broke while everyone else is getting by, your ideas change. You adapt and get by as well. If you remain a *sapeur*, you know that to buy those pants or those shoes, you have to do this scam. Automatically, you have to join in. Nobody tells you you have to join in, but you know it. If you don't join in, how are you going to live? Nobody takes care of you. Everybody's in the same boat. Someone can put you up but they won't give you any money, so it's up to you to get by every day, to figure out how to make money.
>
> (MacGaffey and Bazenguissa-Ganga, 2000, p.58)

Both studies show tensions within and between groups in the places where diasporic communities settle. We can see that when necessary, individuals draw on the resources of their diasporic connections, but the nature of these are fluid. The contact may be a family member, a clan member, a fellow national, or another African living in diaspora. Such flexible use of contacts reflects the uncertainty that many living in diaspora experience, while this uncertainty itself can become a source of common identification. Thus, we must be wary of seeing a fixed and clearly bounded group identity for diasporic communities as they pursue development *in place*.

Summary of Section 3.4

- Development *in* the diaspora entails diasporic members using the connections they find in their new place of residence in order to secure a better life.

- Most research focuses on the economic dimensions of the diaspora which is labelled 'ethnic business' in the sociological literature. Cultural ties underpin economic networks, which over time become 'embedded' in local areas. Such embeddedness facilitates businesses which often face hostility from their hosts and produces distinctive 'enclave economies' such as Chinatowns.

- In the two African cases we saw that people used existing institutions in order to settle in and once established they organized their trade through local diasporic networks.

- The American and Parisian examples clearly demonstrate the very different experiences faced by the African diaspora, largely as a result of class and immigration status differences between them.

3.5 Development through the diaspora

Development *through* the diaspora refers to how diasporic communities utilize their diffuse global connections beyond the locality to facilitate economic and social well-being. This is diasporic development through space and is, in some senses, a geographically 'stretched' version of the first category. However, the very fact of dispersal around the globe opens up new, largely economic, opportunities. This counters the common misconception that the economic opportunities of globalization only benefit transnational corporations. Diasporic connections can enable business people to identify new market opportunities, operate in the flexible (and often exploitative and 'informal') interstices of the global economy and/or effectively serve the fragmented niche markets of their own diasporas.

3.5.1 Trade diasporas

We saw in Section 3.1 that the term diaspora was originally associated with colonization by the Ancient Greeks, and later came to be associated with the experience of exile in general. However, some centuries later the Phoenicians also revived the term to refer to proactive merchants operating along established trade routes (Cohen, 1997). Compared with the 'noble' pursuit of colonization, these diasporas were considered rather inferior and the merchants were treated as outsiders. These arrangements saw traders living as aliens in host communities, but as Curtin (1984, pp.2–3) notes 'a distinction appeared between the merchants who moved and settled and those who continued to move back and forth ... The result was an interrelated net of commercial communities forming a trade network, or trade diaspora.' As we shall see, the choices of settling, endless circulation or repatriation still face contemporary traders in the global economy. Temporary settlement is described as **sojourning**, because the traders wilfully assert their cultural difference and persist with a restless circular migration between suppliers and markets.

In contrast to sojourners, some traders have inserted themselves into their host society and become quite powerful, although in some cases they have never been accepted as true citizens. Such traders fulfil a unique and important role, because while they are outsiders who undertake the rather ignoble art of trade, they service different sectors of the local economy. This 'intermediate' status means that they have acted as a buffer between, for want of a better word, the élites and the lower classes. Hence, despite their difference from the élites, they are welcomed as useful social, economic and political brokers. Indeed, during the colonial period, the British actively encouraged the settlement of the Lebanese traders in West Africa, as described in the case study below.

Case study: The Lebanese in Sierra Leone

Earlier, I discussed the Creoles in Freetown and how they had an ambivalent place in society, being identified as part European and part African, but 'belonging' to neither culture. When the Lebanese traders arrived in Freetown at the turn of the twentieth century they soon carved out an important place in the economy and polity of colonial and, later, post-colonial Sierra Leone. The following two extracts show how this evolution occurred and how, as a trade diaspora, the Lebanese utilized diasporic connections beyond the country, but also became partially integrated with local society.

Figure 3.6 Lebanese diaspora and family businesses: Abdel Hamid Salhab (right) with a friend in the Salhab brothers' textile shop, Dakar, Senegal, 1954/55. The Lebanese emigrated to Europe, the Americas, Africa and parts of Asia to escape poverty and persecution. Family connections were important in helping members of the the diaspora to carve out a living in their new homes.
Source: Collection Ghassan Salhab, Arab Image Foundation, copyright Arab Image Foundation.

This first extract, from Banton's (1957) *West African City: A Study of Tribal Life in Freetown*, captures the mixed attitudes towards Lebanese traders in Sierra Leone during the colonial period. The extract begins with a quotation from Bauer's *West African Trade*.

'The Levantines [people from the eastern part of the Mediterranean] in West Africa represent types of immigrant who have an important part to perform in the economic development of many under-developed countries. Although they are rarely highly educated, they are resourceful, industrious, enterprising and exceptionally gifted in the perception of economic opportunity. They are independent of existing commercial interests, and in many branches of trading activity are important and effective competitors of the large European firms ... as in many parts of the world, the immigrants who could contribute the most to economic development are regarded with the greatest suspicion by influential sections of the Administration, their admission particularly resisted, and their activities under pressure from local sectional interests and from already established expatriate commercial interests' (Bauer, 1954). The Lebanese enter into intimate relations with Africans: the small trader in the country leads a life not so very different from that of his customers, advances loans to peasant farmers, speaks their language and gets to know their outlook. Many have taken a wife under native customary law and then pensioned her off when they have married a Lebanese woman. Thus there is an increasing number of Afro-Lebanese children, some of whom have difficulty in adjusting themselves to their situation. The relations of the Lebanese with the mass of the native population are good though some African leaders resent their success and are able to excite antagonism against them.

(Banton, 1957, p.101)

Later on, some members of the Lebanese diaspora in Sierra Leone have used their place as 'intermediaries' or 'strangers' to shape post-colonial development in Sierra Leone. The following excerpts from Reno's (1995) *Corruption and State Politics in Sierra Leone* show their influence as business partners and intermediaries in diamond trading and local and national politics. The distinctive features of Lebanese business (including family networks and foreign connections) have put them in a strong position to forge profitable links with the post-colonial rulers.

Lebanese businessmen benefited from the rejuvenation of their historic middleman roles. The new 'official' private economy built upon pre-existing Lebanese business networks. Lebanese businessmen provided the 'gateway' for delivering old networks to Shadow State [the informal hidden and often corrupt practices which run alongside the more formal state system] control, a process akin to the colonial imperative to negotiate with chiefs as intermediaries in the establishment of a European alliance with local collaborators ... Like his colonial predecessors, Stevens'* political strategy and fiscal incapacity led to wholesale incorporation of the collaborators' own social networks and networks of exchange, along with all the political dangers to the centre inherent in their pursuit of private interests.

*President Siaka Stevens, who ruled between 1968 and 1985.

Lebanese entrepreneurs, especially Jamil and Yazbeck*, but also about fifty other families with lower-profile international contacts, expanded their own business interests through arrangements with politicians and administrators. Some of these families had long managed diamond digging and buying operations in Kono on behalf of politician partners. However, the impossibility of ever holding state office prevented Lebanese businessmen from seeking further opportunity through formal politics rather than business. Their status as 'strangers' and 'exploiters' in the public eye reinforced Lebanese exclusion from full participation in Sierra Leonean society.

*Mohamed Jamil, a successful businessman and diamond exporter, who was allegedly involved in a *coup d'etat*, and Tony Yazbeck, another successful businessman.

Visible displays of dependence show politicians the importance of Lebanese services, but they also heighten popular perceptions of the privileged and isolated position that the 'strangers' occupy in the Shadow State. When asked what problems he faced, a housewares distributor in the provinces – himself enjoying favoured access to a politician/Lebanese businessman joint venture – replied that 'Our customers do not trust African businessmen. Many people go to the yellow man [Lebanese] because they say that their black brother will treat them like a *bobo* [small, insignificant child]. We have to convince them that they should not always prefer the stranger. But this is difficult when that is what our leaders do.' Such expressions linking [economic] opportunity to ethnicity are common among both Lebanese and African businessmen.

The lack of significant African competition and the flight of European capital also afford opportunities to expand in the formal economy. Lebanese-owned businesses dominate more highly capitalized sectors of the economy. As in Kono, family connections offer alternative sources of credit outside the collapsing formal banking sector. Just as among Kono Lebanese businesses, family access to foreign exchange facilitates illicit imports of goods, thus giving a further competitive advantage over legitimate African businesses, which are forced to rely upon legal (taxed) imports. This business activity takes place as a spin-off of the 'private' economy, but is now virtually the only source of formal state revenue to provide basic services to citizens.

(Reno, 1995, pp.149–152)

Debates exist as to why some trade diasporas have proved so successful (Cohen, 1997). The first explanation is that such communities have a 'pariah' status, because they are different from the host and retain an internal cultural cohesion which facilitates sufficient trust and co-operation for commerce. This cultural cohesion is also crucial in maintaining the necessary dogmatism and persistence which are often required when such peoples face hostile treatment by their suspicious hosts. Some have argued further, in line with Weber's ideas about capitalism and the Protestant work ethic, that certain diasporic communities have cultural traits that predispose them to commercial activity. This parallels arguments made by some scholars that the Confucian ethic of co-operation has been responsible for commercial success in East Asia – see Section 3.5.2 below.

A slightly different interpretation of the success of trade diasporas is that their deterritorialized condition means they are perfectly suited to reading various 'different' cultures and spotting market opportunities. Being a perpetual outsider means that you have to become adept at understanding multiple 'hosts'; something which an arrogant imperialist diaspora might be less inclined to do. In the case of the Lebanese the diasporic traders are intermediaries who promote the economic development of the élite, without the élite themselves having to get their hands dirty; but the danger is that the diaspora remain 'outsiders' who can be blamed for economic exploitation if things go badly.

3.5.2 The 'paradigm' of Chinese diasporic capitalism

Many of the debates about diaspora and development have been driven by the experiences of the Chinese. Whereas the Jewish and African diasporas have for many come to symbolize victimization and the search for an authentic homeland, the Chinese experience has come to signify the innovative and entrepreneurial spirit that can exist within diaspora. In this section, I discuss the 'paradigmatic' case of Chinese diasporic capitalism and the lessons we can learn for diasporas in general and for the experience of the African diaspora in particular. Cohen (1997) discusses the evolution of the Chinese diaspora over the past 500 years, their status as sojourners and their spatial segregation in self-contained 'Chinatowns' across the world. However, I am more concerned with recent, and not unrelated, debates about the success of a specifically Chinese variant of diasporic capitalism.

The key debate concerns why the Chinese diaspora has been so successful. Is it, following the logic of Weber (1989), because Chinese culture has innate characteristics which make Chinese people more effective capitalists? The basic argument here is that the Confucian ethic contributes to economic success amongst Chinese people, wherever they are in the world. In terms of the earlier discussion in Section 3.2, this is an essentialist theory based around a belief in innate and unchanging cultural values. These cultural traits are believed to be based upon two pillars; 'the creation of dedicated, motivated, responsible and educated individuals and the enhanced sense of commitment, organizational identity, and loyalty to various institutions' (Kahn, 1979; quoted in Dirlik, 1997, p.306). This implies that there is a coherent and stable 'Chinese' identity which underpins the desire to succeed and accumulate wealth. It also, apparently, explains the high levels of intra-diasporic commercial flows, because Chinese people (or families) have a strong basis upon which to trust one another more deeply.

However, we have seen that diasporas are rarely as coherent and unified as this argument suggests, and neither is this the case with the Chinese diaspora. In particular, such a theory suppresses class and gender differences as well as the 'dark side of Confucianism' (Dirlik, 1997, p.313) involving such tendencies as exclusion and authoritarianism. More generally, it ignores the 'structural context within which this capitalism has arisen' (p.315). These factors cast 'strong doubt on culturalist claims that represent them as essential, exclusive and unchanging Chinese values' (p.314). Instead, an alternative explanation stands the culturalist argument on its head, explaining this success

Figure 3.7 Chinatown: a dragon procession, Manchester, and Gerrard Street sign, Chinatown in London.

through broader trends in global capitalism. In an era of 'flexible accumulation', multinational capital has decentralized and uses greater numbers of subcontractors. This shift produces complex business networks which exploit dynamic market opportunities and increasingly fluid 'comparative advantages' of multiple sites. As Dirlik (p.309) argues, 'diasporic populations may also be strategically well-placed to deal with some of the demands of transnational production and other transactions that are transnational in scope'. So, existing Chinese diasporic networks are perfectly suited to exploit the new terrain of global capitalism. These networks may be based around certain cultural affinities, but these are differentially exploited at different times and in different places depending on market and political opportunities. As Ong (1993, p.752) observes, 'diasporic Chinese seek a flexible position among the myriad possibilities (and problems) found in the global sphere'. Crucially, class and gender dimensions are both important. Those best able to exploit these flexible opportunities tend to be from the upper classes, while working classes only feature as the 'nimble fingers' exploited in New York sweatshops or Economic Processing Zones in China. And as Box 3.6 explains, the Chinese diaspora depends on male-dominant family relations.

Box 3.6 The Chinese diaspora and global capitalism

These extracts from Aihwa Ong's article entitled 'On the edge of empires: flexible citizenship among Chinese in diaspora', published in *Positions* in 1993, explore alternatives to a culturalist explanation of Chinese diasporic success.

Up until the Tiananmen crackdown, the Chinese considered themselves sojourners/refugees and developed little sense of national identity with Hong Kong as a nation. Hong Kong Chinese experience political freedom as a marketplace phenomenon, and perceive citizenship as the right to promote familial interests and economic gain with no sense of obligation to society at large... (p.742)

...The pervasiveness of material values and the instrumental approach to all facets of social life are key components of the modern consciousness. The fashioning of self is thus almost totally expressed through the power of a personal choice, risk-taking, and flexibility in the local marketplace and, increasingly, in the global economy... (pp.745–755)

...In prominent overseas Chinese family businesses (those with assets of a few hundred million US dollars), the family head is usually the founder of the business. Either a grandparent or (more likely) the father, who became wealthy after amassing a fortune in the Hong Kong real estate market, tightly controls both family and business relations and, over his lifetime, gradually passes management and financial control to his sons. Confucian relational ethics invest sons and daughters-in-law with particular roles and obligations, making them amenable to the biopolitical agenda of the family firm. A middle-aged tycoon, Alex Leong (pseudonym), tells me, 'I remember, even when I was in junior high, my objective was to follow my father's footsteps and be in business ... to take over the family business rather than try to work for someone else or do my own thing. Because I think it is very important for sons to carry on the family business, something that has been built up by your father. To me that is the number one obligation ... If your family has a business, why would you go work for somebody else, and leave a hired man to look after your family business? To me that doesn't make any sense...' (pp.756–757)

...Thus, the subjective masculinity of this very cosmopolitan family is defined primarily in terms of one's role as a *son*, and success in contributing to the wealth accumulation of the family of origin, to which one's *jia* [relations within the family] is economically fused. Unlike daughters, who would inherit a smaller share of the family wealth than sons (30 to 70 per cent, in Alex's family), sons must be *active* in the running of the family business. To be merely a passive recipient is to play a feminine role, like his sisters, who marry out, or his wife, who is not supposed to involve herself in her husband's family business, but to focus on producing heirs and providing for a warm and supportive family life...

...In the 1960s, middle and upper-middle class teenage boys like Alex applied to US high schools and colleges for further education. Alex's father always told him, 'Your future is really going to be outside Hong Kong. So you should be educated outside, as long as you maintain some Chinese customs and speak Chinese.' An entire generation embarked on a transnational strategy of seeking overseas education, thus acquiring foreign 'cultural capital' (Bourdieu, 1987) that would eventually facilitate their manoeuvres in different cultural economies (see Ong, 1992). Wealthy families often use their sons' education abroad, especially in England and in North America, as an entrée into the foreign country. Parents visit to buy homes for the children and to set up bank accounts. Upon graduation, the sons open up a foreign branch of the parent company. Wherever it is located, the family firm operates as the vehicle par excellence for flexible accumulation, that is, the deployment of innovative financial instruments that allow flexible twenty-four-hour responses to a highly uncertain, competitive global capitalism (Harvey, 1989a). Through this mix of individual and family cultural strategies, Chinese entrepreneurs widen the social field of operation to the global arena, thereby attempting to subvert and elude the regulation of particular nation-states. (pp.758–760)

What the debate demonstrates is that diasporic commerce is based around the ability to spot opportunities and exploit these through flexible networks, which have emerged historically and are held together by varying amounts of cultural 'glue' or 'social capital'. Certainly, there is no unchanging and essential diasporic identity and people exercise their agency in a multitude of innovative and proactive ways. However, for various reasons, such as the racism and marginalization that often greets diasporic communities, a strategic common identity may be presented as a means of resisting this subjugation. As the example of African traders which follows shows, they too exploit flexible opportunities, although their class and legal status, as well as the racism they face, affect their relative success.

3.5.3 African trade diasporas

This section further examines the activities of the African traders in our French and American case studies (Arthur, 2000; MacGaffey and Bazenguissa-Ganga, 2000). The economic activities that the African diasporic communities engaged in varied according to class, educational status and legality. While some of those who migrated to the United States were traders, many were professionals engaged in higher education and medicine, whereas those who settled in France centred exclusively on trade and services. In this section we will focus on trading activities.

In general, the traders service their own and other diasporic communities. The most prominent of these trades involve food items, clothing, services such as hairdressing, and venture capital. For example, Arthur details the operation of the Gold Coast Marketing Store in Atlanta.

This store is oriented towards immigrants from Africa and the Caribbean. The owners have relied on family labor and on ethnic and family credit sources to fund the business. The success of this enterprise stems from the diversity of products and services that they provide. Originally, the Gold Coast Market Store sold Afro-Caribbean foodstuffs. Later, its owners began to promote African tourism and started offering their customers electronic message services ... The Gold Coast Market

> Store has become an information center where flyers announcing births,
> deaths, marriages, and the latest news from Ghana are exchanged by
> Ghanaians ... The owners ... have managed to eliminate brokers by
> going to Africa and buying ... items directly. Their reliance on family
> labor works to their advantage because it reduces costs.
>
> (Arthur, 2000, pp.105–106)

Some such ventures utilize truly global connections throughout a loosely
defined diaspora. In MacGaffey and Bazenguissa-Ganga's study a large
number of people had family or kin connections in airline companies,
the diplomatic service or connected to international religious
organizations. While there is no 'typical' pattern to these activities, the
story of Beatrice, an African immigrant to France earning a living
through trading, captures these complex networks.

> Her business consists of importing exotic foods and some other products
> from countries all over the world, to sell in Paris, in Congo–Kinshasa
> and in Congo–Brazzaville. She has been to Los Angeles for fish, to Hong
> Kong and Seoul for other foods, to Johannesburg for the hair extensions
> that it is the current fashion for women to braid into their hair ... The
> airline she works for gives her free tickets when she travels. This has
> been the basis for building up her enterprise ... To deal with the
> problems of doing business and finding her way in strange countries,
> cities, languages and cultures, she takes advantage of her membership in
> the Association for the Reunification of the Christian World.
>
> (MacGaffey and Bazenguissa-Ganga, 2000, pp.100–101)

In both examples, links with home are maintained through circular trips,
either to trade or to visit relations. In this way market signals,
commodities, money and goodwill are continually passing through the
diaspora and benefiting members both abroad and at home.

Picking up Cohen's comment that trade diasporas might be an
'innovatory model of social organization' and Ong's description of the
flexible Chinese diaspora, MacGaffey and Bazenguissa-Ganga see the
Congolese traders in Paris as

> individuals who refuse to abide by the constraints of the global power
> structure and its alliances between multinational capitalism, Western
> governments and African dictators ... [we] do not take the depressed
> view which sees commerce outside the law as a mere coping mechanism
> or survival strategy ... [rather we view it] as a means employed by
> individuals to evade and resist exclusion from opportunity to better
> their lives in circumstances of state decay, economic crisis and civil
> violence...
>
> (MacGaffey and Bazenguissa-Ganga, 2000, pp.3–28)

These traders 'resist' hegemony by operating in the interstices of the
global political economy and take advantage of the opportunities that
globalization offers. Clearly, these are not the mega-corporations that
dominate the global economy, but they are part and parcel of
globalization nonetheless.

Throughout the preceding discussions I have stressed the inseparability of culture from the construction of diasporic communities. However, these cultural representations and relationships are suffused with tensions, especially in terms of constructing a sense of identity that is simultaneously rooted in a commonality and continually in flux, depending on the changing personal and group experiences of the diaspora. Both the American and French studies emphasize, from the outset, that the African diasporas are not homogeneous or monolithic. However, we have already highlighted certain 'shared' experiences that foster a common sense of identity in terms of the motivations for leaving Africa as well as the racism that immigrants often encounter in the largely white host countries. As MacGaffey and Bazenguissa-Ganga (2000, p.10) comment, the traders 'are united in the experience of being excluded by the state from the opportunity to improve their lifestyle, fulfil their ambitions or even to survive'. In this statement 'the state' refers to both the African states from whence the diasporic communities came and the French state in which they currently live. In this sense they have been excluded twice from society and it is this double exclusion, more than some mythical and eternalized cultural traits, that unites such diasporas. However, group cultural affinity does play a crucial part in enabling and strengthening the position of individuals within these diasporas. As one of Arthur's respondents stated, 'The African immigrant must always keep one eye opened to appreciate the realities of being an immigrant. Meanwhile, the other eye is left free to focus on the realities of life at home in Africa' (2000, p.76). This brings us to consider the future for the diasporas in playing a part in development in Africa.

Summary of Section 3.5

- Development *through* the diaspora is an expansion of development *in* the diaspora. Here, the diaspora can utilize connections across the globe in order to capitalize on opportunities in trade.

- Trading diasporas have existed for thousands of years and involve either temporary residence abroad, known as sojourning, or more permanent settlement. Once established, trade diasporas link areas of supply and demand in ever more complex economic geographies.

- The Chinese diaspora has been held up as a key example of a specific cultural identity explaining the success of a particular group. However, I suggest that rather than a fixed cultural identity, we see a group that uses contacts, connections and values flexibly to exploit the fluid and dynamic realities of an integrated global economy.

- Culturally and economically these trades often act as intermediaries between the upper classes and the lower classes, as the example of the Lebanese in Sierra Leone shows.

- However, this in-between status is not always an advantage, as the Paris case demonstrates, with African traders seeking a very precarious living in the 'shadows' of the formal global economy.

3.6 Development by the diaspora

While there is a growing literature on the experience of diasporic communities in exile this is relatively unconnected to practical and developmental questions of home. As we saw in Section 3.2, many discussions of diasporic communities are based upon cultural studies and tend to focus on the symbolic use of home among diasporic communities. While this is undeniably important we want to examine the concrete ramifications of this for development and the flows of ideas, money and political support to the migrants' home country, be it an existing home(land) or one which nationalists would like to see come into being. These flows vary according to the origins of the diaspora, its length of existence, its 'consciousness' forged in hostile 'host' environments and the technological capabilities available to forge linkages between disparate places. In this section we examine these connections to 'home' in a number of ways. I start by looking at the primarily political linkages involved in (re)creating a homeland before outlining a recent framework for classifying more general developmental diasporic connections with home.

3.6.1 (Re)making homelands

In Cohen's (1997) typology of diaspora (Box 3.1) one defining feature is 'an idealization of the putative ancestral home and a collective commitment to its maintenance, restoration, safety, prosperity, even to its creation'. The words 'maintenance' and 'prosperity' clearly tie diasporas into the development of their places of origin, which we shall discuss later in this section. However, the other words in the phrase, 'restoration' and 'creation', give a more profound meaning to the notion of developing a homeland. We have seen in the Sierra Leone example the problems that arose when a group of well-meaning British philanthropists attempted to create a homeland for Africans. The case of Sierra Leone raises vexing questions about who constitutes a diaspora, where is their homeland, what relation does this have to development, and who benefits from it? I want to focus on these issues at a general level, before examining the cases of Africans in France and the United States in more detail.

The idea of a 'homeland' suggests a commonality among the people who are legitimately included in that society. However, the flipside of this can be that inclusion for some is exclusion for others. This is reflected in the metaphors that are often used in the attempt to explain and justify the construction of homelands. For example, discourses of homeland are loaded with gendered metaphors, with motherlands suggesting nurturing and fatherlands evoking the patriarchal protector. On top of these metaphors are those which tie populations to their territories, as if by nature – biological metaphors such as the German

Lebensraum, literally 'living space' in English, implying that those people living in a territory have some fundamental biological tie to that place. Such metaphors associating a people with a specific and bounded territory underpin the idea of the nation-state, as explained in Chapter 2, and can support racial and ethnic exclusivity. Such a desire for exclusiveness can be, as we have seen in Chapter 2, the trigger for the displacement of those deemed undesirable, through ethnic cleansing, for example. In turn those displaced people may seek their own homeland as a source of security and safety. As Cohen (1997, p.106) notes, 'Just as the evocation of "homeland" is used as a means of exclusion, so the excluded may see having a land of their own as a deliverance from their travails in foreign lands.' So, this territorial political vision is closely tied to a cultural imagination of home and a desire to belong.

The imagining and construction of homelands is fraught with difficulties and dangers. Nationalism has been described as 'Janus-faced', that is, two-faced or looking both ways, because a national consciousness looks inwards to its people as the source of identity, yet defines them against outsiders. National consciousness is also structured around looking back and celebrating the past glories of a nation as well as looking forward in protecting its future safety. Nationalism can also be called Janus-faced because it can be both liberatory, in seeking 'freedom' from subjugation, and dominating, because freedom for one group might involve the exclusion of another. Hence, we must be careful about how we view nationalism and be attentive to the different motivations of nationalists as well as the blueprints they have for their putative homelands. In order to make these points clear, I discuss two contrasting examples of diasporic imaginings of homeland. The first is Hindu nationalism, which, while claiming tolerance and pluralism, is hostile towards those perceived as outsiders, most notably the Muslims. The second example is of (pan-) African nationalism which sees the continent of Africa as a single 'home' which the diaspora might return to or influence. It picks up on earlier discussions about the diasporic imagining of a monolithic and romanticized 'Africa' and the various attempts to 'develop' the continent by well-meaning people such as the founders of Freetown and Edward Blyden. While in some cases this vision has become rather exclusionary, the general thrust is towards a more inclusive vision of Africa as a home for all Africans.

3.6.2 Hindu nationalism in the Indian diaspora

Over the past two decades in India there has been a rise in right-wing nationalism, which is so extreme and well organized that Mazumdar (1995) described it as fascism. A striking feature of this extreme nationalism is the active support which this large India-based movement has received from among certain sections of the Hindu -

diaspora, which is scattered world-wide[*]. Mazumdar (1995, pp.1–2) argues that, 'The goal of Indian fascism is to seize political power and redefine India, not as a secular state, but as a *Hindu Rashtra* or Hindu Nation. In this formulation of the nation-state no identity other than the Hindu identity can be allowed to exist.' For the very extreme members of this movement, the exclusion, and even killing, of Muslims is part of this reformulation of the nation. Over the past decade or so the nationalists have become increasingly violent and public, contesting cases in court and standing in elections. This formalized Hindu nationalism goes back to the 1920s. There is no single nationalist organization; however, the most influential contemporary organizations are the Bharatiya Janata Party (BJP), the Rashtriya Swayamsevak Sangh (RSS) and its cultural arm, the Vishwa Hindu Parishad (VHP).

The RSS, for example, aims to embed and strengthen Hindu culture and appeals to a mixture of religious tradition and militarism in which a disciplined and pure body is required for defence of the nation. According to the RSS the innate tolerance and good-naturedness of Hindus explains why successive invaders, the Muslims and the British, have been able to subjugate them. According to an article, 'The story of the Sangh', by a leading RSS member on the RSS website (http://www.rss.org/), 'We fell victim to our own naïve expectations that the aggressors would be fair and truthful' while post-independence politicians, 'infatuated by the lure of power, are perverting our social diversities ... thereby fragmenting our society'. The RSS 'realise[s] that if Hindu society does not stand united as a well organised national personality its very existence will be at stake'. Once this unity is established 'no one can dare challenge it'. Clearly, the imagination of the homeland is one that has continually been threatened by 'outside' influences and only by regenerating a sense of territorial integrity and spiritual unity can future dissolution be avoided. Additionally, the BJP invokes the Jewish experience of expulsion and construction of a homeland to validate its case whereby 'Hindutva successfully took the idol of Israel and made Hindus realize that their India could be just as great' (Meghani, BJP website, http://www.bjp.org/).

The RSS is well organized, with around 50 000 *shakhas* or branch associations, around 2.5 million core members and another 20 million volunteers. It is very active in propaganda campaigns and generates membership through mass marches throughout the length of the country. Such membership reflects the forces which have precipitated its popularity. The uneven development of capitalism in India has generated massive poverty with huge numbers of marginalized rural dwellers. Emphasis on ethnic purity chimes with a perception that foreigners have taken jobs away from working-class Hindus, while belonging to a network of people sharing a common ideal opens up possibilities for employment. Traders also use nationalism as a means of securing gains by calling for the indigenization of the economy, which

[*]British rule in India saw large numbers of indentured labourers move to many different parts of the world (including Sri Lanka, Malaysia, East and Southern Africa and the Carribean), closely followed by traders, family members and others. More recently, migrants have left to follow these colonial ties or pursue work opportunities.

involves expelling Muslim traders and transnational corporations and opposing 'Western' cosmopolitan culture more generally. The important point for our discussion is that sections of the diasporic middle classes have been strong supporters of this nationalist movement. While simple explanations are dangerous and cannot address the complexity of the situation, one reason for this support is that many Indian emigrants fear the dissolution of their cultural values, especially among their children, and so react with fervent support for all things 'traditional'.

The RSS is very active developmentally, whereby 'Rural development forms a most important facet of national reconstruction' (RSS website). These programmes include well known elements such as literacy, micro-enterprise support and disaster relief. Additionally, they encompass cultural issues such as 'cow protection' and support for the building of temples. In all these programmes the diaspora is very active. For example, in the Gujarat earthquake of 2001, members of the Indian diaspora were instrumental in sending aid and equipment to the ravaged areas. But while we should welcome 'developmental' activity which targets the rural poor, we must be conscious of the political motives which underpin these substantial efforts; these 'Non-Resident Indians' (NRIs) and 'Persons of Indian Origin' (POIs) have also been widely influential in the nationalist movement. As Bangaru Laxman, who was appointed the BJP's president in early 2000, exclaimed, the BJP needs to 'actively mobilize the growing economic and political power of the Indian diaspora in favor of India' (Khapre, 2000). Given that the Indian diaspora numbers between 25 million and 40 million, and that in the United States, for example, Indians comprise 1% of the population but control 5% of wealth, their potential contribution to Indian development is massive.

As a result, the Hindu nationalists actively target the diaspora. The RSS argues that 'the loss of their cultural identity ... makes them an easy prey to the vicious propaganda and corrupt conversion tactics of Christians and Muslims' (RSS website). Their activities around the world include a youth camp in Bradford, UK, temple building in north London, UK, and publication of various guides on 'good' cultural practice. To further formalize the links with diaspora and capitalize on its political potential, the BJP is pushing for the NRIs to be given dual citizenship and the right to vote in Indian elections, while arguing that visa restriction for both NRIs and POIs should be relaxed. This case reinforces Scholte's (1996, p.588) assertion that 'global communications have made it that much easier for a people to sustain its sense of national solidarity while being dispersed across the planet'. Indeed, we could argue that such nationalism can be even more intense among diasporas. As the pan-African example which follows shows, diasporic communities have had a much stronger sense of African nationalism than anyone actually residing on the continent.

3.6.3 (Pan-)African nationalism

A very different form of nationalism has been evident among the African diaspora. I refer to it as African nationalism although the 'nation' here is the entire continent rather than discrete ethnic or territorial groupings. In this section I examine the activities of the diaspora in theorizing the idea of Africa as a homeland and attempting to secure its physical well-being. We saw in Section 3.2 that 'Africa' as a whole has been an important anchor for many in the African diaspora for a very long time. In some cases this has involved an essentialist understanding of Africa as home, implying that there is some unique essence that unites all the people of this vast continent, whether living there or in exile. More practically, the settlements of Sierra Leone and Liberia* on the west coast of Africa, from where so many slaves originated, were attempts to recreate and regenerate an authentic and tranquil home that Africans could develop (albeit under the tutelage of 'enlightened' Westerners). Trying to capture the range of understandings of Africa amongst the diaspora is a massive task (Fryer, 1984; Gilroy, 1993a,b; Howe, 1998; Magubane, 1987) so I will focus here on an emblematic period in the 1920s when Marcus Garvey was calling for a return to Africa as a response to white domination in the United States. From there I will touch upon the impacts of such beliefs upon concrete developmental activities across various parts of the continent.

*Liberia was established by the Americans in 1847 as a colony for freed slaves from the American plantations.

In the United States, the period from the latter part of the nineteenth century to the early twentieth century witnessed the civil war and rapid industrialization involving the freeing of slaves and mass migration of black people away from the plantations of the south to the urban industrial centres of the north and east. However, black people in Africa and the diaspora at the time were still denied basic human rights and civil liberties by their white rulers, and in the United States the African-American proletariat still experienced widespread poverty and had grown disillusioned with bold promises of freedom. It was in these political and economic circumstances that Garveyism arose.

Marcus Garvey was born in Jamaica in 1887 and spent his middle years in the United States, before going to England, where he died in poverty in 1940. His ideas and programmes were adventurous and involved consciousness raising, publishing, a return to Africa movement and various pro-black business ventures. Garvey linked the (mis)fortunes of African-Americans with the underdevelopment of Africa. As Magubane notes:

> Garveyism in its various forms becomes a powerful political and ideological protest against the despoliation of Africans and Afro-Americans. Blacks in America, because they shared the same soil with their oppressors, became the forerunners of this movement. Their presence in one of the centers of this world drama sharpened their

awareness of the contradictions between ideal and practice, between the carrying of the white man's burden in Africa and their exploitation in white America.

(Magubane, 1987, p.93)

Garvey appealed to the black working classes in the United States who, perhaps for the first time, began to link their existence in diaspora with their identity as 'Africans' and, with it, the plight of Africans living under colonialism in Africa.

Garvey's prime target was the white hegemony which repressed black people the world over. To this end, he established the Universal Negro Improvement Association (UNIA) which aimed to

establish a universal co-fraternity among the race, to promote the spirit of race pride and love, to reclaim the fallen of the race, to administer to and assist the needy, to assist in civilizing the backward tribes of Africa, to strengthen the imperialism of Independent African states, to establish commissionaries or agencies in principal countries of the world for the promotion of all Negroes, irrespective of nationality, to promote a conscientious Christian worship among the Native tribes of Africa, to establish universities, colleges, and secondary schools for the further education and culture of the boys and girls of the race and to conduct a world-wide commercial and industrial intercourse…

(Garvey; quoted in Magubane, 1987, p.114)

Garvey was very critical of middle-class black leaders such as Booker T. Washington and W.E.B. Du Bois, whom he felt had 'sold out' to the white middle classes. Du Bois gave much of his time to the National Association for the Advancement of Colored People (NAACP) which was established by white liberals. Garvey felt that the NAACP was too accommodatory and nicknamed it the 'National Association for the Improvement of *Certain* People'. Instead, he appealed to the black working class.

The UNIA had a huge following, with a rally in Harlem in 1920 attracting 50 000 people. It also published various journals, such as *The Negro World*. Additionally, Garvey called for a return movement so that members of the African diaspora could go 'home' to Africa. To this end he started the Black Star Line, which was a shipping company which was to transport Africans back home. One of Garvey's main goals, then, related to the restoration of an African nation. The following excerpts quoted in Magubane (1987) show the importance attached to achieving nationhood and, as with the Hindu nationalists, one founded on immutable cultural difference and racial absolutism.

Every American Negro and every West Indian Negro must understand that there is but one fatherland for the Negro, and that is Africa … as the Irishman is struggling and fighting for the fatherland of Ireland, so must the new Negro of the world fight for the fatherland of Africa.

(Garvey; quoted in Magubane,1987, p.104)

Figure 3.8 Marcus Garvey, founder of the Universal Negro Improvement Association.

As four hundred million men, women and children, worthy of the existence given us by the Divine Creator, we are determined to solve our problems by ridding our Motherland Africa from the hands of alien exploiter, and found a government, a nation of our own, strong enough to lend protection to the members of our race scattered all over the world and compel the respect of the nations and the races of the earth.

(Garvey; quoted in Magubane,1987, p.121)

It is perhaps Garvey's racialism that undermined his argument, with some even going as far as to label him a fanatic and fascist.

However, Garvey's impact on both American and African politics was momentous. For African-Americans, as Padmore (1971; see Magubane, 1987, p.124) observes, 'Garvey didn't get many Negroes back to Africa, but he helped to destroy their inferiority complex, and made them conscious of their power.' This inferiority complex is, as Magubane (1987, p.111) notes, a product of racism in the 'host' country resulting in the 'black's lack of integration ... which gives him a pariah status'. His influence on African leaders who were pushing for independence was also important. As James comments,

...in 1921 Kenya nationalists, unable to read, would gather round a reader of Garvey's newspaper, *The Negro World*, and listen to an article two or three times. Then they would run in various ways through the forest, carefully to repeat the whole, which they had memorized, to Africans hungry for some doctrine which lifted them from the servile consciousness in which Africans lived. Dr Nkrumah[*] ... has placed on record that of all the writers who educated and influenced him Marcus Garvey stands first.

(James, 1963, p.397)

[*]Nkrumah became Prime Minister of Ghana in 1952, and under his leadership Ghana achieved independence from British rule in 1957.

In concrete developmental terms, though, Garvey's various activities were limited. For example, very few African-Americans made it back to Africa and the Black Star Line was a financial disaster. Garvey himself never made it to Africa and he knew little of the cultural and economic realities there.

It is difficult to assess the concrete effects of pan-Africanist ideas and activities, but they clearly influenced the thinking of a generation of African leaders who were preparing their nations for independence around the time of the Second World War. As Magubane (1987, p.135) states, by the time Du Bois died in 1963, 'the movement for pan-Africanism had returned to Africa and had become a profound ideology for continental unity'. When African countries such as Ghana, Kenya, Nigeria and Zambia gained independence in the late 1950s/early 1960s, they soon established the Organisation of African Unity which, for better or worse, has worked towards continental integration and a shared response to Africa's marginalization (Ackah, 1999).

While formal support for pan-Africanism has waned, there is still a strong, if implicit, belief among many working for development in Africa that certain responses to underdevelopment must be dealt with on a continental, or at least regional, basis. Some of these remain true to the spirit of radical pan-Africanism, such as the numerous campaigns for reparations aimed at compensating Africa for the damage caused primarily by the slave trade but more generally due to exploitation by the West. Other efforts are less confrontational and work through existing organizational structures. For example, the African Commission on Human Rights argues for the recognition of Africa's unique history in any formulation of rights legislation. This involves acknowledgement of the damaging effects of colonialism and the ways in which African societies are divided along multiple ethnic lines. Another example of African regionalism is the Economic Community of West African States (ECOWAS) which, contrary to its name, is more than an economic community. It sees countries throughout the region as suffering from similar problems that only an international political organization can successfully deal with. One of the recent efforts of ECOWAS has been to promote African-led peace-keeping efforts in Liberia and Sierra Leone. A final example is an initiative called the National Summit on Africa which is a United States-based organization which aims to educate Americans about Africa and to 'further strengthen, energize and mobilize a broad and diverse support for Africa in the United States' ('Mission and objectives', The National Summit on Africa website, http://www.africasummit.org/). Part of this involves lobbying the United States government for an enhanced aid budget, but the list of corporate sponsors and high-profile supporters, such as the television personality Oprah Winfrey, points to an agenda of investment-led development and the promotion of more private forms of aid (Martin, 1998).

Pan-Africanism and other 'Africanist' political discourses have had major impacts on both the diaspora, from where they emerged, and on the African continent itself. They all share a belief in a nationalist or Africanist solution to the exploitation of black people living under white hegemony. However, in finding a common identity around which to do this, there has been a tendency to promote a racialized and culturally essentialist discourse of the type we discussed in Section 3.2.3.

3.6.4 Developing home

Alongside, and at times supporting, such political movements as those discussed above are economic transfers. The most important of these flows is in the form of remittances, but given that arrangements usually take place interpersonally and/or illegally, there are no accurate records of their scale. A proxy indicator of the growing importance of remittances is given in the growth of money transfer companies, like Western Union, which make the movement of finances to family and kin members 'back home' and/or in other parts of the diaspora much easier. Indeed, these financial (as well as human) flows have been made increasingly easy with the technologies of globalization. As Portes observes:

> Airplanes, taxis, fax machines, and electronic mail facilitate contact and exchange among common people on a scale incommensurate with what could be done a century earlier. For this reason, and given the economic, political, and cultural incentives to do so, more immigrants and their home country counterparts have become involved in transnational activities. Once the process begins, it can become cumulative so that, at a given point, it can turn into 'the thing to do' not only among the pioneers, but even among those initially reluctant to follow this path.
>
> (Portes, 1997, p.18)

Not only does this show a form of globalization 'from below', but it also shows how diasporic communities tend to follow relatively well-worn pathways, previously traversed by members of the same community.

In this section we will consider in a little more detail the formal and informal African institutions in the UK which are promoting development in Africa, but before that I want to introduce a framework for classifying these types of activity. A group of researchers has undertaken a project to 'analyse the contribution which exile communities can make to reconstruction in their home countries, without returning permanently' (Al-Ali *et al.*, 1999, p.1). Their analysis of Bosnian and Eritrean refugees is useful for classifying the types of activity aimed at developing homelands, and for assessing the potential of such activities. Despite being relatively recent arrivals, the refugees in this study form part of a wider diaspora and many of them will never go home. A study of their activities, therefore, is valuable in a more general discussion of diaspora and development.

The activities the refugees engage in can be divided into economic, political, social and cultural, and may pertain to either the host country or their home country (see Table 3.1). Clearly, the host country focus, including such things as social gatherings and cultural events, overlaps with our earlier discussion of diasporic development in place (Section 3.4 above), so in this section I will focus on the activities relating to the home country. However, as the whole concept of diaspora stresses, we cannot readily separate out 'home' from 'host' (except in a purely geometrical–cartographical sense), since the lived experience of individuals stretches across both these contexts and incorporates family, loved ones, kin, community, ethnic groups or fellow nationals wherever they may be. This affects the activities of diasporic communities, because 'activities which sustain or support the society and culture of the home country within the exile community are considered by both communities to be equally important in shaping the future of the home country' (Al-Ali *et al.* 1999, p.7). We will see that such matters are equally important for the African diaspora who have left Africa, not as refugees, but for reasons of trade or education.

The study also sought to assess which factors affected the differential capacity of refugees to support developmental activities at home or in the host country. To do this the researchers made a distinction between someone's desire to participate in such activities and their capacity to do so. For example, some political refugees may be opposed to the ruling party and, therefore, are reluctant to support any form of national development which might strengthen that party's grip on power; they have the capacity to support homeland development, but lack the desire to do so. In contrast, the refugees may have the desire to participate, but not the capacity. One of the key dimensions in determining the capacity to support home country activities is the degree of integration within the host society. If migrants lack the right to work and/or face routine hostility from the host state or individuals, they are less likely to express opinions or be able to afford to send financial support home. The legal status of migrants or refugees is also crucial, because if they are illegal or awaiting residency status, they are in a weak position to organize support for others. We have already seen this in the contrasting fortunes of the legitimate middle-class Africans in the United States and the illegal Congolese traders in Paris. A further influence on the ability of individuals and groups to support activities back home is the existence of, or their awareness of, organizations dedicated to such activities. We will see shortly, in Box 3.7, how one London-based NGO is seeking to organize and facilitate diasporic African NGOs seeking to promote development in their home countries.

Members of the diasporic community who have earned wealth and respect away from home may contribute to formal development projects. Remittances are sent within families and kin groups, but financial transfers can be more formalized. The transnational communities are

Table 3.1 A classification of refugee activities

	Economic	Political	Social	Cultural
Home country focus	1 Financial remittances 2 Other remittances 3 Investments 4 Charitable donations 5 Taxes 6 Purchase of bonds	1 Participation in elections 2 Membership of political parties	1 Visiting friends and family 2 Social contacts 3 Contributions to newspapers	1 Cultural events
Host country focus	1 Charitable donations 2 Donations to community organizations	1 Political rallies 2 Political demonstrations 3 Mobilization of political contacts	1 Membership of social clubs 2 Attending social gatherings 3 Links with other organizations 4 Contributions to newspapers 5 Participation in discussion groups	1 Events to promote culture 2 Education

Source: Al-Ali, N., Black, R. and Koser, K. (1999) *Mobilisation and participation of transnational exile communities in post-conflict reconstruction, 1989–1999*, report to Economic and Social Research Council, p.8.

characterized 'by an increasing number of people who lead dual lives. Members are at least bilingual, move easily between different cultures, frequently maintain homes in two countries, and pursue economic, political, and cultural interests that require a simultaneous presence in both' (Portes, 1997, p.16). Among the Chinese diaspora such a duality earns these people the title 'astronaut' because they float in orbit between and above fixed locales (Ong, 1993). In developmental terms, these linkages can become institutionalized. Portes (1997) highlights a case in point:

> Mexican immigrants in New York City have organized vigorous campaigns in support of public works in their respective towns. Smith (1992) tells about the reaction of the Ticuani (Puebia) Potable Water Committee upon learning that the much awaited tubing has arrived and, with it, the final solution to the town's water problem. They immediately made plans to visit the new equipment, 'On first sight, this is no more than an ordinary civic project … Yet when we consider certain other aspects of the scene, the meaning becomes quite different. The Committee and I are not standing in Ticuani, but rather on a busy intersection in Brooklyn … The Committee members are not simply going to the outskirts of the town to check the water tubes, but rather they are headed to JFK airport for a Friday afternoon flight to Mexico

City, from which they will travel the five hours overland to their pueblo, consult with the authorities and contractors, and return by Monday afternoon to their jobs in New York City...'

(Portes, 1997, pp.15–16)

While the scale of such developmental connections is hard to assess, studies such as Al-Ali *et al.* (1999) would suggest that they are increasingly widespread.

Box 3.7 Formal linkages: the case of NGOs and AFFORD

The London-based African Foundation for Development (AFFORD) aims to 'support initiatives by the African diaspora to contribute to Africa's development and challenge mainstream agencies, both governmental and non-governmental, to take the African diaspora's input to development much more seriously' (Chukwu-Emeka Chikezie Fergusson, 2000, p.13). AFFORD makes the distinction between the older African diaspora, inaugurated by slavery and colonialism, and a neo-diaspora relating to the post-independence period. It identifies thirteen types of developmental organization engaged in a variety of activities.

Types of organization: individuals, hometown associations, ethnic associations, alumni associations, religious associations, professional associations, development NGOs, investment groups, political groups, national development groups, welfare/refugee groups, supplementary schools, virtual organizations.

Types of activity: person-to-person transfers of money, community-to-community transfers, identity-building/awareness raising, lobbying in current home on issues relating to ancestral home, trade with and investment in ancestral home, transfers of intangible resources, support for development on a more 'professional' basis, payment of taxes in ancestral home.

AFFORD goes on to highlight the case of the University of Hargeisa in Somaliland:

> Against all odds and to much national and international acclaim, the newly developed University of Hargeisa (UoH) in Somaliland recently opened its doors to the first batch of access course students in preparation for a full start in September 2000. Initiated in mid-1997, this effort united Somalis in Somaliland itself with Somalis in the diaspora as far-flung as Australia, Sweden, Kuwait, the United States, and Britain. The project enjoyed support by the government of Somaliland, a territory still without international recognition. A steering committee in London that combined Somali expertise and leadership with British know-how and experience worked in close collaboration with an interim council in Somaliland. Local businesses in Somaliland took full responsibility for rehabilitating the government-donated dilapidated old-school building that was in fact home to over 500

returned Somali refugees. Somalis in Sweden provided 750 chairs and tables; Kuwait-based Somalis sent computers. In the project's second year, the Somaliland Forum, a cyberspace-based global network of Somalis formed taskforces to tackle specific elements, raised money, maintained e-mail groups and hosted real-time e-conferences.

(AFFORD, 2000, p.10)

This is an example of a 'DIY' transnational development initiative which was driven by Africans for Africans. However, it used institutional linkages, both state and non-state, as well as utilizing the communicative power of modern technology to involve a wide section of the Somali diaspora. Crucially, the establishment of a university for a nation which lacks formal statehood is an important step in staking its legitimacy.

The following excerpt, by the founder and director of AFFORD, demonstrates the importance of remittances in promoting the survival of family and community in Africa. The problem of calculating the size of remittance flows, as AFFORD (2000) notes, is that only about 50% of them go through official channels. However, it has been estimated that for Cape Verde, for example, remittances accounted for around 17% of the gross domestic product.

The collective effort of such associations is combined with people's individual efforts to support families and friends back home through remittances of money through formal and informal channels. Little wonder that money transfer companies such as Western Union and Money Gram have raised their profile among African communities: they are competing for business with the hundreds of African-owned money transfer ventures that are the lifeline for increasingly impoverished families in Africa with relatives abroad.

'Remittances help people in Africa to cope with poverty', says Dr Claude Sumata, an economist who studies remittances from Africans in Europe and their impact back home; 'many people face problems like unemployment, low or no wages and bad state policies.'

Indeed, in the case of his native Democratic Republic of Congo (DRC), where failure to meet donors' conditions [the economic and political conditions attached to their loans] means that there is no inflow of aid, people are even more dependent on remittances from relatives abroad, according to Sumata. Moreover, 'remittances can help people to start businesses', he says, and thus, for the DRC represent the only inflow of capital for small-scale enterprises.

And studying these remittance patterns is important, says Sumata: 'They are a contribution that African people make to their countries. People say it's the IMF [International Monertary Fund] and World Bank that help Africa but Africans abroad set up businesses and promote overseas trade with their countries.'

> This combination of collective community effort and individual remittances means that for some African countries such as Ghana, with significant and well-established diasporas, Africans abroad are indeed probably putting more money into the economy than are official aid donors.
>
> (Chukwu-Emeka Chikezie Fergusson, 2000, p.12–13)

Referring back to our case studies of the African diasporas in the United States and Paris, both sets of Africans link their activities in diaspora to development of home. This may be through remittances, gifts or more substantial investment in new businesses. Tied to this is a strong social obligation. MacGaffey and Bazenguissa-Ganga discuss *lusolo*, which is a Congolese belief that 'success in commerce is a gift that is inherited in the family and that the wealth it brings belongs to the family and should be shared among them' (2000, p.126). These 'pressures for redistribution' are strong and clearly link the diaspora to development. Similarly, Arthur reports of one migrant whose failure to send remittances resulted in virtual ostracization, with his father exclaiming 'When you die make sure you are buried in America' (2000, p.134). Both studies also suggest that diasporic communities, either formally or through 'hidden' dissent, were prepared to contribute to ousting despotic African leaders and addressing the political crises that precipitated their migration in the first place.

A key difference between the two cases is that the Africans in the United States clearly see themselves as sojourners. They prefer a temporary legal status as opposed to full-blown naturalization (that is, the renunciation of their original citizenship to become exclusively American citizens), because 'that enables them to educate themselves, to work, and to save enough money to provide the capital needed to establish a business at home. Most African immigrants expect to return to Africa to live there permanently' (Arthur, 2000, p.127). However, given the relatively recent arrival of most of these immigrants and the continuing uncertainty back home, one has to question how many of them will fulfil this desire. Equally, both studies showed that failure in education, for a variety of reasons, forced Africans into the 'undocumented' realm as their study visas expired. Once in that realm the future is far less certain. For the Congolese in Paris 'The future does not look hopeful' (MacGaffey and Bazenguissa-Ganga, 2000, p.164).

Both studies also show that diasporic communities see business opportunities in Africa. Returning to the trader Beatrice, mentioned in Section 3.5.3, MacGaffey and Bazenguissa-Ganga report how she ultimately wants to establish production units in Congo, but has experienced embezzlement of her money and so is looking at more diverse opportunities across the globe until the situation is more predictable.

> She bought equipment for a medical office with the profits of her trade. It went into operation, but was managed by a Congolese who embezzled

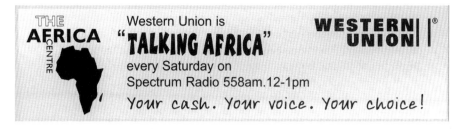

Figure 3.9 The Western Union – used by many of the African diaspora to send money 'home' to relatives.

the funds so that she had to close it down. She plans to sell the equipment to the General Hospital and has the necessary contacts there to do so ... She plans to develop trade with Nigeria because it is a huge country and she has family connections there. She already knows wholesalers eager to buy T-shirts she has seen in the United States. She also plans new lines of business in Switzerland, where she has other connections.

(MacGaffey and Bazenguissa-Ganga, 2000, pp.162–163)

The respondents in Arthur's study recognize the extreme difficulty and riskiness of doing business in Africa (due to political unrest, poor infrastructure and limited markets) but seem more optimistic than those in Paris. Arthur's survey showed that 80% of his respondents intended to return to Africa once they were wealthy enough and the political and economic climate had stabilized. Hence, 'most African immigrants structure their economic decision-making by focusing on the long-term economic potential of their homelands. Participation in the economic development of their countries of origin is paramount' (Arthur, 2000, p.129). As one Ghanaian stated:

Why should I spend over $100 000 for a house in the United States paying an interest of about 8% for thirty years when with only $20 000 I could build a nice two-story building or purchase one in [one] of the exclusive communities in the Accra-Tema area ... We have banks in Ghana now that will allow you to draw your money in dollars once you have a foreign account. Life doesn't get better than this.

(Arthur, 2000, p.128)

Both studies show that diasporic Africans draw on wide-ranging 'ties' which facilitate their economic and social well-being outside of their homes. But these ties also extend back home, through individual connections to family, formal inter-community linkages, or, as with the University of Hargeisa, globally networked co-operation between peoples of the same nation. Hence, the ties and affinities are multi-scaled and may be used flexibly for different developmental activities. As we have already emphasized, these connections may also be used simultaneously, with an individual sending remittances home, attending cultural events organized by their local diasporic organization, participating in efforts to support the physical well-being of a home community, and lobbying for the removal of an authoritarian government.

| Summary of Section 3.6 |

- Most discussions of the diaspora and home focus on the role of imagination and cultural identity. While important and interesting, such studies fall short of analysing the concrete effects of these 'spiritual' connections with home.

- The concept of 'home' has many connotations and is usually linked to a sense of belonging and safety. However, such belonging and safety can be premised on the exclusion of people who are perceived to threaten the harmony and security of home. This means that identification with home can have positive and negative effects depending on who holds the power to shape the homeland.

- In the case of Hindu nationalists the homeland is seen to be under threat so that efforts by more extremist Indian politicians and diasporic Hindus to secure the home involves expulsion or extermination of Muslims.

- In contrast, pan-African nationalism was a defiant response to racism and exploitation, although it should be remembered that it was based on an essentialist view of Africa.

- More recently the African diaspora, either individually through remittances or collectively via organizations, has actively supported the development of home. These obligations to home are strong because of the extreme political and economic hardships which propelled individuals and families into migrating. Indeed, for many, leaving Africa to earn a living abroad was the only available strategy for ensuring the well-being of the entire family.

3.7 Conclusion: the future of diasporas and development

This chapter has shown that diasporas play an important, but often unacknowledged, role in development. The key to their success has been to utilize the cultural ties which bind these far-flung communities. Following our threefold schema identifying development in, through, and by the diaspora, we have shown how these ties facilitate developmental activities and flows in a range of different ways. The first involves the use of cultural ties in the place of exile. These 'embedded' social relations enabled entrepreneurs and migrants to gain a foothold in new societies and to begin to carve out competitive advantages by working with and through their diasporic community networks. The second way in which cultural identity and diasporic connections facilitate development is through exploiting opportunities in a globalizing economy. Contacts across the globe allow entrepreneurs to spot market openings and source commodities cheaply from around the world. The final way in which we noted that cultural ties can facilitate development is through transfers of money, political support or goods to the homelands of diasporic communities.

Overall, the chapter has challenged the view that the motivating forces behind development are necessarily states, international financial institutions or Western-based NGOs. We have seen that the activities of diasporas contribute to development in both formal and informal ways. As such, they represent a form of 'globalization from below' in which 'small' players, as opposed to mega-corporations, can make use of the opportunities offered by globalization.

And what of the future? With deepening globalization there is a series of contradictory forces at work. On one hand, the mobility of people and their ability to communicate and transact have increased so that the developmental potential of diaspora is likely to expand. In the case of AFFORD, for example, more formal developmental linkages are being made alongside longer-standing processes of remittance transfers. For UK-based African NGOs, the future may require more co-ordinated and strategic involvement with the formal development agencies who must, in turn, recognize the vital role that African efforts play in promoting African development (Ndofor-Tah, 2000). On the other hand, social polarization and economic and political exclusion mean that there will be increased pressure on the poor of the 'Third World' to seek their livelihoods elsewhere, even though the movement of 'illegitimate' people is likely to be curtailed through restrictive immigration and citizenship procedures. Hence, the activities and lifestyles of the Congolese traders in Paris may become an ever more important role model for the future.

Diasporic networks are an important component of the deterritorialized social and economic processes which are increasingly challenging development studies' conventional and analytical attachment to territories such as states or localities. They especially exemplify the importance of de-localizing certain key development concepts: in this case, social capital is stretched out across and constituted through dispersed diasporic communities. In addition, alternative forms of development are emerging in the transnational ties that bind diasporic communities to their homelands and to one another. Clearly in all this places and territories have continued to be relevant: it is in new settlements in 'host' countries, for example, that dense ties and opportunities for social, economic and political networks have been facilitated. We will return to review these broader consequences of diaspora for development in the final chapter to this book. The following chapter turns to consider this interplay between place and displacement, territories and flows, in greater detail through the case of urbanization and urban development.

4 City futures: new territories for development studies? by Jenny Robinson

Contents

Introduction to city futures

This chapter will explore the possibilities for urban development in different kinds of cities around the world. In common with the rest of the book, the chapter will be concerned with both displacements – flows or networks, such as the networks of diasporic communities discussed in Chapter 3 – and places, or territories.

It seems obvious that cities might be thought of as territories – any map of a city offers a bird's-eye view that clearly establishes where that city is relative to its surroundings, and encourages us to think of the city as a whole or, a territory. But as discussed in the introductory chapter, viewing development through the lenses of discrete territories – such as states, or in this case, cities – neglects a great deal of relevant social and economic activity which crosses the boundaries of territories and stretches across national and international scales. In conjunction with human movements, which shape the social life of cities, the flows of economic resources and information into, across and beyond cities are crucial determinants of any city's economic future.

In this chapter we will be exploring the consequences for development of understanding cities as distinctive places or territories which are made up of, and shaped by, a whole range of social, political and economic flows into, across and beyond the observable borders.

More specifically, this chapter is concerned with how life in cities can be improved. It addresses the following questions:

1   Given the complex nature of cities, as composed of diverse flows which come together to shape a distinctive and contested territory, how can an equitable and inclusive future for cities be imagined?

2   In the face of diversity, conflicting interests and powerful wider forces, how can individual cities shape their own development?

Section 4.1 of this chapter sets out some background for thinking about cities and development. Section 4.2 then explores different approaches to urban development, outlining various attempts to improve life for people in some of the poorest cities in the world. Section 4.3 moves on to consider the place of some of the wealthiest cities, specifically in relation to the wider economic flows of globalization. Development initiatives in poor cities have often been chiefly concerned with those parts of the city most in need of services, usually peripheral and informal areas. By contrast, many urban development initiatives in wealthier cities (though, increasingly, those in poorer cities too) have focused more on cutting-edge economic activities with a global reach.

Sections 4.4 and 4.5 of the chapter suggest some ways to bring these contrasting sets of concerns together, to promote economic growth in dynamic sectors without neglecting the needs of the poorest urban dwellers. We first consider new approaches to development which aim to negotiate city futures across different parts of the city and amongst the diversity of interests and activities which make up urban economies and city life (Section 4.4). Section 4.5 concludes by looking at the case of Johannesburg, where the post-apartheid moment has opened up opportunities both for addressing the needs of poor people and peripheral areas, and for greater engagement with the global economy.

4.1 Development and displacement in cities

4.1.1 Cities and displacement

It is hard to tell where most cities begin and end. You might think this casually as you travel towards the borders of most cities, where built-up areas become interspersed with open spaces, even countryside or wilderness, and where urban activities can co-exist with rural ones. In some parts of the world, notably in South-east Asia, the blurring of urban and rural areas as cities expand has led commentators to identify a distinct form of settlement which they have called *kotadesasi*. As McGee (1989, pp.93–94) explains, this is 'a coined (Indonesian) word that joins *kota* (town) and *desa* (village) – urban and rural activity occurring in the same geographic territory'.

More than this blurring at the edges, though, there is a sense in which the question 'where is the city?' can elicit an even more profound response. Ecologists have developed the concept of the 'footprint' of a city to capture the idea that cities have an impact on the planet (their 'footprint') way beyond their physical borders – no matter how indistinct they may be at the edges. Cities of necessity draw their resources for survival and production from beyond their borders, whether it be from nearby market-gardening enterprises which supply basic foodstuffs, or via the rail, air and ship links which bring in goods from a hinterland which can stretch all the way around the globe.

Cities are closely associated, then, with many of the processes of deterritorialization which some commentators see as characteristic of 'globalization'. The social, economic and cultural flows and networks which make up the architecture of globalization acquire a greater density as they overlap in cities, bringing resources, ideas and people together in urban space (Massey *et al.*, 1999). Thus, if cities are made up of and shaped by a range of flows into, across and beyond their observable borders, let us think about this for the case of Lusaka, the capital of Zambia. Although Lusaka is one of the poorest cities in the world, like all cities it carries in its physical fabric the traces of its position in a range of networks and associations stretching across to other parts of the country and beyond. From the sprawling informal areas housing people from all over the country, to the grand buildings of international banks which facilitate flows of currency, investment and loans in and out of the country, Lusaka is tied into a range of networks of social and

Figure 4.1 Lusaka, Zambia, showing one of the main approaches to the city from the international airport and suburbs. Adverts and commercial and government buildings illustrate Lusaka's central role in the Zambian economy.

economic relations. Evidence of the city's colonial past and the presence of post-colonial intergovernmental agencies both indicate Zambia's place on the international political stage – Lusaka's symbolic role as capital city draws flows of visitors for meetings, summits, peace negotiations and so on. The immediacy and uniqueness of the city itself is apparent to any visitor, and also to the residents, but without attention to the wider networks which shape what a city is it is difficult to understand what makes that place distinctive. This chapter will argue that appreciating a city's distinctiveness as a place, as well as its role in wider networks, are both crucial to imagining and planning potential city futures. As in previous chapters, our argument is that processes of territorialization and deterritorialization, or place and displacement, are closely entwined.

It follows that not everything about cities is to do with flows into, across and beyond them. In terms of human movements there are, of course, some people who find it more difficult to move than others: disabled or elderly people, who may find it difficult to leave their neighbourhoods, or even their homes, for example; or people in parts of cities which are poorly served by public transport and whose mobility is therefore limited. On another timescale, there are households that might find it very difficult to move, from one town to another, for example, at certain stages of life – children in school, or a limited scope for alternative employment may make some people very dependent on the area or town in which they live. More than this, the built environment of a city represents a huge long-term investment of human effort and capital in a particular place, and can make cities seem very fixed, or immobile.

Cox and Mair (1988) have described this feature of city life, whereby people and institutions are dependent on a local place and find it hard to move, as **local dependence**. They identify a range of actors who are locally dependent. These include the households I have mentioned, but also include local governments, which of course can only be the local government of the city they are in! The same applies to service providers or utility companies – gas and water suppliers, for example, are dependent in some countries on the locally bound infrastructures which deliver their product. Some types of business, perhaps local family firms, or property developers and, in some countries, such as the United States, banks, are established and operate in limited areas, such as major cities or regions. All these actors in the urban scene can be described as 'locally dependent'. Of course remaining in one place is not (always) forced upon people – many people's decisions to remain in familiar areas are influenced by positive aspects, such as family and community ties that encourage them to stay.

So alongside the flows or displacements which come together to shape city life and economies, the territories of various levels of government and the more settled lives of locally dependent people and institutions in places are also crucial features to consider in exploring possible urban futures.

Cities are complex entities to define and to understand, shaped as much by wider flows and networks as by local communities and enterprises. More than this, the range of interests and activities in most cities is vast and not always mutually compatible. Nonetheless, thinking of the many different flows and networks which make up cities, creating distinctive places or territories, brings into view a field of development which is of increasing significance in the contemporary world.

4.1.2 Cities and development

Finding creative and equitable ways of planning and shaping the future of cities is something which has only recently come to be a major concern in development studies. Urban issues have for a long time been very low on the priority list of international development agencies, including that of the World Bank. Since 1972, between 3% and 7% only of its lending has been devoted to urban development, and urban-oriented activities have been spread through the Bank as a whole, rather than being concentrated in any specialist unit. At the end of the 1990s, though, the Bank turned the focus of its attention more firmly on the city (Wolfensohn, 1999), and the historical lack of interest in urban issues is changing dramatically.

There are two reasons why cities are set to be a central focus of development agencies in the coming decades:

1   As some significant milestones in urban growth are reached, cities have become a focus of public attention. It is popularly considered that over half the world's population now lives in cities (although in 2000 some official statistics suggested this was still not quite the case). Moreover, most of these people (almost 70% in 2000), and most of the largest cities, are now in the poorest countries (see Table 4.1), and development organizations have started to pay much more attention to cities as sites of development.

Table 4.1   The world's twenty largest urban areas, ranked by estimated 2000 population

	City	Country	Population (millions)		
			1990	2000	2015
1	Tokyo	Japan	25.0	27.9	28.7
2	Mumbai (Bombay)	India	12.2	18.1	27.4
3	São Paulo	Brazil	14.8	17.8	20.8
4	Shanghai	China	13.5	17.2	23.4
5	New York City	United States	16.1	16.6	17.6
6	Mexico City	Mexico	15.1	16.4	18.8
7	Beijing	China	10.9	14.2	19.4
8	Jakarta	Indonesia	9.3	14.1	21.2
9	Lagos	Nigeria	7.7	13.5	24.4
10	Los Angeles	United States	11.5	13.1	14.3
11	Kolkata (Calcutta)	India	10.7	12.7	17.6
12	Tianjin	China	9.3	12.4	17.0
13	Seoul	South Korea	10.6	12.3	13.1
14	Karachi	Pakistan	8.0	12.1	20.6
15	Delhi	India	8.2	11.7	17.6
16	Buenos Aires	Argentina	10.6	11.4	12.4
17	Manila	Philippines	8.0	10.8	14.7
18	Cairo	Egypt	8.6	10.7	14.5
19	Osaka	Japan	10.5	10.6	10.6
20	Rio de Janeiro	Brazil	9.5	10.2	11.6

Source: Based on United Nations (1995) data.

2   There has emerged a greater awareness of the creative potential of city life. Economic growth is thought to be facilitated by the wide variety of opportunities for interaction and networking which cities offer (we will explore this further in Sections 4.3 and 4.4).

It is not yet the case that most poor people live in cities, but the trends in population growth across poorer countries suggest that these numbers are rising, especially in rapidly urbanizing regions (See Table 4.2). In Latin America, more than 70% of the poor already live in cities (although this high figure is partly the result of relatively small settlements being defined as 'urban'). By all accounts the proportion of poor people living in cities is set to rise in other regions (UNCHS[*], 2001). Moreover, there are strong grounds for suggesting that poverty in cities is often underestimated, as the higher costs of urban living, the hazards of disease and pollution and the costs of access to basic services are not accounted for in most poverty criteria, which are assumed to be uniform for all areas, both urban and rural (UNCHS, 2001, p.16). In addition, many of the impacts of poverty in urban areas are borne disproportionately by women. Meeting household needs in a context of inadequate service provision adds to women's already heavy burden of domestic labour (Beall, 2000). As the UNCHS notes in its *Global Report on Human Settlements* (2001, p.15), 'in the years to come, policy makers need to reckon with the urbanisation and feminisation of poverty'.

[*]United Nations Centre for Human Settlement

Table 4.2 Size and growth of urban and rural populations, by region

Region	Level of urbanization % (2000)	Urban population (thousands) (2000)	Annual growth expected % (2000–2015)	Rural Population (thousands) (2000)	Annual growth expected % (2000–2015)
World	47.0	2 845 049	2.0	3 210 000	0.3
Africa	37.9	297 139	3.5	487 306	1.1
Asia	36.7	1 351 806	2.4	2 330 744	0.2
Europe	74.8	544 848	0.3	184 039	−1.2
Latin America	75.3	390 868	1.7	128 275	−0.1
North America	77.2	239 049	1.0	70 582	−0.5
Oceania	70.2	21 338	1.2	9055	0.9

Source: UNCHS (2001) *Cities in a Globalising World: Global Report on Human Settlements*, Earthscan, London, pp.271–273.

This chapter will explore how the task of planning the development of cities and imagining city futures is presenting itself to city dwellers and city managers around the world. The challenge they face is to consider how to improve the lives of the billions who already live in and around urban areas and to plan for the millions of people who are moving to cities every year. Part of this will involve accommodating the diversity of activities and interests which make up any city. Focusing only on certain areas within cities, or prioritizing certain groups or economic sectors over others can reinforce inequalities within cities or overlook some of the benefits of different economic and social sectors for the city. This chapter will explore the potential for development and growth across the wide range of social, economic and political activities which co-exist in cities and which draw into them the people, investment, ideas, wealth and cultural diversity which shape their futures.

Summary of Section 4.1

- Cities are important targets for development interventions, as more and more people, especially in poor countries, make their homes and seek their livelihoods in cities.

- With the urbanization of poverty, there is a need for development studies to redress the previous neglect of cities.

- Cities can be understood both as territories and in terms of many different flows and networks, stretching beyond their borders – they are places, profoundly shaped by displacements of people, resources and information.

4.2 Urban development challenges

The challenge of meeting the needs of a diverse and often rapidly growing urban population has for a long time faced those who manage and govern cities; if anything, the challenge is becoming a greater one. With larger urban populations and, in many places around the world, increasing inequality and poverty, improving life in cities is an urgent task. The often difficult conditions of city life have encouraged a range of efforts to improve things – and communities, local and central governments and the private sector have all been involved in trying to provide better housing, more efficient transport systems, more employment opportunities and healthier living environments (Beall, 2000). While these issues are the concern of urban dwellers everywhere, there have been important differences in the extent to which they have been addressed in different places. This is partly to do with politics: in some cities and countries the voices of those most in need of improvements in their conditions of urban living may not be powerful enough to encourage interventions. But the extent to which urban issues have been addressed also has to do with available funds – in many wealthy countries it has been possible to address these concerns more effectively than in poorer ones.

4.2.1 Different urban development agendas

Table 4.3 summarizes the extent of provision of some of the basic infrastructural requirements of urban living in different parts of the world. The data indicate that there are, as might be expected, substantial differences between cities in wealthy and poorer countries in relation to their level of provision of such services. As the authors of the UNCHS report 'The state of the world's cities' observed:

> Connection rates to all utilities increase substantially with increasing levels of ... development. In the cities of (less) developed countries, water is connected to about 37% of urban households, 14% have

sewerage facilities, 50% have electricity and 13% have telephones; these are very close to the proportions in sub-Saharan Africa as a whole. In the developed countries, however, on average 78% of urban households are connected to telephones and almost all households to other services. This difference reflects the availability of funds: cities in developed countries have 32 times as much money per person to spend on infrastructure as do cities in least developed countries.

(UNCHS, 2000, p.15)

Table 4.3 Percentage of urban households connected to utility services, by region, from 1993 data

Region	Water connections (%)	Sewerage connections (%)	Electricity connections (%)	Telephone connections (%)
Africa	37.6	12.7	42.4	11.6
Arab states	77.4	58.9	90.2	31.4
Asia	63.2	38.4	86.1	26.0
Industrialized (e.g. US, UK)	99.4	97.8	99.4	89.1
Latin America and the Caribbean	76.8	62.5	91.6	41.2
Transitional (e.g. Russia, Czech Republic)	96.6	88.8	99.2	61.9
All	66.2	51.8	76.6	38.2

Source: UNCHS (2000) 'The state of the world's cities', *Global Urban Observatory and Statistics*, United Nations Centre for Human Settlements (Habitat) website, http://www.urbanobservatory.org [accessed 20 March 2000].

Table 4.4 Local government revenue and capital expenditure, by region, from 1993 data

Region	Revenue per person (US$)	Capital expenditure per person (US$)
Africa	15	10
Arab states	1682	32
Asia	249	234
Industrialized	2763	1133
LAC	252	100
Transitional	237	77
All cities	649	245

Source: UNCHS (2000) 'The state of the world's cities', *Global Urban Observatory and Statistics*, United Nations Centre for Human Settlements (Habitat) website, http://www.urbanobservatory.org [accessed 20 March 2000].

These differences vastly affect the relative quality of urban life in different countries; citizens and governments from one country to another face very different kinds of challenges with substantially different resource levels available to them. The city product per person (like the GDP per capita of the city) in Africa was estimated at US$683; that of industrialized countries, US$22 926 (Auclair, 1998). Disparities in local government revenue and expenditure are even greater. Although variations in the division of taxation and responsibilities between local and central governments make inter-country comparisons rather difficult to interpret, the trends in Table 4.4 are striking.

The differing circumstances present amongst different cities in terms of economic activities and levels of infrastructural investment have shaped the kinds of development interventions which have been considered possible or appropriate in different contexts. Much of the thinking behind urban development planning has approached these differences by dividing cities into categories. Most broadly, cities have often been thought of as either developed (advanced 'Western' cities), or 'Third World', and urban development thinking and practice have taken different forms in poor and wealthy countries.

This split in urban development practice has been reinforced by the rise of a field of development studies specifically concerned with speeding up the economic growth of less developed countries (Hewitt, 2000; Thomas, 2000a). A set of strategies has evolved to help cities in 'Third World' countries address what seem to be their very different concerns from cities in the West – rapid population growth without economic growth, burgeoning informal sector activities, a large poorly housed or homeless population and extensive irregular settlements. In contrast, cities in wealthier countries have had to address issues such as population decline, urban sprawl, economic de-industrialization, urban regeneration, economic growth, inner city decline and homelessness. More recently, the focus of analyses of cities in wealthier countries has been on the impacts of globalization – an issue of growing concern to cities in poorer countries too. We will consider this later in the chapter (see Section 4.3).

First, though, the rest of this section will explore the range of urban development interventions which have been employed to address the apparently distinctive needs of cities in poor countries (see also Beall, 2000). At different times this has involved a commitment to housing provision or upgrading of shelters, informal sector support, improving community participation, securing land tenure, enabling service provision, and improving governance capacities and infrastructure (Beall, 2000; Burgess *et al.*, 1997). We will review some of the ways in which development interventions in so-called 'Third World' cities have changed over time and how they have affected these cities. The key outcomes, we argue here, are that they have helped to shape the form of the city, often encouraging peripheral and sprawling developments, and that they have focused most attention on specific parts of the city, particularly informal areas and poor neighbourhoods.

4.2.2 Development in 'Third World' cities

In the period from approximately 1960 to 2000 urban development interventions in poorer countries have shifted in at least three main ways:

- from concerns about urban bias potentially draining resources from the countryside, to an enthusiasm for urban creativity;
- from a focus on neighbourhood-level projects, to city-wide programmes; and
- from predominantly national-scale economic planning to city-level economic development initiatives.

We will explore each of these in turn.

Beyond urban bias?

One of the strongest legacies of urban development thinking in relation to poor countries is the idea that the growth of cities undermines the development of the countryside, where it is assumed that most poor people are located. This at least partly explains why cities have been a very low priority on the agendas of international development agencies. From the 1970s until very recently, development studies has been influenced by concerns of **urban bias** in national policies, which were thought to have established terms of trade between city and countryside that favoured cities. Rural products were relatively underpriced compared to industrial outputs, imported goods, and the wages of industrial workers. Some felt, therefore, that the countryside was subsidizing urban growth (Lipton, 1977). In response, rural poverty has dominated development interventions in poor countries until recently. This is reflected in the development studies literature, which has had very little to say about cities.

This was in stark contrast to the urban studies literature focused on 'Western' cities, which saw the city as an engine of growth and a site of creative innovation. By the early 1990s these ideas about 'Western' cities were beginning to influence policy makers concerned with promoting economic growth in 'Third World' cities. This new way of thinking saw cities in poorer countries as holding the potential for economic growth, rather than being a drain on the countryside. Under the influence of neoliberalism, development interventions have been encouraged to support the efficient functioning of urban economies, especially in relation to infrastructure provision and urban management (World Bank, 1991). We will explore this further below.

From neighbourhood projects ... to city-wide programmes

In the 1960s and early 1970s interventions were focused on the improvement of informal settlements and the provision of basic services and infrastructure in these areas. Initially, these were provided through government subsidies: shacks were removed and formal housing

*A form of 'housing' delivery where a site, with basic services (water, sewerage, electricity) is provided for residents, who must then build their own shelter.

provided. The substantial cost implications of these initiatives soon became apparent, however, and a new policy consensus emerged in the mid-1970s, which took a more positive view of squatter settlements (Burgess *et al.*, 1997). The provision of **site and service housing*** (with secure land tenure) on the periphery of cities was another common response to the high costs of housing provision and the problems of availability and costs of well-located land. It was usually too expensive to settle or acquire land in the inner city areas, and the peripheral focus of development interventions was also supported by the common understanding, particularly in Latin American cities, that peripheral settlements were the end point of the rural in-migrants' cycle. Although new migrants might initially seek accommodation in inner city slums, they would find more permanent accommodation on the outskirts of the city (Burgess *et al.*, 1997, Chapter 7). Moreover, the long-term under-provision of housing in many poor economies means that it is not only the very poorest or the most recently arrived who live in slums or squatter settlements (see Box 4.2 on Rio de Janeiro, for example). Inadequate housing remains one of the most serious concerns for urban development policy (UNCHS, 2001).

An example of a housing upgrade project in Lusaka, Zambia, is outlined in Box 4.1. Looking at the map in Figure 4.2 (p.154) can you assess what consequences this neighbourhood-level project-based intervention might have had for the city as a whole?

Box 4.1 The Lusaka sites and services and squatter upgrading project

Extract from Rakodi (1988, pp.298–299)

There were in Lusaka at independence in 1964 about 21 300 households, 35% of whom were accommodated in unauthorised or semi-authorised housing. In the years after independence, extremely rapid population growth (13.4% per annum between 1963 and 1969), accompanied by inadequate housing policies, led to the further growth of unauthorised areas, until in 1973, they accommodated 26 300 households, or 40% of the city's population. None of the residents in these areas had formal title to the land, planning or building permission, and as such were officially regarded as illegal residents, although following the establishment and strengthening of the political party organisation in squatter settlements, especially following the declaration of a One Party State in 1971, demands for services were occasionally met, implying a sort of creeping recognition of the better established areas, despite the official policy which was to resettle their residents in serviced plot schemes. However, the slow and problematic progress of serviced plot programmes and the increasing scale of the problem led to a change of policy in the Second National Development Plan (Government of the Republic of Zambia, 1972, pp.145–149), in which upgrading of selected squatter areas was to complement an increased emphasis on sites and services policies, home ownership and removal of subsidies on housing, and decreased emphasis on the construction of complete low cost houses for rent. The offer of a World Bank loan made implementation of the new policy feasible, at least in Lusaka, and, following the preparation of a project proposal by the National Housing Authority in 1973, a semi-autonomous implementation unit, the Housing Project Unit (HPU) was established within the Lusaka City Council and the project was implemented between 1974 and 1981.

The project included plans for providing 4328 serviced plots, the installation of physical infrastructure in three squatter complexes (George, Chawama and Chaisa-Chipata), the provision of social facilities in all the project areas, and associated city-wide infrastructure. The World Bank loan was to cover 48.5% of project costs, including all foreign exchange costs and 23% of local costs and is repayable over 25 years initially at an interest rate of 7.25%, after a four and a half year grace period. The squatter areas to be upgraded were selected according to various criteria, including their large size, the cost of off-site infrastructure provision and suitability of their locations for permanent residential use. At that time, low-income housing projects were a new venture for the World Bank and many of the components, particularly those related to upgrading of unauthorized areas, were relatively untried.

The spatial consequences of site and service and housing upgrade programmes were, in Lusaka and many other cities, broadly a reinforcement of peripheral urban sprawl. For the purposes of urban development, the city had come to be synonymous with the peripheral areas of inadequately housed and poorly serviced populations – those areas which seemed to distinguish 'Third World' cities (unfavourably) from cities in the 'West'. In the case of Lusaka, the diversity of the city's economy and landscape, which we noted in the introduction to this chapter, were lost from view. Moreover, the peripheral location of settlements like Chawama increased the costs of infrastructure provision. Obviously developments like this did improve living conditions for a significant number of those in the city, although the improvements were not always kept for the poor – middle-class households benefited when poor families found it necessary to trade the long-term benefits of residence and ownership for immediate income by selling on their houses (Rakodi, 1988).

While cities had been seen as sites for targeted development projects such as housing upgrades, mostly at the neighbourhood level, until the 1990s urban development interventions seldom took a view of the city as a whole, or reflected on the potential of the city-wide economy. National development strategies such as import substitution industrialization[*] (popular since the early decades of the twentieth century) had substantial consequences for urban growth, as new manufacturing firms and infrastructural development transformed cities and provided

[*]A strategy to replace imported manufacturing goods with locally produced goods. It usually required a tariff barrier on imports to protect relatively uncompetitive domestic enterprises.

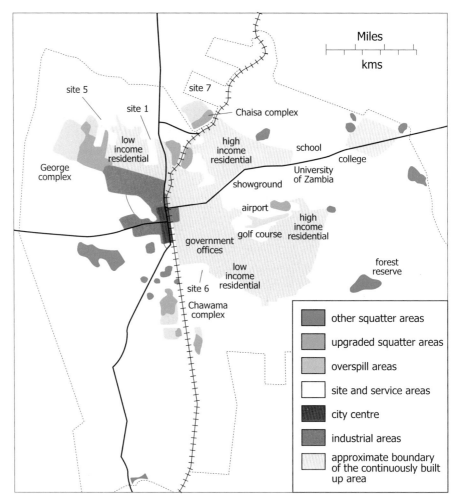

Figure 4.2 Map of Lusaka: site, service and squatter areas. Source: Rakodi, C. (1988) 'Upgrading in Chawama: displacement or differentiation?', *Urban Studies*, vol.25, no.4.

employment opportunities for the growing population. But the field of 'urban development' had for decades neglected what Harris (1992) has called the 'real urban economy'. Economic growth was not considered an important part of urban development planning, and was much more the province of national- and regional-level governments.

However, as we noted above, by the early 1990s, the urban policy consensus established in the mid-1970s, focusing on project-based housing and services provision in poor neighbourhoods, began to be dislodged by a neoliberal-influenced set of policies focusing instead on the broader concept of urban productivity as well as urban poverty. This approach, pioneered by the World Bank, saw cities as 'engines of economic growth' rather than parasitic drains on the national economy. It emphasized private or public–private partnership strategies for housing and services provision (as opposed to state or donor provision) and it highlighted the importance of infrastructure provision and efficient city-wide managerial capacity as essential to support economic enterprise.

Although there were many aspects of urban development which this new emphasis on urban productivity neglected, especially inequality and social needs, the urban imagination of development agencies had begun to stretch. The example of a major city-wide infrastructure provision project in Rio de Janeiro through the 1990s exemplifies this new approach (see Box 4.2). Neighbourhood-level projects continue to be important in improving city life, but urban development initiatives are increasingly taking a city-wide view.

Policy makers interested in promoting development have since come to appreciate even more the potential contribution of urban economies, whose successful management and development are now seen as a crucial determinant of wider economic growth. From the point of view of addressing poverty, too, the stretching of the urban development vision to include the city as it is of a whole is increasingly seen as of key importance. As the UNCHS (2001) notes, addressing inequality is as effective a way of combating poverty as promoting economic growth, if not more so. But for that both poor and wealthy parts of the city need to be considered together.

Box 4.2 Rio de Janeiro: towards city-wide development interventions

Extracts from Riley et al. *(2001)*

The *favelas* [squatter settlements] of Rio de Janeiro have long been recognised as one of the most visible manifestations of poverty in the city and as a symbol of the inequalities between the rich and poor ... While the *favelas* of Rio de Janeiro may not uniformly house the poorest of the city's poor, their residents suffer from sub-standard services and infrastructure, ill-health, low levels of educational attainment, social stigmatisation, violence, insecure employment and low and unstable incomes (Gilbert, 1995). It is in this context that the city-wide Favela Bairro upgrading programme was launched by the Municipal Government of Rio de Janeiro in 1994, aiming to provide the necessary conditions that would enable *favelas* to be seen as neighbourhoods of the city. Favela Bairro is one of many programmes that together make up the housing policy of the city, but of these Favela Bairro has the most resources, the greatest scale, and highest political profile. It aims to upgrade all the municipality's medium-sized *favelas* (of between 500 and 2500 households each) that make up nearly one-third of all *favelas* in Rio, but which house around 60% of the city's total *favela* population ... Favela Bairro can be argued to be one of a growing number of large-scale public sector initiatives currently being implemented with the objective of reducing urban poverty ... Such initiatives reflect the priority that poverty reduction is now receiving from policy makers, international agencies, NGOs [non-governmental organizations] and communities alike... (pp.521–522)

...An important element of the project is the issue of scale, displaying a concern for the project as a means to directly affect people's lives, but also a concern that projects be implemented on such a scale as to impact on the city as a whole, acting as a means to reduce inequalities and disparities between rich and poor neighbourhoods... (p.523)

...During the 1980s, the percentage of people living below the poverty line in Rio increased from 27.2% to 32.5%. Rio became the city with the highest absolute number of poor people in Brazil, standing at nearly 3.64 million... (Cardoso and Lago, 1993). Throughout the decade, the population living in *favelas* on the urban periphery grew by 50.7% (Lago, 1992) and in addition, there was a marked increase in violence within and around Rio's *favelas* associated with the illegal trafficking of drugs and the violent and repressive style of the police forces. Meanwhile the National Movement for Urban Reform was influencing the shape of the new Federal Constitution of 1988, and for housing, new legislative instruments were developed to improve housing conditions and above all, establish local government control over land use. In Rio, the incoming mayor embraced these challenges through a master plan and later, a strategic plan for the city, recognising the need to address the low-income housing problem not through localised interventions but as part of an urban development strategy for the whole city ... Ultimately [the] objective was to work on a huge scale and go beyond the limited and piecemeal approaches which had dominated the 1980s and involved just a limited number of municipal actors. (pp.524–525)

Figure 4.3 A *favela* in Rio de Janeiro, in close proximity to the apartment blocks of the wealthy.

City-level economic development initiatives

The role of city government had by the early 1990s come to be understood to include providing services to ensure labour productivity, enabling shelter provision and maintaining infrastructure crucial to the urban economy. But the economy per se remained the province of national policy in most countries. The thinking behind the World Bank's (1991) new urban policy emphasized the city purely as the place where economic activity happened. It was not seen as a site which held the potential to enhance and promote economic activity in its own right. In addition, cities in most poorer countries were governed within a highly centralized system of administration. In this context, local politicians had more incentive to lobby national government for increased resources than to look to managing or improving the local economy. As Harris summarizes:

> …hitherto 'urban development' has tended to exclude a concern for the underlying urban economy, making it impossible for city authorities to consider directly measures to enhance urban productivity. The agenda has been broadened from the immediate issues of maintaining order and providing services, to a concern with the environment of the poor. It needs now to consider the economy proper, particularly because increased administrative decentralisation and a more open world economy are likely to make the role of city managers much more important (however these are identified). This will require considerable inputs of technical assistance, particularly to identify the city-specific agenda of issues and continuing mechanisms to monitor the changing economy. Hitherto, local authorities have had little incentive to trouble themselves about the economy within their administration. However, decentralisation with greater democracy could enforce on local authorities an increasing interest in the sources of the city's revenues as well as the citizens' income.
>
> (Harris, 1992, p.195)

Harris's predictions have certainly been realized. Urban development initiatives at the end of the 1990s dovetailed with substantial administrative decentralization in poorer countries to produce a set of policy proposals focusing on promoting urban economies at a local level (these are explored in more detail in Section 4.5.2). These initiatives are also reinforced by a growing awareness of the competitive role of cities in the 'global' economy (discussed in the following section). Drawing on and extending the experiences of local economic development initiatives already prominent in many Western cities, urban development policies in poor countries at the turn of this century have started to follow the path which Harris was predicting at the beginning of the 1990s. Urban development initiatives at a city-wide level are advocated by major international agencies and increasingly implemented by cities around the world (UNCHS, 2001; World Bank, 2000).

In sum, urban development initiatives in poor countries have over time been concerned with:

- urban bias;

- interventions at a local community or neighbourhood level addressing infrastructural development, basic services and shelter;

- urban management and infrastructure provision focused on improving general urban productivity;

- city-wide economic development strategies.

Over time, then, the city has emerged as an important new territorialization of development thinking and practice.

Increasingly, development planners suggest that cities which are well organized and managed can attract and direct economic investment and encourage economic growth. As we will see, these strategies are deeply contested in individual cities and are often unsuccessful in their efforts to promote growth and development. But this way of thinking about cities and their potential for development has much in common with other prominent approaches to urban studies which have so far been primarily based on the analysis of Western cities' experiences in the context of globalization. We turn now to consider these in more detail.

Summary of Section 4.2

- Urban development thinking has for a long time been split between urban policy in the West, and urban development in the 'Third World', which have emphasized different parts of cities.

- Globally, however, cities are arguably facing increasingly common problems. Urban development initiatives everywhere face the challenge of acknowledging and incorporating both economic growth, including that with a global reach, and addressing urban poverty.

- Approaches to urban development are now converging on an appreciation of city-wide planning to enable positive engagements with wider global processes and to encourage a focus on city-wide inequality rather than only on poverty. The territory of the city has become a key focus for development interventions.

4.3 Cities and globalization

The previous section explored the ways in which policy makers' views of the 'Third World' city have emphasized certain parts of these cities more than others. In conjunction with rather centralized systems of government, this also contributed to a lack of emphasis on the development of the city as a whole. Until the 1990s, when city-wide development planning began to be encouraged, rural areas, national development and neighbourhood projects were the primary foci, or territorializations, of 'urban' development practice.

More recently, most cities around the world have experienced the widening and deepening of *global* connections of one sort or another

(McGrew, 2000). In both wealthier and poorer cities these global links have had important implications for urban development.

4.3.1 Global cities

If global economic processes are becoming more important in shaping city life, the question arises as to whether these global flows undermine the emerging distinctive role of cities in development strategies which we noted in the previous section. One might expect globalization to diminish the importance of cities in development, but Sassen explains why this has not been the case:

> At the global level, a key dynamic explaining the place of major cities in the world economy is that they concentrate the infrastructure and the servicing that produce a capability for global control. The latter is essential if geographical dispersal of economic activity – whether factories, offices, or financial markets – is to take place under continued concentration of ownership and profit appropriation...
>
> (Sassen, 1995, p.63)

It is perhaps one of the most striking paradoxes of 'globalization' that in an age of great technological innovation enabling rapid communication, travel and interaction across vast distances, the globalization of the world's economy comes to rest upon, and in fact to produce, locally dependent clusters of economic activity. Far from eradicating the importance of place, globalization has arguably reinforced it.

Flows and networks, while central features of globalization (McGrew, 2000), do not tell the whole story: the heightened importance of territories and places, such as cities or parts of cities, is in some cases just as characteristic a feature of processes of globalization.

The headquarters of major transnational corporations have concentrated in areas of key urban centres, such as London and New York, together with the producer services sector (lawyers, finance houses, insurance agencies, management consultants) in order to facilitate the increasingly complex management of their activities, which are stretched across the globe. See Box 4.3 for a longer account of these concentrations of global command and control functions in what Sassen calls 'global cities', a special type of a broader category of **world cities**.

World cities: Sassen's account of global cities is a special case of a more general category of cities, 'world cities', which are broadly seen as hierarchically interconnected 'basing points' for the various components of the world economy. Linked to a sense of the emergence of a global (as opposed to an international) economy, these cities operating on different scales (i.e. some are more regional nodes than globally connected) are thought to organize and articulate global production and world markets. World cities are also locations for national and regional political authority and have distinctive cultural and social roles. This approach to cities often engages in ranking city status according to their functional position within the world economy.

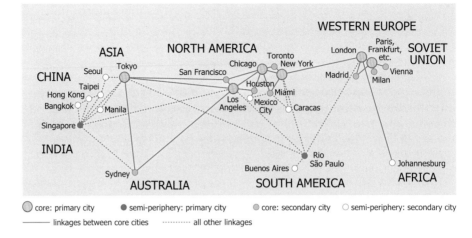

Figure 4.4 The hierarchy of world cities. Source: Knox, P. and Taylor, P.J. (1995) *World Cities in a World-System*, Cambridge University Press, Cambridge.

Box 4.3 On concentration and centrality in the global city

Extracts from Sassen (1995, pp.63, 68)

One of the central concerns in my work has been to look at cities as production sites for the leading services industries of our time, and hence to recover the infrastructure of activities, firms, and jobs that is necessary to run the advanced corporate economy ... At a global level, a key dynamic explaining the place of major cities in the world economy is that they concentrate the infrastructure and the servicing that produce a capability for global control. The latter is essential if geographic dispersal of economic activity – whether factories, offices, or financial markets – is to take place under continued concentration of ownership and profit appropriation. This capability for global control cannot simply be subsumed under the structural aspects of the globalisation of economic activity. It needs to be produced. It is insufficient to posit, or take for granted, the awesome power of large corporations... (p.63)

...According to standard conceptions about information industries, the rapid growth and disproportionate concentration of producer services in central cities should not have happened. Because they are thoroughly embedded in the most advanced information technologies, producer services could be expected to have locational options that bypass the high costs and congestion typical of major cities. But cities offer agglomeration economies and highly innovative environments. The growing complexity, diversity, and specialisation of the services required has contributed to the economic viability of a free-standing specialised services sector.

The production process in these services benefits from proximity to other specialised services. This is especially the case in the leading and most innovative sectors of these industries. Complexity and innovation often require multiple highly specialised inputs from several industries. The production of a financial instrument, for example, requires inputs from accounting, advertising, legal expertise, economic consulting, public relations, designers, and printers. The particular characteristics of production of these services, especially those involved in complex and innovative operations, explain their pronounced concentration in major cities. The commonly heard explanation that high-level professionals require face-to-face interactions, needs to be refined in several ways. Producer services, unlike other types of services, are not necessarily dependent on spatial proximity to the consumers, i.e. firms served. Rather, economies occur in such specialised firms when they locate close to others that produce key inputs or whose proximity makes possible joint production of certain service offerings. The accounting firm can service its clients at a distance, but the nature of its service depends on proximity to specialists, lawyers, and programmers. Moreover, concentration arises out of the needs and expectations of the people likely to be employed in these new high-skill jobs, who tend to be attracted to the amenities and lifestyles that large urban centres can offer. Frequently what is thought of as face-to-face communication is actually a production process that requires multiple simultaneous inputs and feedbacks. At the current stage of technical development, immediate and simultaneous access to the pertinent experts is still the most effective way, especially when dealing with a highly complex product... (p.68)

In some cities, such as Seoul and Tokyo, the significant role of the state in enhancing global competitiveness can also make location in the capital city crucial for large transnational companies in order to ensure them access to the key government ministries which facilitate their operations (Hill and Kim, 2000). Flows of labour, as well as capital, are also co-ordinated and managed through concentrations of relevant organizations in major cities. While the control nodes for transnational capital flows are usually located in cities within powerful economies, the control nodes for labour flows 'are found predominantly in a few key "Third World" cities (such as Manila, Colombo, Dhaka and Hyderabad)' (Tyner, 2000, p.62). The physical layout and location of these globally connected cities enables social interactions amongst government and private recruiters, foreign employers and migrant workers. These interactions promote global labour migration as part of national development strategies.

There has been enthusiastic recognition of the success and status of 'global cities' as basing-points for the management of the global economy and as top class environments for the stimulation of a wide range of economic activity. City managers around the world have taken notice!

As King (1995, p.228) put it, 'After 10 years of circulation, the world city metaphor is used by city governments, the financial élite and the cultural industries as a mirror in which to assess their own fortunes, or to mobilize their competitive image.' Global or world city status has become an ambition for cities around the world. Cities from Istanbul to Singapore want to be global. The territory of the city has become a crucial focus of many attempts to promote economic growth, as part of initiatives to attract international investment or to encourage cutting edge global economic sectors (such as finance, information technology or attracting headquarters functions).

But calculated attempts at world or global city formation can have devastating consequences for many people in the city, especially the poorest, in terms of service provision, equality of access and redistribution (see Box 4.4 below for the example of Istanbul). Global and world city approaches encourage an emphasis on promoting economic relations with a global reach, and prioritizing a certain limited range of prominent sectors of the global economy for development and investment.

Box 4.4 Istanbul between civilization and discontent

Based on Robins and Aksoy (1996, pp.6–33)

Like other cities aspiring to 'world city' status, Istanbul is now struggling to achieve a strategic role in its global region – which incorporates the Middle East, the Balkans, the Black Sea area, and the Turkic republics of Central East Asia. As in all those other cities, urban élites are seeking to adapt the urban infrastructure and economy so as to benefit from the new global conditions of accumulation and competition. There is also an attitude of cultural acquiescence and conformism to the global paradigm – in line with current ideas about city marketing and image creation. The meaning of globalisation is certainly not what it is in London or New York. In Istanbul one also needs to take account of the broader Turkish context (this includes the existence of an earlier orientation to modernisation and to global popular culture as well as massive in-migration to the city from poor areas of the Anatolian countryside).

In this whole process of change, there are certain possibilities for developing a more diverse and vibrant urban culture. At the same time, however, there are dangers of fragmentation, polarisation and confrontation. Either way socio-cultural developments fundamentally contradict and contest the global modernisation project.

There is a gathering consensus about making the 'great leap' to transform Istanbul into a global city. At a time when national economies are being weakened by the forces of globalisation, it is being argued that the significance of cities as players in the global economic field is growing.

Not only Turkey's transnational capital interests, but also the major political parties and much of the media have given support to this 'global city' project. Tekeli (1994) argues that the 'principal objective of a strategy for Istanbul should be to make it a world city', turning it into a global economic, communications and cultural centre of the semi-peripheral part of the world. In the cause of repositioning it as a global city, dramatic changes have been, and are being, wrought in the urban form and fabric of Istanbul. The urban élites have striven to attain the quality of infrastructure and facilities that would make the city attractive to investors, businessmen and tourists. To stay on a par with rival cities – a former mayor of metropolitan Istanbul, Bedrettin Dalan, considered these to be Paris, London and New York, no less – they have sought to upgrade transportation and communication systems; to build hotels, conference centres and executive housing; and to create cultural attractions, theme parks and shopping malls. The new financial district, (for example) that has come into being around the Büyükdere Caddesi has attracted 25 bank headquarters of big companies like Sabanei Holding and IBM, and is now dubbed the Manhattan of Turkey.

But it must also be recognized, Robins and Aksoy point out, that the process of modernization has consequences – a predominantly low-rise city with many historical assets is being transformed by massive high-rise buildings, motorways which tear an 'ugly gash through the urban fabric', a destruction of a cultural and historic resource in what is an historical city. 'Ironically, even tragically, at the same time that they are developing one kind of resource for the global city, they are destroying (irreplaceable) others.'

New immigrants crowded into informal areas or *gecekondu* (estimates put Istanbul's illegal housing stock at 65%) have been part of a resurgence of Islamic and local Turkish culture within the context of the metropolis. Robins and Aksoy see this 'other' Istanbul as offering an alternative to the globalizing élite. In fact, a political organization representing these interests, Refah Partisi, came to power in 1994, promising to improve the quality of life for the poor of the city. Whereas the earlier coalition had subordinated the concerns of the poor to their globalizing initiative, the Refah seemed concerned to take a more pragmatic attitude to the city's global future, and made some headway with meeting basic services in the *gecekondu*. But the momentum of the initiative to make Istanbul a world city was powerful, and continued despite this change in government.

Just as in the case of development interventions in 'Third World' cities, development efforts to create a 'global' city image tend to emphasize certain parts of cities over others (Amin and Graham, 1997). In this case, it is often the centres of cities, rather than the peripheries, which are brought into view:

> The downtown areas of cities and key nodes in metropolitan areas receive massive investments in real estate and telecommunications while low-income city areas and the older suburbs are starved for resources.
>
> (UNCHS, 2001, p.71)

As well as focusing activities on specific areas, the ambition to 'go global' causes city managers to prioritize economic activities and investments with a 'global' reach above those which may be more local or regional, and frequently also above addressing poverty and/or meeting infrastructural development needs in the city.

Most cities in poorer countries do not offer attractive locations for the global economy's command and control functions, although some cities in poorer countries, such as Kuala Lumpur, Malaysia, do have aspirations to become 'global cities', as Sassen calls them. The example of Istanbul, above, illustrates that promoting a global city agenda in cities in poorer economies draws on a different repertoire of economic activities than those associated with global cities in advanced economies. In addition to global businesses the city government in Istanbul was also aiming to attract tourists, business visitors and a range of international investors. Moreover, the aspects of the global economy which require co-ordination and organizing in poorer cities are different from those in cities such as New York, where the co-ordination of transnational finance and investment takes place. Manila, for example, has a concentration of agencies and institutions which facilitate the movement of low-paid migrant labour to wealthier countries. These activities may have a global reach, and they may have positive consequences for development (e.g. migrant remittances can bring in much needed foreign currency to an economy), but they are hardly the high status and highly productive activities usually identified with the idea of a global city.

Thus we see that it is more feasible for many poorer cities to focus on some of the other associated characteristics of global cities, or what Saskio Sassen (1995) calls 'global city functions'. These can include constructing attractive 'global' tourist and business environments, offering strong incentives to inward international investment, or gaining a global profile through hosting major events, such as the Olympic Games or international conventions. They might also act as a 'gateway', co-ordinating investment flows to their regional hinterland.

Another way in which poorer cities have tried to attract global economic activities has been through Export Processing Zones, or Free Trade Zones (Beall, 2000, p.433). Generally associated with a relaxation of labour, trading and environmental regulations, these zones encourage transnational firms to locate aspects of production (usually low wage and low skill) in poorer economies. These may be 'transnational spaces within a national territory' (Sassen, 1994, p.1), but they exemplify a form of competition for global economic activity which can be harmful to cities, rather than assist with their development. Cities and national governments often have to pay a high price in subsidies and infrastructural developments to attract these kinds of activities to their territory. Placing a priority on economic activities just because they have a global reach can have adverse consequences for local economies and the built environment of cities. A classic case of this strategy is found in the metropolitan region of Manila – see the case study below.

Case study: Export Processing Zones in metropolitan Manila, Philippines

Klein suggests that Export Processing Zones 'exist within a kind of legal and economic set of brackets, apart from the rest of their countries – the Cavite Zone, for example (near Manila) is under the sole jurisdiction of the Philippines Federal Department of Trade and Industry; the local police and municipal government have no right even to cross the threshold' (2000, p.207). In EPZs, companies get substantial tax holidays (5 years in the Philippines), regulations are relaxed, and wages are low – unions are not permitted to operate – and import and export taxes are waived. Klein notes that '27 million people worldwide are now living and working in brackets' (2000, p.208). In the Philippines 459 000 people were working in 52 EPZs in 2000. The largest number are in China, where 18 million people are estimated to work in 124 EPZs. In Cavite, the pollution, growing population and urban infrastructure are the problem of the local council – but very few companies pay any tax. The costs of industrialization are borne by the local population, whose chief benefit is the chance of working (along with migrants to the region) for the low wages which are meant to stave off competition from alternative EPZs, like those in China, where the wages are substantially less.

Sixty per cent of the foreign direct investment in EPZs in the Philippines comes from Japan, and over 20% from Korea and the United States. Thus while technically these EPZs are 'global' parts of the city, they are also founded on a few long-standing bilateral economic relations with firms from countries looking for cheap alternatives for production. EPZs in the Philippines are also often not technically part of the city. Efforts through the 1970s to decentralize urban concentration in Manila identified some areas for investment, and those which took off were the provinces immediately adjacent to the metropolitan area. A densely populated rural area based on labour-intensive rice cultivation offered a large potential labour force and market, as well as an 'intense transactional environment … facilitated by relatively inexpensive and varied modes of transportation such as motorised tricycles, becak, trishaws, jeepneys, buses and motorised canal boats. These allow the easy circulation of commodities, capital and particularly people' (Kelly, 2000, p.70). Hence urban agglomeration has not been necessary for effective industrialization.

Administrative decentralization in 1991 encouraged municipalities across the country to promote industrial zones. The province of Cavite has been strongly marketed to attract international investors, 'involving promotional missions overseas, the hosting of visiting trade delegations, and the publication of brochures in English, Japanese and Chinese' (Kelly, 2000, p.70). The local governments were also very involved in the conversion of land use from agricultural to industrial, and also in resisting moves to unionization in order to keep wages low enough.

The result has been an extended urbanization, a mega-urban region in which, beyond suburbs, major industrial concentrations have emerged.

4.3.2 Global success, or structural irrelevance?

So far we have reviewed two types of approach to cities, each of which has come to focus upon the territory of the city as crucial to economic development around the world. We have seen, first, that urban development thinking has shifted from encouraging specific project-related interventions in peripheral areas within the city, to suggest that urban managers should take a city-wide view of the potential for economic growth (Section 4.2). And, second, analysts of global flows and networks have argued that aspects of the global economy depend on certain of the locational advantages which cities have to offer. One of the key territorializations of the global economy is arguably the city, and policy makers are suggesting that opportunities to engage with wider economic processes can be competitively identified at a city-wide level (Brenner, 1998) (Section 4.3.1).

From both perspectives, it is argued that cities should engage with the wider flows of the global economy; economic activities are more mobile now than they were previously, and cities can build upon their own comparative advantages to attract investment, aiming to advance their position within the global economy.

But there are many potential problems which arise from this approach, some of which we have seen above. City managers may be encouraged to follow certain economic strategies which link into dominant global processes, at substantial cost to the city and the more developmental needs of local populations. Examples might involve sacrificing services in shack areas for tourist hotels and conference centres, as in Istanbul, or attracting international investment without generating the resources to cover the heavy infrastructural and environmental costs of these developments, as in Manila. In addition, the substantial inequalities in the global system mean that pursuing these kinds of initiatives may well mean simply reinforcing your city's place at the bottom of the global hierarchy in terms of economic activity, types of job, long-term plans, and capacity to direct the future of growth – as in Manila where 'globalizing' the economy leaves the city to cover the infrastructural costs of powerful transnational companies with no financial compensation.

Even for wealthier cities, focusing on economic activities with a global reach can detract from many pressing development needs (the case of London, UK, is discussed in Section 4.4.2 below). As McGrew (2000) has noted in the context of globalization more generally, 'Western' and 'Third World' countries are increasingly facing similar demands to address poverty alleviation, social and economic exclusion and urban infrastructural decay in their cities. Even in wealthy global cities, global economic activities co-exist with (and indeed might generate) poverty, as well as more local and national enterprises. It has been suggested that:

> ...cities in the North and South are becoming more alike in their most important characteristics: growing unemployment, declining infrastructure, deteriorating environment, collapsing social compact, and institutional weakness. Although the degrees of similarity and the meanings of these shared features differ between any two cities and between Northern and Southern cities ... a common set of critical economic, social, infrastructural, environmental, and institutional problems beset urban areas regardless of level of national development. The assertion that these problems are shared does not imply that urban areas in the North and South also share equal capacities to address and to resolve them. In fact, it is precisely the variations in economic, financial and institutional capacity that account for the differential prospects for improvement over time.
>
> (Cohen, 1996, p.25)

Perhaps even more worrying is the claim made fairly frequently by global and world city analysts that many cities in poor countries have become 'structurally irrelevant' (Castells, 1996). They are not connecting to the global economy, but instead are increasingly marginalized and disconnected from many of the dynamic elements of the global economy. In this case, the prospects for competing with other cities in order to move up the urban hierarchy towards world or global city status seem limited. Cities which grow without a supporting economic base are often referred to as 'mega-cities' (see Beall, 2000): large in population terms, but having few, if any, of the features of economic success of global cities as identified by Sassen. As some of the largest cities are now found in the poorest countries, the assumption is made that these cities are simply left out of the global economy. Writing of the African region, Halfani notes that it:

> ...cannot share in the mostly urban-based technological advances attained in the modern era. The sub-region is virtually cut off from the cluster of innovations associated with the micro-electronic chip technology. The basic structure of the African city, with its reliance on import substitutions industries, resource processing, and primary exports, is obsolete within [the] global economy.
>
> (Halfani, 1996, pp.93–95)

These are very sweeping claims, which while appropriately concerned with the fate of some of the poorest cities in the world in the face of powerful external economic interests, offer little in the way of hope for future growth, or optimism about building on existing resources.

If we return to our initial example of Lusaka, from Section 4.1 we can observe that this city is certainly not a major player in the 'processes that fuel economic growth in the new global economy' (Sassen, 1994, p.198). But copper is still exported, as are agricultural goods, and despite the huge lack of foreign currency (and sometimes because of it) all sorts of links and connections to the global economy persist. Lusaka has strong relationships with other parts of the country, other cities, and other parts of the region and globe – through commercial banks and foreign governments who hold the country's debt; through the World Bank, aid agencies and international political organizations; and through trade in second-hand clothing and other goods and services. The city continues to perform its functions of national centrality in relation to political and financial services, and operates as a significant market (and occasionally production site) for goods and services from across the country and the world. If we are to imagine the future potential of cities like Lusaka (and, in fact, I would argue, even cities such as New York) we have to bring in to view the wide range of economic and social activities which take place in, and stretch out from, any given city. In addition, we need to promote development strategies which pay attention to the diversity of flows and networks that shape cities, and guard against restricting plans for city futures to a small sector of the economy with a 'global' reach.

Section 4.4 explores the consequences of this suggestion in some detail. It aims to address the question as to how the future of cities can be imagined to include the diversity of activities which take place in them.

Figure 4.5 One of many imposing buildings in Lusaka's main commercial street, Cano Road, this houses one of Zambia's commercial banks.

Summary of Section 4.3

- The globalization of the economy has made cities important locations for the co-ordination and management of dispersed global activities.

- Economic activities also cluster in cities (like finance and producer services in New York, London and Tokyo) where co-location enhances innovation and interaction.

- 'Going global' has become an ambition of many cities around the world, and city managers are eager to attract global functions and transnational investment to their city.

- However, over-emphasizing global functions in development plans can have negative consequences for poor people in cities and for the maintenance of the urban fabric.

4.4 Cities and displacement: assembling flows

In Section 4.3 we noted the paradox that in an increasingly global economy the role of cities, and often small parts of cities (such as financial districts), is becoming increasingly important. Storper concurs that:

> A global economy is emerging, then, but it is not about a homogenous space of flows. It is instead a complex meeting of new kinds of globalised flows and new kinds of territorial economies.
>
> (Storper, 1997, p.239)

Thus, even in an age of global flows and networks, the value of locating close to other people, firms and activities has persisted. And it is cities which draw these different activities and actors together and assemble them in different ways within themselves.

4.4.1 Differences gathered together

The benefits of proximity which are enabled by and produced in cities are felt by a wide range of industries, businesses and firms – not only by those organizations which are involved in co-ordinating the global economy (as we saw in Box 4.3 above). All cities concentrate specific activities in some sectors rather than others, and some have more successful clusters of activities than others. However, all large and medium-sized cities offer scope for the interactions which will facilitate both routine economic activity and innovation. The enthusiasm of policy makers for the creative potential of cities builds upon these possibilities for economic growth which inhere in the range of activities that come together in cities.

Storper extends Sassen's argument about global cities to explore how all cities offer opportunities for economic innovation – in his view, 'New York, Tokyo and London economies ... are just particular cases of the general nature of city economies in late modern capitalism' (1997, p.244). Storper draws on the observation that economic transactions involve not only the trade in goods and money, but rely on 'a kind of [social] "glue" which works behind the backs of traded linkages' (1995, p.405). He refers to the interactions (social, informal, trust-based and learning) which take place in and between organizations as 'untraded interdependencies'. Co-location in cities, or parts of cities, not only facilitates the trade of goods, it also enables these intangible aspects of production and innovation. The examples of the new media industry in New York (Box 4.5) and the local economies of Bangalore (Box 4.6) both explore in some detail what this might mean.

Clustering of firms in different parts of major cities encourages the formation of dense social and business networks, in turn encouraging informal interactions which facilitate innovation and effective negotiation of business deals amongst firms. We have seen that the effective co-ordination and management of the global economy are enabled by co-location within the city, and other kinds of industrial clusters (such as Silicon Valley, California) also facilitate innovation through dense networks of interaction which are enabled amongst producers and suppliers. Clusters can also be identified in the centres of major cities, similarly benefiting from proximity and opportunities for interaction; these include the long-standing concentration of the financial sector (e.g. the City of London, or Wall Street in New York) and more recently the so-called 'new media' companies and other IT firms (see Box 4.5).

Box 4.5 New media, New York (Silicon Alley)

Extracts from Pratt (2000, p.429)

New York has emerged as a contender to be the world node in the production of 'new media' ... New York, or rather Silicon Alley in particular, is actively being 'made' into a new media centre ... Networks exist within, without, and across firms, financiers and clients ... In the new media community developers and financiers have sought to 'grow' the community ... The New York New Media Association [NYNMA] began as a series of soirées and dinner parties of those involved in the arts and technology; as a cultural link between MIT [Massachusetts Institute of Technology] (Boston) and New York. At such occasions, business and pleasure mixed with the exchange of knowledge. Investors developed the knowledge and insight that made investment possible. In time these parties grew from what became 'cybersuds' meetings ['CyberSuds™' is now one of NYNMA's signature events], to huge 1000-plus attendee events. The role such events play is still as a point of the exchange and updating of knowledge, as well as acting as a crude marketplace of ideas and business options; additionally, they have developed into a community support and labour recruitment fair. This is the process by which the NYNMA was created. Subsequently, it become the 'public face' of the New Media community, able to act as a 'third party' to pressurise the City for concessions for its members; it has also acted as a publicity machine...

Silicon Alley was initially a construct of NYNMA, but one eagerly taken up by the community, the City and Real Estate developers. It is true that many new media companies do cluster between midtown and downtown around the locale of the intersections of 5th and 6th Avenues, and 18th and 21st Streets. The connection here is with the availability of relatively cheap loft space for developers to live and work; also within close proximity to street and restaurant life (SoHo); and not so far from Madison Avenue (advertising) and Midtown (old media), and of course, the Downtown (finance and city government).

Interestingly, much of the promotion and construction of Silicon Alley has been carried out through an alliance of the City and NYNMA, and its actual focus has been on the Downtown area. Two influential reports carried out by accountants and management consultant Coopers and Lybrand (1996, 1997) sang the praises of the economic contribution that the nascent new media was making to the New York economy. These reports were circulated free of charge, were made available online, and became the subject of news reports the world over. It was a successful example of an advertising and booster strategy for the city as well as announcing that Silicon Alley was the 'place to be'. In effect, it was seeking to mobilise a virtual community and to attract it to, and weave it into, the community and fabric of New York.

It is not only in successful economies, or economic sectors with a global reach, that co-location in cities can benefit economic activity. The example of Bangalore, India, is instructive here. An emerging concentration of information technology firms, many foreign, has received substantial state support in terms of infrastructure investments, cultural facilities and urban design. Alongside these highly desirable (and very costly for the Indian government) transnational investments, clusters of local economic activity persist, benefiting from proximity, dense social networks and close ties to the local government. Box 4.6 describes this in more detail. It is also worth noting that although the enclaves of international firms were largely developed in isolation from the rest of the city, there are still some links between so called 'informal' economic activities and these formal corporations.

Box 4.6 Local economies in Bangalore

Extracts from Benjamin (2000, pp.41–42)

What really drives Bangalore's economy? How do the poor and middle-income groups who form the bulk of the city's 6 million inhabitants survive, get jobs and possibly progress in life? Local economies form the employment base of most urban areas in India. Detailed research on these reveal a startling scale and diversity of employment generation.

The local economy of Valmiki Nager is made up of weaving and waste recycling activities ... The diversity of land types plays a critically important role in that it allows for groups of various income levels to locate in close physical proximity ... Close physical proximity and high densities allow economic and other linkages to develop between various local (both income and ethnic) groups. For instance, Muslims from the north Indian state of Uttar Pradesh form the worker-weavers of handloom saris and cluster to work in one area of the *vattarams* (old, tiled row houses or old compounds divided into small houses). The master-weavers, who live in revenue layouts across the road, provide them with job orders. The revenue layouts also house weaving enterprises with two types of loom. The first type, producing art silk *jari* (an input for gold brocade), are manually run by workers in the art silk industry belonging to the traditional weaving caste called Devangas. The second, which are electrically powered looms, weave synthetic materials and are operated by Tamil migrants. Most of these looms are small scale and are operated from within the home. ...The weavers say the main advantages of being located here are cheap land and access to the city market which allows them to purchase and procure inputs such as raw yam, and also to sell finished products. Clustering also helps attract agents who visit them to pick up finished produces and also allows them to price their products more accurately and draw on the benefits of agglomeration. In recent times, Marvaries (one of India's ethnic business communities from western India) have moved here from Gujarat and are investing in these enterprises; they also act as financiers.

Another group occupying the *vattarams* are small traders operating in the city market or in KR Road. Despite the dilapidated condition of their houses, the cheap rents and the proximity of economic opportunities in the city market area make this a valuable location. Many trade in waste materials: recycled plastic slippers, paper, plastic and metal, salvaged computer and electronic parts. Both wholesale and retail dealers of recycled materials locate close by – an ideal setting for trade. For instance, one of the main purchasers is a prominent waste trader, Asgar, who lives across the road in the revenue layout. Asgar has a contract with some five-star hotels and large companies to buy their outdated televisions and other electronic equipment which are discarded every two years. After repairs, he sells them to various low-income groups.

Such neighbourhoods also provide access to informal credit and finance. For instance, Asgar, in addition to his waste and recycling business, also organises *chits* – a form of group credit scheme – and membership includes 50 of his own waste product suppliers. Such financial groupings have important political links. Asgar claims that his credit linkages have 'spawned' 1000 votes. This encouraged one of the candidates for councillor to seek his support in return for benefits and city council 'connections', if elected. Asgar, although illiterate, also operates a local *kannada* newspaper with a circulation of 2000. It seems very likely that this too has a role in shaping political interests and in building up pressure groups. The settlements in and around the wards of Mysore Road are known for several such local newspapers. This is not surprising when political pressure is critical for obtaining services for squatter settlements and *vattarams*, and for regularising revenue layouts.

Box 4.6 reminds us that cities such as Bangalore are shaped by a diverse range of social and economic influences, with widely varying reaches across and beyond the built environment of the city. This includes local and national economic and political networks, as well as networks of economic activity which stretch beyond the city, state or country, and draw on transnational links and investments. What this example demonstrates, though, is that links between sectors or networks within the city can be as helpful to economic growth as the interactions within a specialized cluster or economic sector. The recycling of computer equipment from transnational computer firms is one small example.

As Storper observes, it is not just the clustering of individual economic sectors which makes cities productive – it is the generalized opportunities for social interaction which can play an important role in facilitating economic exchange and innovation. Different networks of economic activity overlap in the space of the city (Amin and Graham, 1997; Massey *et al.*, 1999), and, as Storper (1997, p.255) puts it, 'the city is a crucible in which the ingredients, once put in the pot together and cooked, often turn out very differently from what we can deduce from their discrete flavours'. In the terminology of this book, the place of the city assembles and brings together the various kinds of 'displacements' – of people, resources, ideas – which flow into and across the city.

In the next subsection we will demonstrate this more fully. The question that we will be addressing is whether an appreciation of the wider range of social and economic activities which come together in the city – and not just activities with a global reach – might encourage different ways of thinking about city futures. Rather than being tied to competing in the limited range of sectors considered significant to the global economy, or lamenting exclusion from these sectors, can cities of all kinds find opportunities for imagining better futures through their existing diversity? Rather than emphasize the 'global' or 'world' city, can we propose creative alternatives relevant to all cities – for 'ordinary' cities (Amin and Graham, 1997) from Lusaka to London, or Nairobi to New York?

It is not, of course, feasible to offer generalizations about cities everywhere – they vary so much in terms of historical influences, nature of migrations, local and national economic activity, to name but a few distinguishing factors. With that caveat, though, we can make some inroads into considering the general significance of cities as places where different kinds of social and economic activities are gathered together. Cities are pre-eminently sites where social differences are assembled and shaped in particular ways. The distinctiveness of individual cities, or groups of cities, say within a region or country, lies in who and what they draw together, and in terms of what is done with those different social and economic elements once they are co-present within the space of the city. The challenge for urban development planning is to find ways to respond positively to the distinctive assemblages which make up particular cities. This includes the contribution of human movements (urbanization) as well as the coming together of different flows of resources, social practices and ideas.

Let us consider the example of urbanization – the displacement of people from rural areas to urban areas. This has varied considerably in different parts of the world in terms of timing, extent and social characteristics (such as gender, ethnicity and age). The nature of the movement has also varied. In some places, circular migration patterns mean that many urban migrants retain close links with their rural homes; in other times and places the form or duration of urbanization has meant greater disconnections between rural and urban kin. These different forms of migration shape the potential for urban development in at least two ways:

1   Human migrations create different kinds of linkages, or *social and economic networks*, between rural and urban areas and sometimes across national borders. They are one of the ways in which we can imagine the city to be spread way beyond its physical borders.

2   The diverse backgrounds, experiences and economic activities of urban city dwellers together add up to the city as a whole and collectively determine how a city's future development can be imagined and how it might be contested. Negotiating the future of a city across the social and economic divides within it is one of the greatest challenges of planning urban development. We will return to consider this challenge in some detail in Section 4.5.

Closely related to the human movements, or displacements, which shape the social and economic life of cities, the flows of economic resources and information into, across and beyond cities are crucial determinants of any city's economic future. The rest of this section will explore two aspects of these wider influences on city life and city futures: firstly, their *diversity*; and secondly, their *varying geographical range*. For cities around the world, extending the scope of urban development planning in these ways could be an important step towards longer-term and sustainable city growth more inclusive of all citizens. We consider in turn the case of a wealthy, 'global' city and the case of cities in economic crisis. In both cases, a range of social and economic networks is important to planning improvements for life in these cities.

4.4.2 The diversity of economic networks in cities

London, UK, is one of few cities in the world which do not need to aspire to world city status. Rather, those responsible for London's urban development are confident of their city's status as one of the world's most successful cities:

> Measured on a wide range of indicators such as financial services, government, business, higher education, culture and tourism, London holds an established position as a World City. It is a role that underpins the economy of the city as a whole. London is a globally successful business location paralleled only by a small number of the world's other great cities such as New York, Paris, and Tokyo.
>
> (London Development Agency, 2001, p.12).

The concern here is to sustain the city's pre-eminent position in the face of growing competition from other aspirant global cities. Although global financial and business services are at the core of London's economic activity (38% of employers and 32% of employees in 1998, double the figures for 1988), for London as a whole 'about 70% of employment is in firms whose main market is national rather than international' (LDA, 2001, p.18). The concern, nonetheless, is that growing dependence on the international finance and services sector increases London's vulnerability to external global influences, over which as a city it has little control (LDA, p.45). The temptation to neglect the rest of the city's economy in favour of global links is one that city policy-makers wish to avoid.

The city's economic managers are eager to seek out existing and potential opportunities for interaction, or synergy, between different sectors. This invites closer attention to the diversity of economic activity in the city, and discourages an emphasis on only those activities with a global reach, or those obviously indicative of London's world city status. Tourism and creative industries, retailing and concentrations of cultural activities may not themselves be 'global' but they all enhance London's world city status, attracting global firms to locate there and feeding innovation, especially in fields of creativity and design. Such activities are also important, though, in supporting London's ongoing manufacturing industry (7% of employers, 8% of employees), as well as new Information and Communication Technology (ICT) activities and other potential growth areas, such as environmental technology, and an emerging social economy. They can also play a role in fostering greater social inclusion, as demonstrated by London's substantial and diverse ethnic minority population which supports a cosmopolitan urban culture – definitely an asset in the cultural industries.

London's policy-makers are grappling with ways to manage a city where some of the world's most prosperous global businesses compete for space with some of the country's poorest citizens. Living in London is expensive, sometimes unhealthy and usually crowded. Ensuring a functioning and efficient transport system and general urban infrastructure is something which is important for all London's residents. It is possible that investing in this aspect of sustainable urban living could support ongoing productivity gains for business and at the same time maintain satisfactory urban lifestyles for the poor, improving accessibility to employment and services. But as the elected London Assembly notes, opening up new parts of the city to efficient transport links could mean successful businesses outbid local firms and residents for well-connected locations.

Real challenges face London's relatively new (2000) metropolitan-wide authority, the Greater London Assembly, and its popularly elected Mayor, in implementing a vision for development of the city as a whole. This vision needs to include: central parts of the city engaged in global business activity; the poorest inner city areas; extensive suburban economies and residential areas; commuters pushed beyond the formal city borders in search of affordable housing; and the wider regional economy which is an integral part of London's economy.

So even in a city which claims global status, and which can devote substantial resources to planning its economic future and supporting the poorest residents, building a vision for the future of the city across the range of economic flows is not easy. National, global, European and diverse cosmopolitan links stretching out from London's many ethnic communities all offer potential contributions to a future growth path for the city. Building on London's long history of economic links through Europe and the British Empire and beyond, the global reach of the city is undisputed and a valuable resource. But policy-makers are eager not to lose sight of the substantial contributions of nationally and locally

Figure 4.6 North London's Green Lanes is home to a vibrant Cypriot economy, with Greek and Turkish Cypriot shops side by side.

oriented activities, and there is a strong awareness of the potential exclusion of London's poorest and poorly educated residents from dynamic economic sectors, which rely on highly educated and skilled workers. A broad and inclusive strategy, which aims to exploit 'the connections and interdependence which increasingly exist between previously separate business sectors' (LDA, 2001, p.46), is being conceived to direct interventions to meet the needs of the city-wide economy.

Finding these synergies between different sectors of the urban economy and exploiting or encouraging their potential interactions within city spaces are just as much of a challenge for cities at the other end of the world cities hierarchy. Important here are the ways in which the co-existence of economic sectors within cities can be a source of opportunity for the very poor in times of crisis.

4.4.3 Urban poverty and economic diversity

Approaches to urban poverty stress that in times of crisis, urban households are faced with the demands of finding new ways to manage their particular mix of capabilities and assets, often within powerful constraints. The resourcefulness of poorer urban residents within the context of the urban environment is not something which can be assumed, but there are aspects of urban living which can make it more or less possible to navigate these times of crisis (see Beall, 2000, pp.434–435). These include:

- individual and neighbourhood household resources;
- the diverse and overlapping economic and social networks of the city; and
- more extensive country-wide and transnational networks.

We will consider each of these in turn.

Individual and neighbourhood resources

The incomes available to poor people are likely to decline severely in times of economic crisis (because of price inflation, rising unemployment, growth in casual or flexible work, or decreased ability to work as a result of poor health due to deteriorating wider conditions, such as health services). Thus, in times of rising poverty, poor people in cities have to consider how to make best use of their particular range of assets, often simply to maintain basic levels of consumption. In cities, these assets seldom include land for food production (although vegetable gardening and peri-urban farming can be significant in some places), but they do include a familiar range of stocks of human and social capital, household and kin relations. In addition, in urban areas poor people might have access to what is often a significant productive asset, especially for women – a house. Matching child care and household chores with income generation can mean home-based work is crucial to poor women, even when it is poorly paid and involves long hours of work. This can be particularly important when in times of economic crisis more women and children join the labour force. Owning a house can help extended households add on structures for young or elderly family members, although this can in turn undermine the capacity for rental income. Home-based enterprises, though, do depend on the provision of wider infrastructures, such as electricity and water, making these basic urban needs potentially crucial to supporting the economic activities of the poor.

In cities, local community networks can also make a big difference to coping strategies, but these are also potentially under threat as more people need to work longer hours and have little time and fewer resources for community engagement. 'Reciprocal relationships and social networks, originating in rural–urban networks, based on kin and place of origin, and on more recently formed local networks, are important in the [community] consolidation process' (Moser, 1998, p.13). However, the social life of cities can equally deplete social capital – crime, violence, drugs and alcohol all take their toll on the potential for sociability, making the streets dangerous and night-time meetings unattractive. Stressful and violent social relations, including those within households, might have to be endured to attempt to sustain economic viability.

City-wide networks

So, urban communities and the dense networks of local areas can be significant in supporting poor families through times of economic crisis. But forms of sociability in the city are seldom entirely associated with one neighbourhood, nor are urban dwellers likely to be part of only one single community. The city, as we have seen, brings together many different communities, and many different networks which stretch not only across, but also beyond, the city. In times of crisis, and at other times too, poor people are potentially able to move between different networks and neighbourhoods and perhaps to try out new kinds of identities or ways of belonging in the city. Just as a move from the formal sector to the informal sector in the face of unemployment can see urban households making use of the co-existence of different networks of economic exchange in a city, the diversity of the social life of the city can also be a flexible resource. The rise of religious enthusiasms, or the revival of older ethnic identities or social practices are all indications of these flexible attempts to create or renew social capital (see the definitions in Chapters 1 and 3). De Boeck describes some of these dynamics in relation to urban Zaire, against a backdrop

Figure 4.7 Formal and informal aspects of city life co-exist in Mumbai (Bombay), India.

of disillusionment not only with the local plundering élite, but also with the former colonial rulers and current international capitalist forces:

> The current politics of identity, usually stressing one's independence and self-supporting qualities, is evidenced by the proliferation of 'popular' painting, theatre and local newspapers as chronicles and commentaries on the urban context ... by the proliferation of spiritual healing in urban, and to a lesser extent also rural, contexts ... by the (re)emerging and (re)inventing of ritual as exemplary enactment of co-operative sociability, whether or not it is actually realised outside the time of the performance itself; by a renewed stress on ethnic identity; by the emergence of new forms of reciprocity in church-connected grassroots organisations that play an increasing role in the promotion of people's self-awareness ... by actions such as the *radio tableau* in the *cités* of the city of Kikwit [in Zaire] where international radio news (RFI, BBC, Canal Afrique, Afrique No. 1) is spelled out and commented upon by the owners of small portable radios on a blackboard in the street while the whole neighbourhood contributes batteries to keep the radio working, as a way of escaping interpretations and representations imposed upon them from elsewhere.
>
> (De Boeck, 1996, p.95)

The co-existence in cities of many different economic and social activities suggests that thinking about city futures, whether in so-called global cities, or in some of the poorest cities of the world, should involve attention to how quite different social and economic networks are accessed and entwined through the energies of city dwellers. This requires a focus not only on the located social and physical assets of neighbourhoods and homes, but invites an approach which 'finds ways to traverse the networks, pathways and routes along which a wide range of the city's productive capacities and potentials are made' (Simone, 1998, D8). Far from being excluded from the global economy or from formal elements of the cities in which they live, the poor residents of the world's poorest cities are compelled to work tirelessly to secure what advantage they can from linking in to opportunities wherever they come from, whether it be through family or acquaintances, those with money to spend, those with contacts in the official world, or organizations of all kinds with security or information to offer (as Giles Mohan discusses in some detail in Chapter 2 of this book). In relation to cities in Africa, Simone comments:

> In a fundamental way, the question of where African cities are going could be answered by a consideration of where African urban residents are going, pursuing their own objectives, within their own time frame. While it is true that urban poverty is growing worse, and that African urban life is increasingly ghettoized, urban residents are not standing still. There is something going on, people are trying to come up with new ways of earning a living, of helping others out, of making interesting cities.
>
> (Simone, 1998, D8)

And as we have seen in this section, where the residents of cities are going in the course of their search for livelihoods and opportunities, is both across different sectors and areas of the city, and beyond its borders.

The varying reach of city economies

The process of cultivating opportunities for survival, or livelihoods, stretches not only across cities apparently divided by inequality, formal and informal activities and economic opportunity. Like all economic activities, the spatial reach of the livelihood strategies of poor people is varied and extensive. Households in many parts of the world can be characterized as 'multi-local' or 'translocal' – stretching across the urban–rural divide, or even across national boundaries, as individual members and the household collectively seek opportunities to improve their position. Prior rural networks can continue to be a vital part of the lives of urban dwellers; whether it be in helping newcomers to settle in and to find jobs and homes or just some company, such networks can perpetuate rural social relations in urban areas. Children might be sent to relatives in rural or urban areas to help with their education, provide labour for extended or shrinking households, escape violence or ensure a proper upbringing, for example.

Like all social relations, those which stretch across urban and rural areas are subject to change. In times of economic crisis, relations with rural kin might become more important to older urban dwellers facing a costly urban retirement with little in the way of pension and few locally based family members. Cultivating these relations can be a demanding and risky business. Some striking cases of this have been recorded in Zambia, where after many years of working in copperbelt mines, mineworkers face the dilemma of where to live in their retirement. Many plan to return 'home' to rural areas, and in a time of severe economic crisis even those who had invested heavily in urban living and lifestyles find that they have to turn to their rural kin for opportunities to continue to earn a living. But these returns are fraught with conflicts over access to rural resources of land and long-neglected kinship networks, sometimes even involving accusations of witchcraft and murder (Ferguson, 1999). Re-establishing links beyond the city is not always easy.

Moreover, the nature of urban–rural networks varies considerably. In some places, strong trading and social networks can help household members in both places, as Moser notes for one town in the Philippines, 'In Commonwealth [city], for example, complex urban–rural reciprocity systems have remained strong, reducing vulnerability for both urban and rural households' (Moser, 1998, p.13). In other places, such as 1990s' Zimbabwe after structural adjustment, simply keeping in touch with rural kin can become impossible as costs of travel and communication become prohibitive (Potts, 1999).

Beyond negotiating between different economic sectors within the city, or across rural–urban kinship networks, urban dwellers often also seek to establish or pursue linkages which stretch from one city to another, often across national borders. Moser summarizes some of the ways in which these livelihood strategies with different spatial reaches can work differently in different places:

> To maximise returns, households have responded proactively to changing labour demands. In Cisne Dos (Guayaquil, Ecuador), workers have migrated to rural areas to take advantage of new opportunities in shrimp aquaculture, sending remittances home; in Commonwealth (Philippines), households have been able to partially offset vulnerability in the formal labour market through remittances from household members working overseas and through expanding opportunities in the informal sector. In Chawama (Lusaka, Zambia), however, limited informal sector opportunities for a few male traders have been insufficient to compensate for retrenchment in formal sector service employment.
>
> (Moser, 1998, p.9)

One of the informal sector activities popular in all areas of Lusaka is trade in second-hand clothing. Called *salaula* (a Bemba word meaning 'to select from a pile'), second-hand clothing is the eighth largest US export to Zambia (about US$3.5 million in 1991) and used clothes are also imported from Canada and Europe. The trade itself is not new, but previously most used clothes were imported from Zaire. Since the late 1980s, however, traders with experience in this area from Tanzania (including Asians and Lebanese traders) have entered the business, acting as 'middle-men' and utilizing large warehouses to store the bales of imported used clothing before selling them on to informal street traders. 'The *salaula* section in markets is many times larger than the food section in Lusaka … *Salaula* traders are young and old, women and men with different educational and employment histories and from many ethnic groups. Women slightly outnumber men' (Hansen, 1994, pp.511–512).

Figure 4.8 *Salaula* traders in Lusaka.

Street traders came to be involved in *salaula* in different ways, some through the earlier Zairian trade, some through trading clothes bought from expatriate households, door to door. Others have started more recently, turning to this trade when they hit difficult times due to unemployment or the death of a partner, for example.

These very locally focused informal markets, then, and a popular local clothing style associated with remodelling the second-hand garments, are closely tied in to activities in those localities in the West where exporters bundle clothes, originally made in factories in poor countries around the world and now donated by rich Westerners to charity shops. Zambians make the goods bought in these markets the source of their own livelihood or sense of modern style, confirming that even in the humblest economic sectors of the poorest cities, transnational economic processes are an important element of city futures.

If city futures are shaped as much by wider connections as by local initiative, as much by links between different economic sectors as by processes of clustering, and as much by rural-based networks as by urban neighbourhoods; then where exactly can interventions for effective urban development be made? Supporting rural–urban trade or social links through transport services might be just as important for improving urban living as community-based service delivery in city neighbourhoods. Facilitating the meeting up or interaction of people involved in different sectors of the economy might be one of the most significant enabling features of city life – whether it be 'schmoozing' in coffee bars in the heart of 'global' parts of cities; or encounters in street markets near national and international transport interchanges in some of the poorer parts of cities.

Recognizing the diversity of a city's economic and social life, and the varying geographical range of these activities, is one thing. Building a consensus across these diversities as to what a city's future could be is quite another. While cities assemble social and economic diversity, there are often good reasons to keep some kinds of activities apart. Petty thieves and global business travellers, for example, would have quite different ideas about the possible value of meeting on a city street! And city managers may be anxious about how crime, or a sense of disorder, might damage a city's international image and discourage travellers and investors from extending the range of global ties flowing into that place. All sorts of conflicts arise in the space of the city – conflicts which have to be negotiated and played out in the urban political arena as part of the process of planning how to improve life in any city. The following section considers how visions and plans to shape the future development of cities can, or could, emerge out of contests and negotiations amongst the different interests and activities gathered together in any city.

Summary of Section 4.4

- Cities assemble flows and networks in distinctive ways, and facilitate social and economic activities as well as innovation.

- The diversity and varying range of these networks offer distinctive opportunities for urban development in both wealthy and poorer cities.

- The co-existence of different activities in cities is a source of potential for development, and for flexibility in urban livelihoods in times of crisis.

- But this co-existence is also the source of potential conflict between different, even incompatible, interests and activities.

4.5 Negotiating urban futures across diversity

We noted in Sections 4.2 and 4.3 that urban development planners have come to draw on a view of the city as a whole – as a territory – whether it be in developing the city to compete effectively to become a key location for global business or to address urban poverty. In the former case, a city's image and its perceived existing strengths can serve as an effective platform for further engagement with wider economic flows. In the latter, the residents of a city make claims to belong to a single political community with rights to share the benefits of its economy. In these and other ways, the diverse flows of people and resources combine to produce the city, a territory which has the scope to emerge as a key agent in shaping the global economy, as well as determining elements of local well-being.

This section considers the dynamics of city-wide local economic development initiatives. It will explore how it is that local development comes to be organized around the scale of the city (or how cities are 'territorialized'). And it will consider whether the flows (of people, resources and ideas) which shape cities can be harnessed effectively through local initiative at a city-wide level. One of the major dilemmas facing cities engaging in local economic development is how to balance their ambitions for economic growth (and at times 'global' status) with the demands of poorer citizens for locally sustainable growth paths, provision of basic needs and poverty alleviation. Particularly challenging, then, is drawing all sections of the city's population into a shared vision of that city's future which balances their often divergent needs. The politics of urban development, therefore, is a crucial component in shaping city futures.

4.5.1 Local economic development: competition, conflict and coalitions

Competing cities

Harvey (1989b) argues that as businesses of various kinds have become increasingly mobile, or 'footloose', in the globalizing economy, cities around the world such as Istanbul, Bangalore and Manila have been disciplined into competing to offer the most attractive environment for capital investment. As national states have become less able to direct or protect economic investment in the face of globalization, local governments have entered the competitive terrain of influencing local economic development. Some would argue that the political dynamics of the world economy have been increasingly territorialized at a local urban, rather than national, scale (Brenner, 1998). Under threat of losing their economic base, city governments are competing with one another to keep the businesses they already have, and working hard to persuade others to choose to locate in their city. Cities eager to promote local development are vulnerable to losing investments to places which volunteer more attractive arrangements for firms. In this sense, city managers can be said to be 'disciplined' by global capital into development initiatives which suit them rather than the city's residents.

Disciplining of quite another, but not unrelated, form affects cities in poor or highly indebted countries. This is the promotion of neoliberal decentralizing and privatizing initiatives at all levels of government by International Financial Institutions (IFIs). These processes have also given rise to local governments eager to promote competitive urban development in their cities (as we noted in Section 4.3). Decentralization and democratization in many poorer economies, often under the direction of the IFIs, have started to encourage elements of local economic development initiatives in a wider range of countries.

Local authorities, or local growth coalitions, around the world have been prompted to become more entrepreneurial, actively marketing the city, seeking out new investments or encouraging the growth of existing businesses. The consequences for weaker and poorer cities can be substantial. More desperate for growth, yet less able to afford to support it, poorer cities are likely either to be passed by in the competition, or to pay more in the way of subsidies, or relaxed labour or environment regulations (as in the case study of Manila that we met in Section 4.3.1), than richer cities to attract any given investment. As we have seen, the costs of pursuing development initiatives which prioritize global investment can be substantial. This strategy is also risky and unstable in that it relies on powerful external interests with little local dependence or loyalty, and which are always on the lookout for better opportunities elsewhere.

While this is especially the case for the vulnerable poorer cities (as Jakarta discovered in the late 1990s – see below), it is also true for the wealthiest cities, as we noted for the case of London in Section 4.4.2. In Jakarta, Indonesia, a development ambition to 'globalize' the city's economy led to an over emphasis on transnational economic activities. A general financial crisis in the region plunged the city into a massive economic downturn – and forced a rethink about the balance between emphasizing 'global' and national or regional economic processes in planning for the city's future.

Case study: Jakarta – from global city to city of crisis

A strong push for global city status in Jakarta led to substantial expansion of the city, as peripheral areas saw massive construction projects for suburban housing developments and industrial estates. The central city also witnessed a building boom, as the number of businesses rocketed. Between 1986 and 1996 the number of financial establishments increased from 913 to 3729, and the number of businesses involved in trade increased from 336 772 to 519 655 (Firman, 1999). Office blocks and condominiums transformed the skyline of the city, and many slum areas were removed for these and other developments, including numerous shopping malls. Transnational and Indonesian businesses located themselves in the city, attracted by the superior infrastructure of this city compared to others in the country, and commentators declared that Jakarta was at least on its way to becoming a 'global city'.

Figure 4.9 Halted construction in Jakarta.

And then the financial crisis of 1997 struck. An overvalued currency, excessive dependency on imports and a speculative run against the currency all meant that the boom came to an end. As in other Southeast Asian countries, Indonesian banks had overextended their credit and the resultant crisis saw numerous bankruptcies, departure of some of the transnational companies which had only recently opened for business in Jakarta, and an end to the construction boom. Capital outflows from Jakarta were estimated to reach US$8 billion in December 1998. As in other cities, such as Kuala Lumpur, unfinished buildings stood out against the high rise office blocks – demand for office space was down by half – and economic growth in the city fell from around 9% in the mid-1990s to an estimated minus 7% in 1998 (Firman, 1999). Now dismissed workers had to battle for an income in the overcrowded informal sector. As Firman notes:

> …a large number of dismissed workers have shifted from industrial, construction and services to the 'informal' trade sector, such as

> food trading. Vendors and itinerant traders who operate on the sidewalks (Pedagang Kaki Lima) increased rapidly, from about 95 000 in 1997 to 270 000 in October 1998 ... At present (early 1999), most intersections in Jakarta City are swarming with street singers and beggars who ask for small change from passing motorists.
>
> (Firman, 1999, p.456)
>
> City government coffers are also strained as taxation, based on business transactions, has yielded considerably less income. From an aspirant global city, Jakarta metropolitan region (JMR) has become what Firman calls, a 'city of crisis', and remains a 'city of the poor'. Firman draws some conclusions from this experience:
>
> > The severity of the economic crisis has nevertheless given a lesson on how vulnerable economic development which is heavily based on external forces, including short term foreign investment ('hot money'), can be for Indonesia and other countries in South-east Asia. Therefore, in the future ... development [in Jakarta] as well as urban and regional development in Indonesia, should be substantially based on local resource utilization with greater popular participation in order to achieve a resilient socio-economic development which in turn could prevent the undesirable impacts of globalisation...
> >
> > ...For the moment, urban poverty becomes the most pronounced issue of JMR development...
> >
> > (Firman, 1999, pp.461, 464)

As we noted in relation to the idea of 'global cities', subordinating a city's future development to the demands of economic sectors with a global reach can have negative effects on local living environments and on the possibility for pursuing alternative livelihood strategies. The dangers of Jakarta's globalizing strategy are all too painfully apparent after the event.

Conflicting interests

The costs and risks of global competition are not borne equally by all city residents. Different development paths impact differently upon different communities, and urban development is often fraught with conflict, as we saw in the case of Istanbul (Section 4.3.1). Harvey (2000) outlines some of these different interests in the case of Baltimore, in the United States. After describing the decline of the city's economy and the growing impoverishment of the poor, especially the African-American population, he notes how the city has poured money into private capital initiatives, rather than addressing the needs of the poor:

> There has been an attempt of sorts to turn things around in the city. Launched in the early 1970s under the aegis of a dedicated and

authoritarian mayor (William Donald Schaeffer) it entailed formation of a private–public partnership to invest in downtown and Inner Harbour renewal in order to attract financial services, tourism and so-called hospitality functions to the center city. It took a lot of public money to get the process rolling. Once the partnership had the hotels (Hyatt® got a $35 million hotel by putting up only half a million of its own money in the early 1980s), it needed to build a convention center to fill the hotels and get a piece of what is now calculated to be an $83 billion a year meetings industry. In order to keep competitive, a further public investment of $150 million was needed to create an even larger convention center to get the big conventions. It is now feared that all this investment will not be profitable without a large 'headquarters hotel' that will also require 'extensive' public subsidies (maybe $50 million). And to improve the city image, nearly a half billion dollars went into building sports stadiums for teams (one of which was lured from Cleveland) that pay several million a year to star players watched by fans paying exorbitant ticket prices. This is a common enough story across the United States (the National Football League … calculates that $3.8 billion of largely public money will be poured into new NFL stadiums between 1992 and 2002). The state spends $5 million building a special light-rail stop for the football stadium that will be used no more than twenty days a year.

(Harvey, 2000, pp.138–141)

Of course, some of these initiatives might make the city a better place for people to live in, with more places for recreation and physical improvements to previously rundown areas, such as disused industrial areas or harbour fronts. But the use of public money to attract private investment that might otherwise have gone elsewhere (often called **leverage**) is very controversial, especially in a context of increasing poverty within the same city. In other cities, campaigns to contest this kind of public expenditure have forced city governments to pay attention to the needs of the poor and of outer areas of the city. In Glasgow, Scotland, for example, the well known 'Glasgow's Miles Better' campaign of the 1980s, which aimed to regenerate the central city area, attracted strong community opposition, leading to a redirection of some of the initiative's energies to addressing the needs of peripheral housing estates and promoting employment generation.

City governments often attempt to place their city in the public eye, as a way of making it noticeable as a desirable location for new investment, for tourism, or sports visits, all of which could boost the local economy in different ways. So attracting a football stadium, hosting a major event, or being 'European City of Culture' of the year (as Glasgow was in 1989), can all help to put the city on the map of relevant investors and travellers and enhance its international profile. But whether these strategies represent value for money is deeply contested, and community groups can often think of better ways to spend public money. The dilemma, then, is how to find a balance in the trade-off between an international profile (assumed to be important for attracting economic investment) and local needs, or better still, to promote both in ways which do not undermine the other. In the case study below we see how a local economic development initiative in Durban in 1991 exemplifies attempts to balance these competing agendas.

Case study: 'Operation Jumpstart', Durban

In 1991 a convention of local government, political organizations, community groups, non-governmental organizations (NGOs) and business interests, gathered together in Durban, South Africa, to attempt to 'jumpstart' the local economy.

Behind the scenes the local branch of an international management consultancy company, Arthur Anderson, had astutely been suggesting to the local authority that there was scope, since the release of Nelson Mandela in 1990 and the expectation of a post-apartheid government, for South African cities to re-engage with the global economy. Companies looking to reinvest in South Africa at the end of the boycott of apartheid could find in Durban an excellent location for manufacturing and trade and a large market for general business. Durban, located in a warm subtropical region of South Africa, also has a large tourist infrastructure, which could possibly now expect more in the way of international visitors. Durban had a big image problem, though. A civil war had been raging in the province of KwaZulu-Natal for a decade, and many hundreds of people had been killed. The city badly needed a new image to market, one of a peaceful and industrious workforce, and a politically harmonious citizenry. Durban was looking over its shoulder at Cape Town, which had a much stronger image as a destination for international tourists, and at Johannesburg, always the preferred location for headquarters of national and international companies. If Durban was to improve its economy, the thinking was that it had to be competitive with these other major South African cities.

When the convention met, the city hall was packed with excited participants, including the local authority, white residents and businesses, all of whom had been involved in local government before. New to the scene were the African National Congress (ANC) representatives (crucial for ensuring international political legitimacy for what was still an apartheid local government venture), local community groups and some local NGO representatives. Later on, the trade unions and a wider NGO community were to complain that they had been left out of these plans. Clearly the meeting could have been more representative, but for a divided city like Durban this was a substantially new kind of initiative.

An energetic local businessman was elected to front the organization, and the management consultants received a contract to see through some of the planning and reporting. Subgroups were formed and a series of priority plans developed. The plans spanned the spectrum

Figure 4.10 The International Convention Centre, Durban, built as part of 'Operation Jumpstart'.

from an international convention centre (ICC) (on the basis of expected support from the local council in the form of a land grant and some investment funds) to a major housing development on a well-located and politically significant piece of land from which African shack dwellers had been removed under apartheid. It appeared that a balance had been reached, accommodating the concerns of businesses for a high profile initiative like the ICC (which turned out to be a great success, and is now being extended) and the interests of community groups in housing, services and local employment. Deals were consciously struck across this divide: the community groups and the ANC negotiated access to the convention centre for their own meetings; and the consultants saw the housing development as the price they had to pay to get the pro-business investment in the ICC. Of course, not everyone was happy. Trade unions and NGOs complained at the profligate use of the city's resources to support a private venture, in the ICC and the linked Hilton Hotel. The consultants complained that the housing development didn't amount to a 'hill of beans' in respect of the economic growth of the city. But the forum had created a space for a set of development strategies which stretched (for a while) across these diverse interests, and most of which have in fact been realized.

Building alliances

The case study of Durban gives an example of a city-wide development plan which has successfully gone some way to improving things for the residents of the city and businesses alike. Some of the wider preconditions for the emergence of city-wide development alliances might include the following (which were all present in Durban in the early 1990s): increasing autonomy or decentralization in local government; dynamic personalities who can mobilize a range of constituencies; and a break in political and economic organization which offers new opportunities for both alliance-building and engagement with wider processes. Other catalysts can be experts or consultants who present this as an option for enabling local development (as we will see for the case of the World Bank's City Development Strategies, Section 4.5.2); or perhaps a period of crisis which élites and community organizations wish to overcome in some way (such as the political violence in KwaZulu-Natal during the 1980s).

It is not easy to hold a development coalition together. In Nairobi, a charismatic leader initially drew different constituencies together, but without him, the initiative faltered:

> The First Nairobi Convention was held early in 1994. It brought together people from the private sector, voluntary organisations, community groups, academic institutions, civil servants, council officers, elected representatives, and concerned individuals. The goal of the convention, under the rallying cry 'The Nairobi We Want', was to develop a vision and a strategy for the development of the city that its people can relate with ... [It] was short-lived. The dynamic mayor who initiated it resigned less than 6 months after the convention.
>
> (Halfani, 1996, pp.102–104)

These examples highlight the difficulties of negotiating a basis for alliance-building and finding stable ways of co-operating amongst the different agents, businesses, communities and government. The Nairobi example shows how reliance on one charismatic individual is not enough. The Durban case illustrates how finding a common agenda can involve some serious trade-offs amongst different constituencies: housing development for community groups as opposed to the public funding of a convention centre to support a business–tourism initiative. And alliances can be dominated by the powerful, to the detriment of community interests, as in the case of Baltimore, discussed earlier in this section.

One of the dangers of organizing urban development interventions on a city-wide scale is that large-scale investments and ambitions dominate agendas, and more organized constituencies are able to be more vocal and influential. In addition, the benefits of local participation, often a valuable source of knowledge and capacity crucial to the effective support of development, might be lost. The question arises, who is in a position to pass judgement on the need for and nature of a comprehensive development strategy at the metropolitan or city-wide level? Locally based community groups and NGOs often lack such a wide perspective, and business interests are likely to be partial, or spread out beyond any individual city. The suggestion has been made that:

> Only governments have the legitimacy and capability to steer and integrate the activities of multiple stakeholders by acting beyond single purposes ... Integrating tasks include managing diverse interests to ensure that wider public goals are met by putting more narrowly defined interests in a larger context.
>
> (UNCHS, 2001, p.62)

But as the case of Hong Kong, discussed below, exemplifies, governments themselves are not necessarily unified when it comes to development plans. In this case, different government departments found different proposals more attractive in terms of their own goals. The Industry Department, for example, found the plan to promote a 'Made in Hong Kong' growth path synchronized most readily with their own efforts to promote industry in the city. Nonetheless, the state has played a role in trying to negotiate across the competing interests in the city as it plans future growth paths for Hong Kong.

Case study: Competing growth paths in Hong Kong

In late 1990s' Hong Kong, competing growth paths emerged as the city–state faced a continuing decline of production within its own territory (as opposed to co-ordinating production activities stretched across the region) and a rise in the costs of residential and office rents as capital investors sought speculative gains in property investment. One potential development strategy was associated with industrial-based interests, inclined to reinvigorate a 'Made in Hong Kong' growth path, associated with producing high-tech goods in Hong Kong. 'This report is sponsored by industrial capital with the support of certain parts of the bureaucracy (most notably the Hong Kong Government Industry Department and the Hong Kong Productivity Council)' (Jessop and Sum, 2000, p.2302). The other strategy was associated with a group of property and finance capitalists who wished to reinforce Hong Kong's position as a regional hub, capturing, co-ordinating and managing flows of capital and investment around the region, in places such as China, Asia and the Asian-Pacific Region – a 'Made by Hong Kong' strategy (Jessop and Sum, 2000, p.2302). These competing strategies were each formulated and written up by prominent US university-based consultancies – one from MIT (Massachusetts Institute of Technology), the other from Harvard.

The Hong Kong government and a range of private and public actors coalesced around a highly visible project which for a while seemed set to bring the two strategies together. This project was variously named Cyberport, Cyber Harbour or, more critically, Cyber Villas by the Sea (indicating it would just be a property development, rather than a sound productive initiative). The project had the potential to link together the services sector's emphasis on Hong Kong as managing information flows, with the high-tech production sector's interest in information-based enterprises, and also responded to the property sectors interests in constructing the project and the Hong Kong government's dependence on property tax for 40% of its revenue. But there was resistance from opposition political parties and from capitalists left out of the initiative, as well as from developers concerned that land for housing development was to be lost. This initiative, and more recent ones, were designed in the context of wider efforts to promote Hong Kong's competitiveness with other potential hubs in the region (Singapore, Kuala Lumpur, for example) and also with other world cities.

> More recently (February 2000) the Commission on Strategic Development [CSD], with the approval of the Chief Executive, has reinforced the importance of the financial and business services sector. This is illustrated by an official blueprint for transforming Hong Kong into Asia's 'world city' that would rival the positions of London and New York in Europe and North America, respectively. This would involve strengthening Hong Kong's links with the Pearl River delta and other mainland regions (such as the Yangtze delta and basin and key central and western regions) as well as enhancing its ability to exploit China's imminent entry into the World Trade Organisation and position itself as a 'knowledge-based economy'. This blueprint envisages a complex array of private–public partnerships and networks co-operating under Hong Kong's leadership to promote the overall competitiveness of an emerging multicentred city-region, not only in economic terms but also in cultural and community matters.
>
> (Commission on Strategic Development, 2000;
> quoted in Jessop and Sum, 2000, p.2308)

When negotiating growth paths for their localities, as in Hong Kong, local states do not come into the process as innocent referees. They have strong, if varying, interests in the outcomes of these negotiations. Aside from the common goal of local authorities to promote employment and jobs for local people to ensure re-election, or to enhance their standing on the national or world stage, the balance of political power on a local council could demonstrably influence development plans. Local authorities' interests also vary with levels of autonomy and decentralization, and with their sources of income. Local states with less discretion to act are less likely (or may be unable) to become involved in initiating and promoting local development: very often this area might be the responsibility of higher levels of government (as is the case for high-tech industries in Bangalore; see Section 4.4.1).

Local states whose sources of income are largely national or regional will be less inclined to attempt to promote the local economy. They do better spending their time lobbying regional and central government for more input than they do trying to raise production or incomes locally. However, where local authorities earn a large proportion of their income from local incomes or sales taxation, or, most especially, from local property taxes, then their direct interest in encouraging local economic growth is most apparent.

Whatever their motivations for action, or varying levels of interest in local development, compared to other urban development agents the local state is the most strongly territorialized around the city scale. Whereas communities might promote the interests of their own neighbourhood, and business is usually most concerned with commercial and industrial zones, and possibly with other cities or countries, the local state usually has responsibility for the city as a whole and faces some pressure to address the diverse range of needs. Often, however, the local state will pursue governance and development in association with only selected community or business organizations, to the detriment of other interests. Urban analysts have identified examples of stable local alliances promoting certain growth paths, and have labelled these 'urban regimes' (Jessop and Sum, 2000). Coalitions might stretch across the private and public sectors, but often only draw in a limited range of community interests, and will promote certain kinds of urban development strategies. The example of Baltimore, discussed earlier by Harvey, signifies a long period in which a pro-business initiative aimed to regenerate declining areas of town with large inputs of public money, and indicates a long-standing alliance between local government and business, but a deep rift with local community interests.

The following sections consider the potential for establishing governance structures and imagining urban futures across diverse interests and activities at a city-wide level. We first review a recent policy initiative from the World Bank and its partners in urban development, called 'City Development Strategies', part of their broader 'Global Urban Strategy' (World Bank, 2000). This approach to urban development builds on a view of the city as a whole, and on the distinctive and diverse characteristics of individual cities. It draws on the idea of coalition-building and promotes the value of generating a city-wide vision for future development. We then draw this chapter to a close with a look at the diverse, and sometimes divergent, social and economic processes shaping the city of Johannesburg, and how they are being managed there.

4.5.2 Development strategies for ordinary city futures?

As we noted earlier in Sections 4.1 and 4.2, urban issues were for a long time very low on the priority list of international development agencies, including that of the World Bank. Only at the end of the 1990s did the Bank turn to focus its attention more firmly on the city. In May 1999 James Wolfensohn, then President of the World Bank, welcomed delegates to the first 'World Competitive Cities Congress', part of the Bank's new initiative to promote urban development in association with other international agencies, like the UNCHS and major Western donor governments. Wolfensohn noted some basic facts about the growth of the size of the world's urban population, and the size of the cities in which that population lives, and suggested that:

> We can be sure that wherever we work, whatever we do, our futures will be inextricably linked to the futures of our cities in a way not experienced by previous generations ... Cities can be the engines of national growth, propelling economies as they compete with other global cities. The World Bank is no mere spectator in this global revolution. We are working in over 6000 cities and the experiences of our past efforts now form the vision for future assistance.
>
> (Wolfensohn, 1999, pp.12–13)

At the heart of the new strategy lie four principles, which bear a close relationship to those underlying other Bank initiatives – in some senses the Global Urban Strategy holds few surprises! The policy document describes them as follows:

> If cities and towns are to promote the welfare of their residents and of the nation's citizens, they must be sustainable, and functional, in four respects. First and foremost, they must be *liveable* – ensuring a decent quality of life and equitable opportunity for all residents, including the poorest. To achieve that goal, they must also be *competitive*, *well governed* and managed, and financially sustainable, or *bankable*. The strategy proposes an agenda for helping cities develop along these four interrelated dimensions – a comprehensive development framework for the urban arena ... The urban policy agenda outlines some broadly common goals for all cities and local governments. But it would be implemented very differently in different places, with the pace, priorities, and operational instruments depending on the political commitment and capacities of the local and central government and other key stakeholders.
>
> (World Bank, 2000, p.8)

This broad policy approach is in some ways likely to be as controversial as some national-level World Bank initiatives, including structural adjustment policies, have proved to be. The emphasis on bankability, for example, supports widespread cost-recovery initiatives in service provision for the poor, and also encourages cities to look for sources of private sector and foreign financing for infrastructural investments. As the UNCHS (2001) notes, 'the connection between the logic of the market and the logic of liveability is anything but automatic' (p.xxxiii). We might rightly express some concern that a structural adjustment policy for cities might be smuggled in through this programme, especially if we notice that the processes of decentralization and local autonomy (partly promoted by earlier Bank strategies) have multiplied the potential client base for the Bank. The Bank now sees the move to urban development as 'good business for the Bank. There is growing demand for Bank assistance in this area ... from a newly empowered set of clients – municipalities themselves' (World Bank, 2000, p.40). The involvement of the World Bank in the controversial process of corporatization and partial privatization of municipal services in Johannesburg (see Box 4.7), for example, has led local trade unions to raise these kinds of questions.

Box 4.7 Johannesburg and the World Bank

The City of Johannesburg is in the process of restructuring itself as a metropolitan government. Labelled iGoli 2002*, the plan includes fundamental changes in the overall governance structure of the city and involves a radical restructuring of the fiscal, institutional and regulatory framework for the delivery of municipal services. In addition, the city is undertaking bold reforms in the areas of local economic development and the establishment of metropolitan health and policing districts. Underpinning each of these areas is a plan to address the problem of urban poverty on a sustainable basis. The City has asked the Bank to provide a comprehensive package of technical assistance in support of iGoli 2002 and assist in donor co-ordination. The engagement with Johannesburg raises the possibility of implementing the approach of a Comprehensive Development Framework [CDF] at the city level – an issue that is pertinent in an era of decentralisation and urbanisation. Furthermore, the engagement with Johannesburg draws solely on the Bank's ability to co-ordinate the international experience of urban development. No lending relationship is expected. The engagement will test the limits and possibilities of a pure knowledge bank as the basis for a city level CDF.

*iGoli is the vernacular name for Johannesburg, meaning 'place of gold'.

(World Bank, 2000)

Trade unions and a new organization, the Anti-Privatisation Forum, strongly oppose these initiatives. With the cry, 'Phantsi nge-iGoli 2002, phantsi! Away with iGoli 2002, away!' the South African Municipal Workers Union (SAMWU) and a range of other organizations joined forces to oppose the process of corporatization and privatization initiated by the Johannesburg Metro Government. They write on their website:

Since January 1999, SAMWU has been involved in an intensive struggle against a privatisation plan that will radically restructure the city of Johannesburg. The plan, known as iGoli 2002, aims somehow through privatising more than a dozen services, through cleaning hawkers off the streets, paying top executives millions of rands, building thousands of drop toilets with no flush facilities on top of the water table, and through selling off profitable assets, to turn Johannesburg into a 'world-class city'.

(Congress of South Africa Trade Unions, 2001)

But there are many different aspects to the new approach of the World Bank, and while there are concerns about the implications of spreading neoliberal forms of local governance, if we were to end the discussion of the World Bank's new strategy there we would be overlooking potentially important contributions of these policy initiatives to urban development. In terms of the arguments we have been making so far in this chapter, the Global Urban Strategy, and specifically the policy tool it promotes, City Development Strategies, reinforces several elements of our approach. It identifies the need to:

- negotiate across the diverse sectors and needs of the city;
- adopt a city-wide perspective;
- appreciate that urban economies spread beyond the city's borders.

To maximize the potential of the strategy, the four principles at the heart of the strategy, described earlier, need to be balanced against one another. Bankability and competitiveness need to be traded off against liveability, especially for the poor. And effective forms of governance involve substantial interface with communities and civil society groups. City Development Strategies (CDSs) aim to draw together people from different constituencies to assess the potential for future growth of the city as a whole. This represents a significant new phase in urban development policy. As one of the key World Bank advisers in this field notes, 'To help civic leaders articulate a shared vision for the city's future, CDSs aim to set out community visions, priorities and actions and help guide the allocation of resources' (Campbell, 1999, p.19). Box 4.8 summarizes the Bank's perspective on promoting economic competitiveness within the framework of the four dimensions of sustainable development identified above, and outlines the first city-wide development initiative undertaken by the Bank within this framework in Vietnam.

Box 4.8 City development strategies and the case of Haiphong, Vietnam

Helping cities define proactive strategies to exploit and strengthen their comparative advantage represents a relatively new agenda for the Bank, but one for which there is increasing demand from local government clients. Such strategies must avoid misguided efforts to simply attract investments from other locations with tax or public investment incentives ('a race to the bottom'). Local economic development is better served by mobilising the city stakeholders to identify local strengths, bottlenecks, and market opportunities and to commit to appropriate joint actions. The Bank can facilitate city-wide economic analysis and strategy development with urban clients and help ensure that the process includes the perspectives of the small-scale and informal sector, explores the potential for non-traded as well as traded production, and finds ways to share the benefits of growth with the poor and unemployed. The Bank can also help to develop and disseminate analytical instruments to support the process, such as urban regulatory assessments and policy-relevant urban indicators. And it can maintain a strong macroeconomic dialogue to ensure that the basic country conditions for local economic growth are in place.

(World Bank, 2000, p.15)

In late FY98 [Financial Year 1998], the Bank responded to a request from the Government of Vietnam and local authorities of the city of Haiphong to provide technical inputs to, and facilitate a process of, defining an economic development strategy for the city ... The essential message from this activity is that the city is lagging behind a rapidly evolving economic transformation. The initial report recommends a 'small bricks' strategy focused on small-scale improvements in neighbourhoods, by which both governance and physical improvements can be achieved. A city development strategy for Haiphong begins with an understanding of its rapidly changing productive structure – one that is moving from hard industries to labour-intensive light manufacturing exports. The most important finding of this report is that Haiphong's future lies as much in promoting light manufacturing exports and a stronger service base, as in promoting an export processing zone and industrial parks (the initial interest of the city authorities). Policy should therefore support the creation of jobs in labour-intensive export of shoes and garments and in the development of 'softer' services to support future growth. At the same time, environment and governance are inextricably linked to successful investments and measures need to be taken on both these fronts. A key strategy for all these objectives is for the city to become more actively involved directly at the neighbourhood level where the public infrastructure is undercapitalised and where the city has already demonstrated excellent results in service delivery (for instance, in improving water supply).

The analysis in this first stage concludes that the city has ample scope to broaden its development strategy to include components beyond, perhaps even more important than, the special economic zone. Further, the city has the financial and revenue base to greatly increase its capital investment to support new components, but it should weigh trade-offs in spending on a few large infrastructural investments in contrast to many smaller ones, like streets, drainage, and other neighbourhood improvements.

(World Bank, 2000, p.110)

Of course, as Section 4.5.1 explored, the politics of the negotiations amongst the different local organizations are likely to be profound, with different groups having different priorities and perspectives. A common vision for a whole city must be achieved in the face of conflict and division.

The following section looks at initiatives to generate a vision of city-wide development in Johannesburg, South Africa. The challenges of negotiating the diversity of interests and economic activities which face any city wishing to embark on a development strategy are well exemplified by the case of Johannesburg.

4.5.3 Johannesburg: an African world-class city?

Figure 4.11 iGoli 2010 logo.

This is the slogan adopted by Johannesburg's metropolitan council to describe the imagined city of 2010: 'an African world-class city'. The skyline of central Johannesburg dominates the profile of the sprawling metropolis and, as in many cities, symbolizes the economic achievements of the city as a whole. But Johannesburg is a city of cultural diversity, deep racial divisions and social inequality, and brings together a range of different economic activities.

The challenge to manage and enhance the many different kinds of economic activity and sociability in this city is matched by the need to overcome a long history of organized racial discrimination, impoverishment and exclusion under apartheid. Added to these challenges, the local authority has been through a protracted period of post-apartheid local government restructuring, culminating in the creation in 2000 of the Greater Johannesburg Unicity (an integrated metropolitan-wide government). Moreover, financially, the city has been facing ongoing budgetary deficits, partly a result of decades of poor financial planning, as well as large outstanding payments for services (some inherited from anti-apartheid boycotts, some from continued unwillingness or inability to pay for poor levels of service provision).

In 1999 the city embarked upon a process of organizational restructuring in an attempt to draw together and address all these concerns. This initiative was known as iGoli 2002 (see Box 4.7 above), and a longer-term plan for the city's future development was known as iGoli 2010.

Although based on broader cost-recovery and business principles associated with neoliberalism, which have generated a lot of controversy, the council's restructuring under iGoli 2002 was, according to Beall *et al.*, urgently needed to address the racially based administrative fragmentation and chaos inherited from the apartheid era. As they note:

> There is a very clear sense across the city that, without success in the technical transformation of local government, the pro-poor goals of reconstruction will not be achieved, and this is the fundamental premise of iGoli 2002...

> (Beall *et al.*, 2000, p.118)

As part of the iGoli 2010 process the city initiated a city-wide 'partnership' of key stakeholders: government, labour, community and business. It also drew on 'international experts experienced in transforming major cities around the world into world-class, globally competitive cities' (Greater Johannesburg Metropolitan Council, 2000). The World Bank carried out a major study of Johannesburg's large firms, and a branch of the international urban development consultants, the Monitor Group, based in Johannesburg, was given a brief to carry out a major study of the city's existing and potential contribution to economic growth. Historically the local government of Johannesburg, like so many

Figure 4.12 Johannesburg. From the heart of the central business district (a), to the new business centre of Sandton (b) and the dense informal areas on the outskirts of the city (c), Johannesburg is a diverse city with many challenges to face in creating a vision for future development.

(a)

(b)

(c)

local governments, has not been very involved in promoting economic growth, and has focused more on service delivery. Now, the council needs to face the challenge of contributing directly to planning and supporting economic growth in the city. Based on the study by the Monitor Group and surveys of residents' opinions, as well as more qualitative assessments of the concerns of different sectors of the city (labour, communities, business) the new city council, elected in December 2000, held informal consultations to outline a preliminary version of its' strategic vision for the city (this is still being finalized at the time of writing, 2001). It concluded that:

> Johannesburg has a vision of becoming an African world-class city defined by increased prosperity and quality of life through sustained economic growth for all of its citizens.
>
> (Greater Johannesburg Metropolitan Council, 2001, p.29)

The city council identified six key strategic priorities for 2001/2. Four general ambitions were: economic development and job creation; by-law enforcement and crime prevention; service delivery excellence; and good governance. Two other more specific priorities were identified as being the inner city, long a source of concern because of ongoing economic decline there, and the need to respond to the HIV/Aids epidemic, which is a growing problem.

Johannesburg's city council faces an enormous challenge to meet these goals. With life expectancies of African women projected to fall from 67.4 years (1995–2000) to 44.4 years (2005–2010), largely as a consequence of Aids, the most vulnerable groups in the city will be struggling to meet increased health and family care needs in very difficult conditions. In this context, the ambition to be 'world-class' needs to be carefully balanced against the substantial need to address poverty and ensure basic health care and an effective response to the Aids epidemic.

Thus the city development strategy as outlined by the council's priorities looks to balance service delivery across the city with the attainment of economic growth and job creation. This ambition comes partly from the responsibilities placed on South African local governments by the national legislation which requires 'developmental local government'. Whereas local economic development initiatives has usually been divorced from issues of poverty alleviation in many parts of the world, South African municipalities are required to address both at the same time. A range of initiatives around the country have seen creative efforts to link growth promotion, including global competitiveness, with pro-poor policies (Rogerson, 1999). The challenge for governments and community representatives alike is to come up with imaginative ways of negotiating these different priorities on behalf of the future of the city as a whole.

The slogan, 'Building an African world-class city', has been important in expanding the priorities of economic growth for Johannesburg's city development strategy. The aspiration to be world-class matches Johannesburg's achievements with those of other cities prominent on the world stage, especially those which are part of the cutting edge of 'global' economic functions, notably finance, services and IT. But, as we have seen above, following these approaches for city development has had serious adverse consequences in many other poor and middle-income countries, so there is room for caution.

Moreover, service-level comparisons for historically disadvantaged areas and communities are established across quite different urban comparators than those which are used for infrastructure for IT and business services. Ambitions for a 'world-class infrastructure' and 'technological capability' (Monitor Group, 2001, pp.8, 10) are clearly drawing on central and successful areas of highly developed cities like New York's financial district (but not the Bronx), the City of London (but not neighbouring Tower Hamlets), Hong Kong or perhaps new developments in places like Kuala Lumpur and Singapore. Overall, the world-class ambitions of the city have been interpreted in this report to emphasize economic interventions to support a bundle of globally prominent activities which have been identified as growing rapidly in Johannesburg over the second half of the 1990s, labelled, 'the knowledge economy'. Given the job creation, skills profile and locational dynamics of these sectors, this emphasis is quite likely to exacerbate the trends towards a divided city, which the Monitor Group report itself identifies as damaging. But council ambitions to promote skills development in the city could be one way to avoid this. More problematically, supporting the infrastructural development needed for a world-class knowledge economy sector will almost certainly mean fewer resources for extending service delivery and addressing poverty in predominantly African areas. The city council is faced with some stark choices.

Are there alternatives to ambitions to be world-class, or to 'go global'? In this chapter we have emphasized the interaction amongst different elements of the city's economy as potentially productive, rather than as involving trade-offs. Are there lessons which Johannesburg could learn from developments in a city like Bangalore, where emergent clusters of diverse economic activity seem to offer an example of different sectors, as well as formal and informal economies working productively together?

While the knowledge economy may be the fastest growing economic sector in Johannesburg, it is relatively poor at job creation. Other sectors, while perhaps not so fast-growing, may contribute more to employment creation, and thus meet some of the other goals identified by the council. Furthermore, the council's city-wide perspective could also draw it to encourage flows across the city to enable the poor to access centres of wealth generation.

Quite positively, the evidence for existing interaction across different elements of the local economy is strong in Johannesburg, if the World

Bank research is considered. Strong linkages, forward and backward, between large, small and even informal firms speak well of the potential for tying dynamic sectors more closely into other parts of the local economy. A further possibility for the city is to consider (in both developmental and welfare terms) how it can support the resilient survivalist sector. Practical support in the form of affordable access to retail spaces for all types of trader, and a political commitment to encouraging a more positive view of these traders could help a lot here. The council has committed itself to support entrepreneurialism in the informal sector, but has shown less interest in the survivalist sector which has very little potential for contributing to growth but much potential to ensure day-to-day survival of the poorest.

These are a few of the issues which the discussion in this chapter might direct us towards. But one final concern, which we considered in Section 4.5.1 above, is the difficulty of accommodating diverse interests, and of proposing a vision for the future of cities across conflicting needs and concerns. Johannesburg exemplifies that well. Not only were there serious conflicts over the privatization and corporatization of services, but these spilled over into the longer-term strategic visioning process. Trade unions and civic groups withdrew from iGoli 2010 as a protest against the restructuring of service delivery, although later consultations over the city development strategy have been more inclusive. But forging a common vision in which choices have to be made between infrastructural development in formerly white areas, now also rapidly growing business centres for the dynamic 'knowledge economy', and investment in informal and former township areas, is not going to be easy. Similarly, until a strong alternative set of policy advice is available, the appeal of going global and being world-class may prove irresistible for Johannesburg's leaders.

Summary of Section 4.5

- City-wide development initiatives have to confront deep divisions within urban society, in a context of severe competition between cities for success in a global economy.

- Building alliances across competing interests in cities is a challenge which cities are being encouraged to meet as part of a broader international policy initiative to promote urban economic development.

- Agencies like the World Bank are encouraging the 'City Development Strategies' initiative, which takes a city-wide perspective and tries to accommodate different economic sectors, and also to promote both economic growth and poverty alleviation.

- The case of Johannesburg illustrates how contested such initiatives can be, and how difficult it is to focus on global competitiveness alongside addressing inequality.

4.6 Conclusion

Building on the role of both place and displacement in the making of city life and city economies, this chapter has proposed a framework for thinking about city futures. We have suggested, along with other writers (Amin and Graham, 1997; Massey *et al.*, 1999; Storper, 1997), that cities are produced out of the many overlapping networks and co-existing activities which take place there. For an equitable and inclusive future, city dwellers and city managers need to balance the competing demands and needs of the many different interests and groupings which find a home in the city.

The process of negotiating city futures is fraught with conflict, as we have seen, and the imbalances in power relations between community groups and international business ensure that there is no easy route to an equitable development strategy for any city. To suggest otherwise is probably to enhance the ability of the powerful to promote their own agendas. The conclusions of this chapter do not establish any kind of blueprint for urban development; but the arguments presented here have set out a way of thinking about cities which lays the groundwork, we hope, for the creative planning and hard work of debating and contesting alternatives in cities, and for finding ways to enable an inclusive envisioning of city futures.

One of the important outcomes of the arguments pursued here is that while cities everywhere face the challenges presented by diverse communities, it is also the case that cities in all regions of the world can aim to harness the potential which is represented by the range of social and economic activities found there – economic activities with disparate reaches, some global or transnational, others regional, national, or city-based. But all of these components of the city benefit from and add to the dynamic interactions which take place in cities. As we have shown, to prioritize activities with a global reach, either analytically (as global city theorists do) or in practice (as many city managers have), is to miss so much of the potential for economic growth and development which cities offer. More importantly, it is potentially to divert energy and attention away from the huge challenges which the 'urbanization of poverty' presents. Addressing poverty means addressing inequality, and for this too, all areas and activities in the city need to be kept in view.

The territorialization of development at the scale of the city has emerged very clearly from the discussions in this chapter. Whether it be to address poverty, to compete in global markets, or to assess the potential for future development across the city as a whole, cities as frameworks and sites for development interventions are increasing in importance. This suggests, indeed, that urban development may well represent new territories for development studies, redressing the long neglect which ideas of urban bias have imposed on the field. More than this, in the creative way in which cities combine the distinctiveness and potential of place with the opportunities invested in 'displacements' – the way in which they are both territories and combinations of flows – the field of the urban represents a significant challenge to the broadest intellectual foundations of development. The opportunities for refocusing development on both flows and territories, on both places and displacements, rather than a monochrome view of either territories (states and nations) or flows (as in 'globalization'), are exemplified in the space of the city. We will return to explore this more fully in the final, concluding, chapter of the book.

5 Think local, act global: transnational networks and development by Helen Yanacopulos

Contents

Introduction to transnational networks and development

Development may be thought of as a general process of social and economic change, with profound effects for particular individuals in places. Thomas (2000a, p.25) has called such processes **immanent development**. At the same time, development is an international, or perhaps global, project concerned with mobilizing resources, markets, capital and ideas – a process of **intentional interventions**. Whether immanent or intentional, though, the development process has generally been understood to be taking place within bounded territories which are clearly defined and internationally recognized – that is, on the scale of the nation-state. Although there have also been conceptualizations of development along thematic lines, such as gender, health or rural development, these have still been addressed in terms of their taking place within bounded territories. However, both conceptually and practically, it is increasingly evident that states are just one (albeit still important) actor in the development process. Development does, certainly, take place in local areas, or within nations, but many aspects of development are also associated with flows across the borders of such territories. Increasingly, neither local areas nor the territories of states can contain the variety of actions and actors which influence the development process.

Transnational networks that are non-governmental and transcend state boundaries defy the traditional notion that developmental actors are bounded by local or national scales. While development always affects individual places, transnational networks of development actors are not necessarily restricted by their location. These networks can be seen as part of the broader process of displacement – the rising significance of flows and networks – which make up the phenomenon of 'globalization'. Such networks are not particularly new, but they are becoming more prominent, and what makes them exciting is that their expansion and operation are facilitated by new technologies. *The aim of this chapter is to explore the role of these transnational networks in challenging, influencing and working both within and across bounded territories of states and local areas.*

The first section of this chapter sets out some of the key terms which will help us to understand the significance of transnational, non-state actors in development, and how this relates to displacement. Section 5.2 explores the extent to which territories continue to be important within the context of transnational networks. Sections 5.3–5.5 each consider one example of transnational networking, exploring some of the range of forms of organizational associations which I suggest are contributing to the emergence of 'deterritorialized' forms of governance in the field of development.

Overall, the argument of this chapter is that *although development-induced displacements and dominant forms of globalization may signal 'displacement' to be a set of processes undermining the potential for development, some aspects of displacement, flows of information and networks of association, are also changing the architecture of development in ways which could offer hope for future improvements.*

5.1 Transnational networks and the association revolution

This section sets out some of the background and theory behind networking and the rise of associations outside the realm of the state. It offers a way of thinking about the role of these new organizational forms in development, through the concept of governance. It is suggested that forms of 'deterritorialized governance' co-exist alongside more familiar political forms (such as states and international agencies), and are reshaping the landscape of development.

5.1.1 Transnational networks

'Transnational networks' is a broad term used to describe activist networks that transcend national boundaries and consist of members often motivated by shared values rather than professional or material concerns. Such networks sometimes share information on issues and frequently lobby for changes in legislation, policies and international agreements. While these networks may involve various types of political actor, they are generally non-state in nature. The level of cohesion between members of transnational networks varies, as does their organizational appearance. However, they do have distinct similarities and are generally focused around a specific issue, such as abolishing landmines, lobbying for debt relief for Highly Indebted Poor Countries (HIPCs), or advocating for the rights of indigenous groups, to name but a few.

These networks differ from many other development actors in that they are non-governmental *and* operate in more than one country. Typically, their efforts embrace transnational issues (which also always have a local and national relevance) and target not only international institutions, but also local and national governments, as well as corporations. Transnational networks are not necessarily 'inter-national' groups working together; they are 'trans-national' in the sense that they operate across state boundaries and their members are not necessarily defined by their national identity. While an *international* organization, such as the International Monetary Fund (IMF), is composed of a number of nationally based organizations (for example the UK Treasury), a *transnational* network is made up of individuals and groups from a variety of locations – national identity is not a defining feature of membership. Members are not restricted by location, either their own or their target's; their strength is that they work on a multitude of levels, or across a range of scales, frequently simultaneously. For example,

Oxfam International, which is comprised of the various national Oxfams, lobbied the World Bank and the IMF on debt relief in the late 1990s. Each national Oxfam also lobbied its own government (many of which sat on the board of the World Bank and IMF). Additionally, the same Oxfams worked with 'Southern' partner non-governmental organizations (NGOs) to lobby their governments, and co-ordinated campaigns in various countries to heighten awareness of debt relief needs.

Transnational networks are not new; there have been value-based non-state transnational networks, such as the Anti-Slavery Network, the Women's Movement and the Peace Movement, since as early as the mid-nineteenth century, and many would argue that the Labour Movement, which has been in existence for over a century, is also a transnational network. But what is striking about more recently established transnational networks is that technological advances in Information and Communication Technology (ICT) have meant that such networks can now thrive. Consequently, there have been many more transnational networks emerging over the last decade. Print media, the radio, television, fax and the Internet have altered the way we exchange information and communicate with each other, and such technology has been an essential element in the rise of these transnational networks. Individuals and groups have increased their ability to systematically communicate quickly and cheaply with more people than ever before. In addition, our ability to travel vast distances that may have been inconceivable only a generation ago has changed our perception of space, and encouraged a sense of responsibility for what happens to others around the world, in response to what O'Neill (1986) has called the 'needs of distant strangers'. While the ability to utilize these technological advances may be unequally distributed between individuals and regions, they have had a global impact nonetheless.

This increase in access to ICT has created political opportunities, rendering bounded territories such as states more porous to flows of information, ideas and people. (However, it must be recognized that ICT creates political opportunities not only for 'good' causes, but also for those less worthy causes, such as criminal, terrorist or racist groups.) With the excitement surrounding such technological advances, it is frequently suggested that the importance of the state and the value of local action are no longer significant. But is the relationship between sub-state, national and transnational development actors as simplistic as this? I suggest not, and through the discussion which follows and the examples later in the chapter I will consider how flows of information and networks of association co-exist with states and international agencies. More than this, this chapter will argue that together states and transnational networks co-produce the field of development policy and practice. Before we move on to that, though, it is important that we establish the relationship between such transnational networks and the core concept of this book, *displacement*.

5.1.2 Displacement and networks

What do these new development actors, transnational networks, have to do with the focus of this book, displacement? In the field of development, the term 'displacement' conjures visions of refugees and forced migration (as discussed in Chapter 2), or sometimes refers to the shifts of populations migrating to unknown lands and cities to create a better life (as explored in Chapters 3 and 4). Displacement has, by definition, been a fairly negative term, referring to dislocation and a lack of embeddedness in a place. However, as we have been exploring throughout this book, there are other aspects to displacement – one might dare to say, a more positive view of displacement, involving a range of human movements, as well as flows and networks of all kinds.

Flows of information, possibilities for travel and the potential for organizational networking can enable individuals and groups to take forward issues that often transcend any particular location. Development action can then be seen to take place not only in familiar, or traditionally defined, political spaces (such as states), but also in other types of emerging 'global' spaces, created through these transnational networks. In some senses, then, it could be argued that these networks are (at least to some extent) 'displacing' the state as the primary arena where development actions occur. This chapter will examine these new kinds of 'political spaces' generated by transnational networks involved in development – the new kinds of territories, or spaces, which they create, perpetuate and operate in.

This form of 'displacement', or the creation of new forms of political space beyond the state, has been called **translocality** by Mandaville (1999), who goes as far as to say that 'the very nature of political territoriality may be under-going certain transformations'. Mandaville argues that translocality is not that new, but has certainly increased markedly with the prevalence of new technologies; it has always existed, but during the last two decades of the twentieth century it has expanded and been recognized and accounted for in ways it was not in the past.

Translocality: This represents an abstract space, brought into existence through connections being forged between individuals and groups situated in places. Thus, translocality is a conception of politics taking place not within bounded states, but in the context of what flows between, across and through localities. Mandaville (1999, p.654) emphasizes the difference between 'translocal' and 'international' activities by stressing that translocal activities happen across state boundaries, whilst simultaneously challenging the very nature of these boundaries. 'These are people and processes which do more than operate across or between the borders of nations; rather they actively question the nature and limits of these boundaries by practising forms of political identity which, while located in geographical space, do not depend on the limits of territory to define the limits of their politics.'

Mandaville uses the term 'translocal', as opposed to the term 'transnational' in order to emphasize that these networks are not just working across states, but also challenging these boundaries through their very existence. Stretching as they do from one local area to another, arguably some of these connections render the nation-state redundant as a point of reference. Thus, Mandaville claims that their actions can be interpreted as a challenge to the state system. Even so, Mandaville does not see this as indicating or leading to the demise of states in the near future. Rather, *Mandaville is attempting to bring into focus and account for movements – displacements – across boundaries, flows and networks which have often been ignored in past conceptualizations of politics and, in this case, of development.* Following Mandaville encourages us to re-examine the 'architecture' of development by looking at flows, or networks, across territories. Viewing interactions in this way makes us aware of the complexity of the world, and of politics and development in particular. Flows, or networks, are much more difficult to explain (or to contain) than the neat categories of scales or territories, whether they be local, national or international.

This approach to re-examining or 'reframing' development is not without its critics. It could be argued that while non-state and international institutions play a role in development, states are still the structures that matter; while non-state actors and transnational organizations exist, they do so only because states have always allowed them to do so. Also, it could be argued that the fact that transnational networks exist does not mean that they are important; states are still the most powerful actors in development (albeit that the capacity and abilities of states varies greatly). The gross national product (GNP), human development index (HDI) and other indicators of development are measured through states, and states are still central to much development thinking. Furthermore, the image of the strong state or, as Thomas and Allen (2000) discuss, the developmental state, even gained currency during the 1990s. But the most compelling argument of critics of transnationalism is that the state is still the most accountable system of politics available.

The prevalence and growing significance of transnational networks and international institutions, such as World Bank, IMF, United Nations and the World Trade Organization (WTO), do not mean that states have become irrelevant.

Brenner (1998) makes the point that the state itself is not being eroded, but re-articulated and re-territorialized in response to the importance of both sub- and supra-state scales. For example, the IMF, which is comprised of state members, may seem to be challenging the autonomy of states by imposing conditions on how governments structure their economies – but it is at the same time perpetuating the view that the state is an appropriate vehicle of development. Brenner's point is more powerful if we consider that the bounded territories of states are not absolutes – that states have been socially constructed since their inception. They have been constantly re-negotiated, re-articulated and re-territorialized. The bounded territories of states are reflections of historically specific power relations. There are countless illustrations of this: the changing boundaries between France and Germany in the first half of the twentieth century; the creation of new countries such as Eritrea and Bangladesh; and the break-up of the Soviet Union in the early 1990s, to name but a few. Therefore, the idea that states are currently being re-negotiated and re-articulated through the rise of transnational political and economic processes should not surprise us.

An examination of transnational networks should not, therefore, deny the importance of territories in the form of states. Nonetheless, focusing on transnational networks engaging in development action allows us to explore many important aspects of how development is being influenced and negotiated today, both outside the realm of states and in association with them. Exploring the interface between flows and territories, in this case transnational networks and states, gives a more accurate reflection of the changing global arena in which development occurs. It also brings into view a wider range of opportunities for promoting (or challenging) development initiatives.

This chapter suggests that both territories and flows, both place and displacement, need to be kept in view if we are to capture the dynamics of development at a global scale. Considering the interaction between flows and territories, how they operate and how they challenge, influence and interact with each other, is a complex way of looking at the world, but it is argued that it is a more useful explanatory framework for exploring contemporary development processes than the approach of considering discrete and separate territories.

Section 5.2 below considers the relationship between transnational networks and territories in more detail, and Sections 5.3–5.5 each develop examples which together highlight three aspects of the relationship between transnational networks and territories:

1 Transnational networks can challenge bounded territories through **scaling-up**. This is defined as expanding the impact and organization of NGOs and Social Movement Organizations (SMOs) beyond the local level. To illustrate this, the Zapatista Movement in the province of Chiapas, Mexico, will be examined.

2 Transnational networks can attempt to influence the rules of engagement amongst nation-states through **campaigning**. The formation of networks is often inspired as a reaction of groups to 'global' issues – issues which individual groups could not hope to influence or affect independently. An example of how transnational networks attempt to influence 'global' and structural issues through lobbying and global campaigning is the anti-Multilateral Agreement on Investments (MAI) campaign. Here, groups banded together to

attempt to influence the nature of agreements amongst states about the rules of foreign investment – in the past this domain has typically been closed to non-state, non-commercial groups.

3 Transnational networks can also attempt to influence other development actors by **bridging**. Such networks are comprised of member groups which are located in different places, and the networks act as a bridge from one level or scale of decision-making to the other. To illustrate bridging, we will be examining the organization Oxfam. Oxfam works frequently at the grass roots or at the local level, but builds on this to lobby and campaign at the national level (with national governments), and at the international level, in centres of power such as Washington, New York and Geneva. The nationally based Oxfams have formed Oxfam International, a transnational network, for this purpose.

Before moving on to look at the dynamic relationship between place and displacement both generally and in the context of these examples of transnational networking, the rest of this section explores two key concepts which will assist our analysis of these processes – the 'association revolution' and 'governance'. Section 5.1.3 considers the idea of the association revolution. It establishes the range of organizations which are involved in these various forms of transnational networking, and describes their rise to prominence in the international political arena. Section 5.1.4 explains and defines the concept of governance. Transnational networks interact on many different levels to shape development policies and thus participate in the governing process. This concept of governance, as opposed to government, is fundamental to the ideas explored in the rest of this chapter.

5.1.3 The association revolution

Something quite extraordinary has been occurring on the world scene over the past two decades ... A striking upsurge has taken place in organised voluntary activity, in the formation and increased activism of private, non-profit or non-governmental organisations in virtually every part of the world ... People are forming associations, foundations and other similar institutions to deliver human services, promote grass roots development, prevent environmental degradation, protect civil rights, and pursue a thousand other objectives ... A veritable 'association revolution' now seems underway at the global level that may constitute as significant a social and political development of the latter twentieth century as the rise of the nation-state was of the latter nineteenth...

(Salamon, 1994, p.109)

New configurations of actors across issue areas, organizational divides and levels of power are all features of Salamon's 'association revolution'. Within the development literature this 'revolution' has been explored from various perspectives, and is reflected in an increase in the discussion of civil society, NGOs and social movements – it denotes a proliferation and reconfiguration of actors in world politics. Simai (1994, p.348) describes this shift as an increasing citizen awareness 'of international problems, especially problems related to poverty, human rights, gender issues and the environment … [Associations] have introduced a new dimension into the functioning of the international co-operation system'. Driving this revolution are both the organizations' shared goals to effect large-scale change and a conducive technological environment which allows groups to do so. Non-state organizations, such as NGOs and SMOs involved in development issues, represent a large proportion of Salamon's 'association revolution'.

There are various perspectives on the association revolution. These range from those who dismiss it, claiming that it is 'no revolution at all', to those who see it as a challenge to states and to the prevailing system of politics. Strange (1996b, p.199) advocates the latter perspective, claiming that the increasing number and scope of SMOs and NGOs represent a shifting of loyalties that can no longer be contained (however much they ever were) within national boundaries. Strange asks, 'Where do allegiance, loyalty, identity lie? … Sometimes with the government of a state. But other times, with a firm, or with a social movement operating across territorial frontiers.'

Of these non-state organizations, NGOs have received the most attention within the field of development. NGOs consist of durable, bounded, voluntary relationships amongst individuals, with the aim of producing a particular outcome, using specific techniques. The term generally refers to organizations that are not-for-profit and are usually independent of the government. In the field of development, this umbrella term covers a variety of different types of organization. As Thomas and Allen (2000, p.210) outline, development NGOs have generally started by running localized projects and providing welfare and relief services, and their role has broadened to include advocacy at national and international scales.

Quantifying the association revolution is difficult. The Union of International Associations recognizes over 15 000 international NGOs which operate in three or more countries and draw their finance from more than one country. In 1994, over 10% of public development aid, US$8 billion, was channelled through NGOs, surpassing the volume of the combined United Nations system of US$6 billion. About 25% of all assistance from the United States is channelled through NGOs (Weiss and Gordenker, 1996). Not only has the number and scope of NGOs increased since the 1970s, but so too have the expectations placed upon them. Between 1970 and 1985, the total development aid disbursed by international NGOs increased tenfold. Additionally, development NGOs have been put in the position (frequently as a result of their own publicity) where they are seen as the vehicles of development success, where states and international organizations have failed.

While NGOs have been receiving a great deal of attention in the development literature, social movement organizations (or SMOs) have also been important players in development, and are part of the association revolution. SMOs are typically formed to promote specific social changes, traditionally involving localized collective action. Within a development context, they sometimes articulate an *alternative vision of development* to that which is currently taking place in their local area. Social movements are often both locally focused and a reaction to issues which have a wider 'global' purchase. Their battles have usually been fought at local and national levels and often their utilization of technology has been difficult (and remains so) as they are generally comprised of localized and marginalized groups. However, in recent years there have been various movements that have successfully taken their cause outside of their local area or state – the dam movements, such as the 'Save the Narmada Movement' (see Chapter 2, Section 2.3.3), being prime examples, as well as the Zapatistas, which we will discuss in Section 5.3. These transnational social movements have been effective in identifying the importance of solidarity groups outside of their country to foster change, and have a network of supporters internationally.

5.1.4 Governance

As with other chapters in this book, this chapter is concerned with exploring ways in which displacement and development are integrally related. In this case, we are exploring how development is changing due to the emergence of transnational networks, which have been enabled by flows of information and networks of association. Our suggestion is that transnational networks, states, and International Financial Institutions (IFIs) interact on many different levels to shape development policies and outcomes through contesting, negotiating with and influencing each other. These networks, states and institutions are all taking part in transnational, or deterritorialized, forms of governance.

Governance describes the process by which issues are defined, steered and negotiated. Governance is not just about how governments govern, but also about how a variety of institutions and networks, such as those discussed in this chapter, are involved in influencing and participating in the governing process. The definition of governance below will help to explain the term. As you read the definition, take note of the distinction made between *governance* and *government*. This is particularly relevant for our purposes, as it indicates that the use of the term 'governance' is an attempt to capture a deterritorialized process occurring outside of national boundaries.

Governance: The term 'governance' is not new, but has gained currency in the last decade. There are two aspects to governance. The first aspect is *governance as purposeful activity* – what Rosenau (1995, p.14) calls 'steering mechanisms', such as the framing of goals, issuing of directives, pursuing policies, and changing norms. A consideration of norms is particularly relevant in situations of power asymmetries, such as those between NGOs and IFIs, where framing and steering can to some degree be facilitated by normative appeals by the less powerful to influence the more powerful. While governance may resemble government, it is not equivalent to it. Governance and government 'both refer to purposive behaviour, to goal-oriented activities, to systems of rule; but government suggests activities that are backed by formal authority ... whereas governance refers to activities backed by shared goals that may or may not derive from legal and formally prescribed responsibilities' (Rosenau and Czempiele, 1992, p.4).

The second aspect of governance is *governance as an explanatory tool* – in explaining the rise of examples of state and non-state actors working together. Thus, governance refers to a looser and wider distribution of political power within and beyond the bounds of the nation-state, 'the crazy quilt nature of modern interdependence' (Finkelstein, 1995, p.267). Governance 'embraces governmental institutions, but it also subsumes informal, non-governmental mechanisms whereby those persons and organisations within its purview move ahead, satisfy their needs and fulfil their wants' (Rosenau and Czempiele, 1992, p.4).

Thus, governance describes both a range of disparate but related activities and behaviours, and offers a theoretical framework for understanding the larger, albeit nascent, patterns they are giving rise to.

From the above, then, we see that the term 'governance' has two aspects to it. The first, and the one that we are most interested in, is that governance can explain *how change is orchestrated*. In this chapter we are looking primarily at the 'intentional' aspect of development – of development as purposeful action (Thomas and Allen, 2000). Using the concept of governance helps us identify how this action takes place through relationships amongst different kinds of actors and agencies. The concept of governance also helps us to *examine the arenas where governments, IFIs and transnational networks negotiate*. The growing range of interactions which are taking place between transnational networks and territorial governments, as well as international agencies, will become evident through the course of this chapter. Fowler (1997, p.127) calls this a growing 'trilateral collaboration' at a global scale between states, NGOs and IFIs. Governance does not discriminate between state, non-state or intergovernmental actors, as all are involved in the process of influencing the others and shaping policy outcomes. However, this does not assume that power imbalances do not exist. Using governance as an explanatory framework enables us to examine how political change is occurring by investigating not only transnational initiatives novel in their content or form (or both), but also what lies beneath these changes and their likely consequences.

Governance captures essential elements in the changing relations and dynamics amongst a diverse range of actors and their collective role in shaping development, both immanent and intended. Governance is about relationships that are not usually dependent or coerced, but that may be voluntary, temporary, ad hoc, and conceived under the pressure of events (Rosenau, 1990). Relationships that take place within transnational networks, such as those fostered by the Zapatistas, the Multilateral Agreement on Investments campaigners, and organizations working on debt relief, all share these characteristics. These relationships amongst groups are possible because they are based on shared goals and common understandings, and similar perceptions of costs and risks. Transnational networks reflect the fluidity of such relationships, as they work across as well as within territories, and affect the operations of territorial entities, such as the state. The relations between these networks and territories will be discussed in greater detail in the following section. Here, we can draw our discussion of governance to a close by returning to the key distinguishing feature of 'governance' as opposed to 'government' – its deterritorialized character.

There have been vigorous debates about whether a form of 'global governance' is emerging to replace territorial forms of government through the state. What we are suggesting here is not an either/or position, but rather that *state (and other) territories, and emerging forms of transnational civil society organizations, are interconnected, and all contribute to emerging forms of 'deterritorialized' governance.*

A useful starting point here is with one of the most prominent theorists of global governance, James Rosenau. He claims that while governance may be occurring on the transnational level, it does not mean that it is *global* governance – the agents and structures engaged in this governance do not necessarily always have a global reach. Rosenau (1997, p.10) proclaims that 'the organizing perspective is that of governance *in* the world rather than governance *of* the world'. As there is no central authority on the global level, the *governance of the world* is a difficult idea to defend. However, *governance in the world* suggests that governance and influence are originating from communities, non-governmental organizations, states, and other non-state actors, all of which operate in and across existing localities and territories.

The following section explores in greater detail the nature of the interactions which are emerging between transnational networks and territories or local areas, in the context of the governance of intentional development efforts.

Summary of Section 5.1

The relationship between development and transnational networks, states, and IFIs has been discussed in this section. Three key points were made:

- Transnational networks are not new, but the advent of Information and Communication Technology has facilitated their increase in numbers and influence.

- These networks of association and flows of information (or displacements) which enable transnational networking are increasingly shaping decisions and politics, and leading to a shift from the association of development with the territories of states or local areas, to an emphasis on transnational political arenas.

- One approach to understanding this process, governance, draws our attention to how governments, IFIs and transnational networks influence each other and together shape development outcomes.

5.2 Transnational networks, territories and development

We have seen that transnational networks of non-state organizations are increasingly being recognized as important actors in development. These transnational networks are not only cutting across local, national and international scales but are also affecting the ways in which development is conceptualized and is practically occurring. These transnational networks are very much a part of what McGrew (2000, p.348) has described as a process of 'globalization'. McGrew describes globalization as 'a process (or a set of processes) which embodies a transformation in the spatial organization of social relations and transactions – assessed in terms of their extensity, intensity, velocity and impact – generating *transcontinental or interregional flows and networks of activity, interaction, and the exercise of power*' (my emphasis).

In this chapter, as in previous chapters of this book, it is argued that although networks and flows may be becoming more significant in contemporary life, they do not replace territories. And as in the examples discussed in the previous chapters of this book, we should expect that our discussions in this chapter will find close relations between places, or territories, and what we have been calling displacements (or flows and networks).

In this sense, then, when speaking of global campaigning and transnational networks, it is not to suggest that politics has been rendered irrelevant to local places or territories such as the state. Even 'global' campaigns start somewhere and end somewhere; they are based on issues that affect people's lives and are often rooted in specific places. And as Chambers (1998) notes, even powerful institutions with a claim to global operations are, by necessity, localized in places, and can attract criticism and opposition there – as in the case of the anti-globalization protests outside the World Bank's offices in Washington, DC, in April 2000.

As we explore the three case studies of transnational networking in Sections 5.3–5.5 (scaling-up, global campaigning and bridging) we will see specific examples of how local areas, territories and localizations of powerful institutions all shape the outcomes and operation of organizations. First, this section explores in general the influence of transnational networking on the changing territories of international politics.

5.2.1 Changing centres

In order to examine the ways in which development actors are organized and located, or territorialized, this section explores the idea of centres of *allegiance, competence* and *power*. For example, throughout the ages, individual political allegiances have been based upon kinship groups, religious affiliations and territories. Centres of competence and power have also shifted – for example, the centre of political power in the UK shifted from the church to royalty, and then from royalty to parliament. Advances in Information and Communication Technology have facilitated further changes in centres of competence and power as more organizations are able to shape policy and governance.

Shifting allegiance

An illustration of shifting centres of allegiance can be found in the rise of NGOs and SMOs. For example, there are over 1 million Amnesty International members, committed to human rights issues, in 162 countries (see Amnesty International Online website). Amnesty membership groups in all of these countries work on various campaigns, such as releasing political prisoners or advocating the ending of the death penalty in countries such as the United States. Amnesty members from all over the world have voluntarily joined because they have an affinity with the values of the organization. However, Amnesty International is very aware that an individual's change of allegiance might involve taking a position against their government on a certain issue and could potentially cause problems for that individual. Therefore, in order to avoid governmental repercussions to its members, Amnesty has a policy of not allowing individuals to participate in campaigns in their own country through their Amnesty group.

Transnationally, the networks of members of Amnesty International have considerable political leverage and normative force in the field of human rights. This influence escalates when Amnesty International works with other groups involved in rights, thereby creating a transnational network of human rights activists.

Strange (1996b) has described changes or challenges to allegiances in terms of an increase in the conflicting loyalties of individuals. Strange argues that the ending of the Cold War has resulted in an absence of absolutes and a situation where allegiance and loyalty are not always to a government of a state. Multiple political allegiances are not necessarily

Figure 5.1 Amnesty International members in 162 countries around the world work on various campaigns to promote human rights.

a new phenomenon; but the availability of information and the increased ability to link with others who have similar allegiances is making multiple associations more likely. This 'shrinking political distance' has resulted in what were thought of as domestic issues increasingly appearing on international agendas. Awareness of the injustices and needs of 'distant strangers' has established connections and allegiances beyond the state.

While many agree with Strange's views concerning changing allegiances, loyalties and identities, do these changes indicate that states are decreasing in importance? Sceptics of Strange's perspective would claim not. They argue that the changes in centres of allegiance are merely the result of states delegating their workload to non-state developmental actors. Non-state actors are not a genie that has been let out of its bottle, but are allowed to exist, or even brought into existence, through states themselves, through the funding, regulation and, thus, the legitimacy that states bestow upon non-state organizations. As Krasner (1995, p.279) claims, 'even the very existence of certain kinds of non-state international actors reflects state institutions. In a world dominated by Nazi regimes, Amnesty International would not exist' – or it would have to be an underground organization. Nevertheless, the increase of non-state organizations over the last two decades is undeniable; it is their relative political importance, especially in relation to states, that is contested.

Shifting competence

Allegiances are extending and multiplying, and so too are perceived 'centres of competence' (the institutional nodes or networks which carry out certain delivery and decision-making functions). The relationship between the state and other groups in society has been changing, as has the allocation of social and economic responsibilities. States in both developed 'Northern' countries and developing 'Southern' countries have been increasingly subcontracting services, and in some cases NGOs have been contracted to provide services which 'weak' or 'failing states' cannot provide. For example, the prominence of foreign NGOs in countries such as Rwanda and Bangladesh illustrates the shift of service provision from state to NGOs. However, the changing development architecture under examination here is not just about the 'hollowing-out' of the state and the use of NGO services and expertise by governments. What is important here is that through such 'hollowing-out', NGOs' competence on a wide range of development and policy issues is increasing and often challenging that of states.

Shifting power

Strange has also proposed that in recent times the focus of power has moved from states to international organizations, where a degree of authority over some issues has shifted upward, from the political institutions of national capitals 'to the scattered headquarters of international bureaucracies'. As she notes, 'International organisations – IGOs or intergovernmental organisations – are certainly more numerous and more visible than they were a generation or more ago. The annual meetings of the World Bank and the International Monetary Fund draw literally thousands of journalists every year' (Strange, 1996b, p.161). And, more recently, such meetings have drawn thousands of protesters too, as in Figure 5.2, which shows protesters outside the World Trade Organization meetings in Seattle in 1999.

International organizations such as the World Bank and the IMF have become truly global institutions, with very few countries exempt from their influence. An increase in technological and economic

Figure 5.2 Anti-globalization protesters outside the World Trade Organization in Seattle, 1999.

interconnectedness has made these IFIs centres of power. However, these 'centres of power' are also often associated with specific places where the IFIs are based and important decisions are made. Washington, New York and Geneva, homes of the World Bank, United Nations and International Labour Organization, amongst others, are becoming increasingly important places in the world of development, frequently more important than state capitals. This is a reflection of the rising prominence of the multilateral institutions generally, and the IFIs, such as the World Bank and IMF in particular, in development issues. Transnational networks of development, including NGOs and social movements, are therefore also locating in centres of power, in order to better engage with and challenge these multinational institutions.

Thus, even as governance and political allegiances are becoming deterritorialized, older forms of territorially based political entities persist (like states and international organizations) and new kinds of important places or territories are emerging. Centres such as Washington, or places where significant international meetings have been staged, like Seattle or Genoa, are important re-territorializations of the global political economy. Moreover, transnational networks and organizations now compete with territorial entities such as states for the political allegiance of individuals and groups.

5.2.2 Different kinds of networks

The term 'network' is notoriously vague – and in this chapter we are using it to describe a range of different kinds of organization and communication. Before we turn to explore the case studies of transnational networks, and try to assess their broader significance for development, it will be helpful to examine the meaning of the concept of 'network' itself in more detail. There has been much ambiguity surrounding the term, which stems from the fact that it has been used in two distinct ways.

1   *Networks as information exchanges*: For example, NGOs belonging to a network to exchange information on debt relief, environmental issues or big protest meetings. Warner (1995, p.3857) talks about viewing the network as a metaphor, and sees such networks as *functional connections, set up for the exchange of information, with no structural organizational linkages.*

2   *Networks as distinct organizations*: This is where individuals or organizations join together (in varying degrees) in order to achieve their aims, whether social, economic or political. Warner (1995) states: '[these] relationships ... possess characteristics indicating that they may be seen as some kind of quasi-organizations' (p.3857). Thus, in this second description, Warner sees networks as *organizational structures where members agree to work together and consequently give up some rights in pursuing their own interests for the interests of the group.*

These two definitions could be thought of as opposite extremes of the continuum of different forms which groups might adopt when choosing to work together as part of a networked organization. Various terms have been used to describe the degree of interconnection between such individuals and organizations, such as 'collaboration', 'coalition' and 'alliance'. 'Collaboration' includes all aspects of the information-exchange type of networking, and also involves altering activities and sharing resources to enhance each other's capacity for mutual benefit and a common purpose by sharing risks, responsibilities and rewards. Both the discourse and the practice of 'collaboration' have become increasingly common in both for-profit and not-for-profit circles. Collaboration is taken to imply a very positive form of working in association with others for some form of mutual benefit. 'Coalitions' are more formalized groupings, where members have formed a secretariat and where there are commitments to the coalition from its members (Huxham, 1996).

So while there are various degrees of cohesion and organizational difference amongst the different types of grouping we will be examining, the broad term – network – is generally used to describe all of them. It has been used as an umbrella term to describe various types of groups and individuals working together.

There are, of course, both advantages and disadvantages in the various organizational forms that groups adopt. For example, a global campaign that is based on addressing a single issue and which requires a broad degree of support, such as the Jubilee 2000 Debt Relief campaign, is better suited to the loose information sharing network form. However, a transnational network where members are required to have a great deal of trust and commitment, and which requires a collaborative secretariat and works on a broader range of development issues, would be better suited to the more structured coalition form. One such example is Oxfam International, which will be discussed later in this chapter, which also works on debt relief, but in conjunction with a much broader spectrum of development issues.

With respect to Warner's second category of networks, more formalized transnational networks usually have a higher level of commitment amongst member organizations, as they have been created to last beyond a single issue. Transnational networks can also have a multi-level or cross-scale functioning where members might have connections to the grass roots, but the network operates at the international level. More formalized transnational network structures reflect that these groups have moved beyond Warner's first category of information sharing networks. Many transnational networks have now become institutions with norms and practices of doing things, with their main objective being to influence governments and IFIs.

Table 5.1 Classifying and refining networks

Type of network and structure	Example
Functional/metaphor: No organizational structure Person-to-person or organization Links/flows of information Sharing information	Anti-globalization protests (Figure 5.3)
Quasi-organizations/collaborations: Give up some rights Collaboration Effective new grouping	Jubilee 2000
Coalitions: Formalized Secretariat Membership-based	Oxfam International

Figure 5.3 Anti-globalization protesters gather in the heart of London, May 2001, closing down Oxford Street, the symbolic centre of consumerism.

In the following sections of this chapter examples of both of Warner's two network forms will be considered. Warner's first description is illustrated by the loose networks of the Zapatista and anti-MAI campaigns, showing how the network form has served as a functional connection for sharing information and co-ordinating groups' strategies. Warner's second description of the network form is illustrated through Oxfam International, which is a network of NGOs, as well as an organization in its own right, where the Oxfam members have made a more formal commitment to the group.

5.2.3 Transnational networks and development

With respect to development, transnational networks are defined by Fowler (1997, p.115) as groupings that can be either short or long term, and involve national, regional, continental and/or global associations of NGOs and SMOs. They come together to promote mutual interests, creating a distinct entity for such a purpose, which may or may not formally register as a separate legal body. They are usually established around specific development issues rather than the concerns of the NGO sector per se. Any work required is done by its members; frequently members will take on the secretariat function either permanently or on a rotational basis. A crucial organizational feature of transnational networks is the active control of the organization by the members. Mandated by members to adopt and voice positions on their behalf, transnational networks serve as platforms for the articulation of members' interests, but do not exercise any formal authority or sanction over individual members. There is also no joint liability for operational performance beyond the shared risk of losing credibility. Therefore, if the transnational network fails in its objectives, the individual members are not affected. The cost involved for members is the time, human capacity, information and investment in the processes needed to reach collective decisions on issues, and then mandating the secretariat and office bearers accordingly. Just as with other transnational networks, the benefits for transnational networks working in development include greater strength when voicing shared positions, together with enhanced access to information.

Sharing information is probably the most common benefit of belonging to a network. The sharing of information and research helps members of a transnational network to articulate clearly a position when speaking to those they wish to influence. Access to information is also invaluable for developing ideas to put to governments and IFIs as a credible alternative to existing policies, and increasing the transnational network's standing as a centre of competence. Technological changes, particularly in the area of communications, have greatly improved the accessibility of research resources and have made communication and conferencing amongst NGOs and SMOs much less expensive and more frequent.

Information sharing involves not only bringing valid and up-to-date data together, but having the expertise to distinguish what should be considered important to the organization, and deciphering the information the members should be aware of. Thus, good dissemination of information is crucial, particularly as the potential for information overload is high. One of many examples of this is the NGO Working Group on the World Bank. This organization sees its annual meetings as a means of disseminating information using documentation, policy papers, and newer forms of information co-ordination such as the Internet. The Africa region of the NGO Working Group on the World

Bank has started a website, 'Afriline' (http://www.afriline.net/), in an attempt to bring information about regional members, as well as information on the World Bank, to one accessible virtual 'place'.

This is only one example of how the Internet has changed the availability of information and allows instantaneous access to it. The Third World Network, a transnational network based in Malaysia with members in Latin America, Africa and Asia, equates the 'network' form of organizing with the Internet itself, stating that:

> It's very much like the Internet – you punch a word and see who else is interested … rather than a formal organization … The strength is that you're flexible with less structure and so in a sense, it's open in that there are many open parts of activity that people can take part in…
>
> (Third World Network, 1998)

In writing about transnational networks engaged in advocacy, Keck and Sikkink (1998, p.200) reiterate that the increase in transnational networks may be attributed to 'faster, cheaper and more reliable information technologies'. In the following description, they outline how information is used by transnational networks in their attempts to influence others.

> A transnational advocacy network includes those relevant actors working internationally on an issue, who are bound together by shared values, a common discourse, and dense exchanges of information and services. Such networks are most prevalent in issue areas characterised by high value content and informational uncertainty. At the core of the relationship is information exchange. What is novel in these networks is the ability of non-traditional international actors to mobilise information strategically to help [increase] leverage over much more powerful organisations and governments. Activists in networks try not only to influence policy outcomes, but to transform the terms and nature of the debate. They are not always successful in their efforts, but they are increasingly relevant players in policy debates … Transnational advocacy networks must also be understood as political spaces, in which differently situated actors negotiate – formally or informally – the social, cultural, and political meanings of their joint enterprise.
>
> (Keck and Sikkink, 1998, pp.2–3)

In this chapter so far, we have identified a range of development-related networks, such as advocacy coalitions, social movements, and NGO networks. While there are differences between these, there are also some similarities. They all describe groups that are: non-governmental; operating across territories; forums for association around issues; and have a differing perspective from the prevailing one of governments and IFIs. Keck and Sikkink, (1998, p.1) summarize this when they state that these networks are 'significant transnationally and domestically. By building new links among actors in civil societies, states, and international organisations, they multiply the channels of access to the international system.' In the remainder of this chapter, we will be looking at three examples that illustrate how these different forms of transnational networks have acted, interacted and negotiated aspects of development within and across territories. As noted in Section 5.1.2, these case studies cover three different forms of transnationality: scaling-up from the local to the global; joint campaigning across national borders; and bridging scales or levels of operation through close organizational co-operation. The following three sections explore each of these in turn.

Summary of Section 5.2

- Transnational networks are giving rise to changing centres of allegiance, power and competence. These changes are challenging what many have seen as the exclusive role of the state in development, although the extent and success of this is hotly debated.

- Although transnational networks are establishing a new architecture to global politics, places and territories continue to be important features of development and global governance.

- Transnational networks can take various forms (looser alliances, or closer collaborative organizational associations), in order to better influence states and IFIs working in development.

5.3 Scaling-up

In this section we will look at the case study of the Zapatistas, and how they have used scaling-up to try to achieve their aims. By first examining the motivations behind scaling-up, we will see how transnational networks can develop around what may be seen as very 'local' issues – such as those raised by the Zapatistas.

Many NGOs and SMOs have increasingly identified the causes and reasons for the perpetuation of poverty as stemming from a globalizing economic system. These groups claim that the IFIs have promoted the ideology of open international markets and argue that this has negative consequences for the poor. They argue that the IFIs are attempting to integrate developing economies into the global economic system, a system that is not always fair to these developing 'Southern' countries, communities and individuals. Thus, in order to target the IFIs, NGOs and SMOs have elevated their advocacy work to the transnational level by either creating or joining transnational networks – for NGOs and SMOs to address such 'global' systems issues, they too have to scale themselves up to the 'global'. Edwards prophetically outlined this in the following statement:

> Most UK development NGOs accept that significant improvements in the lives of poor people around the globe are unlikely to be achieved solely by funding 'projects' at grass roots level. This is because local initiatives can easily be blocked, undermined, or co-opted by more

powerful forces, whether economic or political. Development work which fails to address these forces can expect to have an impact only on the short-term welfare of a small number of poor people. Those forces which emanate from the national or sub-national political economy must be addressed by indigenous institutions; others are international in character and include the structure of the world trading system, financial and investment flows ... and the policies of multilateral and bilateral donor agencies. The increasing internationalisation of decision-making in economic and political fields and the limited accountability of global institutions have increased the power of these interests.

(Edwards, 1993, p.163)

So transnational networks such as SMOs and NGOs are 'scaling-up' their efforts from the local to the transnational scale. This process is described as follows:

NGOs can expand their impact by increasing their size; taking on new activities; influencing the behaviour of other organisations; and assuring their own organisational sustainability ... Perhaps the most obvious method by which to increase impact for an NGO is to become a larger organisation, manage more funds, employ more skilled personnel, and foremost, cover a larger number of beneficiaries, typically in a larger geographical area.

(Uvin *et al.*, 2000, p.1411)

The impetuses for scaling-up are varied – scaling-up for political impact seems to be an important purpose of groups forming transnational networks. Political scaling-up is done in order to build a political power base for the achievement of the goals of local communities through the wider political process. It is based 'on a recognition of the need to attack the root causes of poverty at the macro-level' (Uvin and Miller, 1996, p.348). Political scaling-up has been broken down into a number of components – information, mobilization and networking being the most significant. Information is collected and disseminated to generate awareness of an issue or a problem. The approach is designed to raise sympathy for an issue or organization, thereby putting pressure on politicians to act. Networking, in this context, aims to bring together groups who are sympathetic and have similar objectives. These alliances are issue-dependent and could be made between 'North' and 'South' or between for-profit and non-profit associations, and they could be formal or informal. The links between groups and individuals are developed through any means available, be they face-to-face meetings, e-mails or conferences. We look at this in more detail in Section 5.4 on global campaigning.

One of the benefits of scaling-up, according to Keck and Sikkink (1998), is what they have called the 'boomerang effect'. The boomerang pattern of influence is a tactical approach used by transnational networks such as NGOs and SMOs, where an organization bypasses the national government and forges links with international allies in order to pressure their national government from the outside. The international allies are not necessarily only other NGOs and SMOs, but could be governments or IFIs. This tactic would not be possible without the scaling-up of groups.

In the following subsection, the case of the Zapatistas will be examined. This is an SMO which has scaled-up and used the boomerang effect, challenging the Mexican state by using international pressure. The Zapatistas have taken a local issue and, using Information and Communication Technology, have managed to bring world-wide attention to their struggle.

5.3.1 Zapatistas

The Zapatistas came to public attention in 1994, when they declared war on the Mexican state, fighting for the liberation of the people of Chiapas, a southern region of Mexico (see Figure 5.4). Their struggle has become synonymous with a new type of political movement, one where a localized struggle has scaled-up from its territory, in this case the region of Chiapas, to attain global attention. As Uvin (1995, p.495) outlines, the Zapatistas have scaled-up like other 'grass roots organisations and local non-governmental organisations [who] seek to expand their impact and move beyond the local level. In doing so, they are becoming players, often reluctantly, at the national and international levels.'

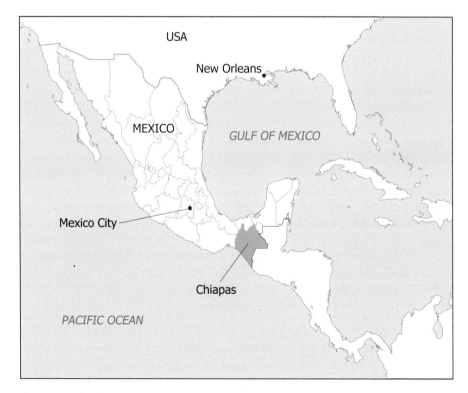

Figure 5.4 The Chiapas region in Mexico.

Figure 5.5 The Zapatistas and their leader, Subcomandante Marcos.

The causes of the Zapatista rebellion are complex. Castells (1997, p.77) observes that there are two aspects to the uprisings. First, the Zapatistas see themselves in what Castells describes as 'historical continuity with five hundred years of struggle against colonization and oppression'. In addition to this, Castells claims that they see themselves reliving this oppression through new forms of the global order – specifically, in the form of the North American Free Trade Agreement (NAFTA) which took effect on 1 January 1994. The Zapatistas felt that the liberalization of the Mexican economy, and Mexico's entry into NAFTA failed to benefit Chiapan peasants and indigenous peoples. The Mexican economic liberalization policies ended restrictions upon imports of corn, and eliminated price protection on coffee. Consequently, it was claimed, the vulnerable Chiapan economy was devastated. In Castells' view, the Zapatista rebellion was also about opposition to the market-based new global order, or 'neoliberalism'.

On 1 January 1994, 3000 lightly armed men and women took control of the main towns in Lacandon, Chiapas. When the Mexican army sent troops to the region, the guerrillas withdrew to the rainforest, but this was after a number of casualties amongst both the guerrilla and army troops. There was widespread sympathy for the movement, and the Mexican president declared a cease-fire on 12 January of the same year.

The Zapatistas are not the only group to be affected by a government's economic policy – what made their struggle distinctive and their response worthy of world-wide attention? The answer to this is in their use of ICT and the media to scale-up their struggle. The Zapatistas have been called 'information guerrillas': through their use of the Internet they have mobilized support within Chiapas, have ignited solidarity amongst other groups within Mexico, and have also tapped into international networks of solidarity. While the Zapatistas' concerns involved issues of land and space in Chiapas itself, they utilized the creation of a transnational network to present their case and increase pressure on their national government – they used the boomerang effect and put their case into the international political arena. This is not to say that their struggle has occurred exclusively outside of Chiapas. The Zapatistas are well grounded in the area – this is very much a local struggle. Their strength has been to make this struggle evident to the rest of Mexico and the rest of the world, and to build a transnational support base. Not until the Zapatista Movement, have the tools of ICT – including the Internet and the media – been used so strategically. What follows in Box 5.1 is Castells' description of the movement.

Box 5.1 The communication strategy of the Zapatistas: the Internet and the media

Extracts from Castells (1997, p.79–81)

The success of the Zapatistas was largely due to their communication strategy, to the point that they can be called the *first informational guerrilla movement*. They created a media event in order to diffuse their message, while desperately trying not to be brought into a bloody war. There were, of course, real deaths, and real weapons, and Marcos [Subcomandante Marcos, the Zapatistas' leader] and his comrades, were ready to die. Yet, actual warfare was not their strategy. The Zapatistas used arms to make a statement, then parlayed the possibility of their sacrifice in front of the world media to force a negotiation and advance a number of reasonable demands which, as opinion polls seem to indicate, found widespread support in Mexican society at large.

...The Zapatistas' ability to communicate with the world, and with Mexican society, and to capture the imagination of people and of intellectuals, propelled a local, weak insurgent group to the forefront of world politics. In this sense Marcos was essential. He did not have organisational control of a movement that was rooted in the Indian communities, and he did not show any signs of being a great military strategist, although he was wise in ordering retreat every time the army was to engage them. But he was extraordinarily able in establishing a communication bridge with the media, through his well-constructed writings, and by his *mise en scène* (the mask, the pipe, the setting of the interviews) ... the mask that played such an important role in popularizing the revolutionaries' image: all over the world, everybody could become Zapatista by wearing a mask. Furthermore (although this may be an over-theorisation), masks are a recurrent ritual in pre-Colombian Mexican Indian cultures, so that rebellion, equalisation of faces, and historical flashback played into each other in a most innovative theatrics of revolution. Essential in this strategy was the Zapatistas' use of telecommunications, videos, and of computer-mediated communication, both to diffuse their messages from Chiapas to the world (although probably not transmitted from the forest), and to organise a worldwide network of solidarity groups that literally encircled the repressive intentions of the Mexican government; for instance, during the army invasion of insurgent areas on February 9, 1995. It is interesting to underline that the origins of the Zapatistas' use of the Internet are two developments of the 1990s: the creation of *La Neta*, an alternative computer communication network in Mexico and Chiapas; and its use by women's groups (particularly by '*De mujer a mujer*') to link up Chiapas' NGOs with other Mexican women, as well as with women's networks in the US.

...Extensive use of the Internet allowed the Zapatistas to diffuse information and their call throughout the world instantly, and to create a network of support groups which helped to produce an international public opinion movement that made it literally impossible for the Mexican government to use repression on a large scale.

...This was the key to the Zapatistas' success. Not that they deliberately sabotaged the economy. But they were protected by their relentless media connection, and by their Internet based worldwide alliances, from outright repression, forcing negotiation, and raising the issue of social exclusion and political corruption to the eyes and ears of world public opinion.

But how does the Zapatistas' scaling-up relate to the idea of displacement? The creation of new kinds of political space beyond the nation-state is very much a part of the scaling-up of NGOs and SMOs. The Zapatistas used the media as a political strategy and they were very adept at using strategic images and words – through networks established across borders and scales (Routledge, 2002). A war of words is not a new feature in political struggles. However, using the right images and the right medium in order to appeal strategically to international interests helped the Zapatistas to create a transnational political space in which their struggle could be heard.

The scaling-up effect has also enabled other solidarity groups to form around similar issues to those raised by the Zapatistas. In Box 5.2 the excerpt from Routledge outlines the emergence of the People's Global Action (PGA) network as one such example.

Box 5.2 People's Global Action

Extracts from Routledge (1998)

The PGA owes its genesis to an encounter between international activists and intellectuals that was organised by the Zapatistas in Chiapas in 1996. In a meeting in Spain the following year, that sought to build upon the Zapatista encounter, the idea of a network between different resistance formations was launched by ten social movements including Movimento Sem Terra ('Landless Peasants Movement') of Brazil and the Barnataka State Farmer's Union of India. The official 'birth' of the PGA was February 1998 ... [and its] purpose was to facilitate the sharing of information between grass roots social movements without the mediation of established non-government organisations ... However, the PGA is not an organisation. Rather, it represents a convergence space of social movements, resistance groups, and individuals from across the world. Its main objectives are: (i) inspiring the greatest number of persons, movements, and organisations to act against corporate domination through non-violent civil disobedience and people-oriented constructive actions; (ii) offering an instrument for co-ordination and mutual support at the global level for those resisting corporate rule and the capitalistic development paradigm; and (iii) giving more international projection to the struggles against economic liberalisation and global capitalism.

Scaling-up, as illustrated in the Zapatista case study, has been one primary objective of transnational networks. However, scaling-up is only part of the story. It might be more accurate to say that organizations have been moving, or 'jumping', scales – not just upwards, but in all directions. We see IFIs focusing on the grass roots, as well as grass roots organizations lobbying states and IFIs. What we are witnessing is not only a scaling-up, but an increasing interlinking of scales with the help of technology. Thus, transnational networks are not only cutting across scales; their strategy is to target specifically all these levels or scales. It is not that NGOs and SMOs are simply changing their scale of operation from the local to the national or international, but that all these areas are being targeted simultaneously, are inter-related, and are affecting each other.

Summary of Section 5.3

- Transnational networking can take the form of 'scaling-up' local movements in association with external partners in order to attempt to influence local or state territorial institutions. This has been called the 'boomerang' effect.

- The Zapatista Movement in Chiapas, Mexico, has drawn on transnational political networks and wider media coverage to pressure the Mexican government from without. 'Jumping scales' from the local to the global, the Zapatistas have come to symbolize this new form of political networking.

- Information and Communication Technology has played a key role in facilitating this form of mobilization, bringing local struggles to a wider audience.

5.4 Global campaigning

The Zapatista case study demonstrates how a locally rooted dispute was scaled-up to a transnational scale. Frequently, disputed issues are not rooted locally, but are instigated by international organizations and concern the international system. These disputes, such as those over the Multilateral Agreement on Investment (MAI; see Section 5.4.2 and Box 5.3), revolve around establishing international rules and forms of regulation. While it is essential to remember that these international rules and systems have ramifications for people's lives (and thereby have a local impact), the battles surrounding them are fought at an international level, frequently in symbolic centres of power such as New York, Washington or Geneva. For NGOs and SMOs to fight 'global' battles in and against the institutions and organizations which set these rules, they need specialist skills in order to advocate their perspectives. Thus, as well as scaling-up, transnational networks must also hone their skills in lobbying, campaigning, mobilizing, and co-ordinating action transnationally in relation to intergovernmental agencies. Many of these tactics have long been important at a national level, but they are increasingly important in responding to issues on a global scale.

5.4.1 Lobbying and campaigning

Professional lobbying is a relatively new aspect of NGO work, necessitated by the need for effective advocacy at the highest levels. While the terms 'lobby' and 'advocacy' are sometimes used synonymously, lobbying is, in fact, a narrowly defined process that relates to the practice of influencing the formal political process (Jordan and Van Tuijl, 1998).

> **Lobby:** An attempt to influence, or steer, formal decisions being made by government officials, though the term has been extended to include actions directed at those outside of the formal political process, but who have decision-making powers.
>
> **Campaign:** With a purpose to mobilize supporters by using the media to put pressure on decision-makers, this requires a clear and simple message and objective. It is typically adversarial, requiring a villain or an injustice.
>
> **Advocate:** To promote the causes of others. Jordan and Van Tuijl (1998, p.6) describe advocacy as 'action that attempts to rectify unequal power relations and rectify power imbalances'. It is a broad term used in development studies to encompass activities such as lobbying, campaigning and educating publics and institutions on development issues, in particular issues concerning the poor.

In contrast to lobbying, campaigns provide a form of public education and can mobilize people around an issue; they can be part of a broader advocacy strategy that may also support an organization's more specific programmes. Keck and Sikkink (1998, p.27) argue that in a campaign a 'causal story' must be established, so that a villain and responsibility for an injustice are obvious, and 'the causal chain needs to be sufficiently short and clear to make the case convincing'.

Lobbying and campaigning require different tools and tactics. Lobbying is a much more targeted process, requiring the art of persuasion, expert knowledge and negotiating skills. In lobbying, vilifying is ineffective. NGO and SMO lobbyists (usually in conjunction with the policy departments and programmers) can provide the groundwork for campaigns and contribute to the articulation of the organization's position. Lobbying and campaigning can be mutually supportive if done in association with one another.

There have been numerous successful NGO advocacy campaigns. Clark (1992) provides a list of successes of NGO advocacy, which range from debt relief to a code of conduct for the marketing of baby milk. One recent 'success' was the international rallying of NGOs and SMOs to stop the Multilateral Agreement on Investments.

5.4.2 The anti-Multilateral Agreement on Investments (MAI) campaign

The MAI was an agreement negotiated in secrecy within the Organisation for Economic Co-operation and Development (OECD) over the course of two years. The OECD is comprised of 25 'developed' countries and has sometimes been called a 'rich man's club'. The proposed agreement was designed to bring about a new set of investment rules that would grant corporations the right to move their operations anywhere in the world without being bound by national governments' regulations. The MAI sought to create a world where capital could be moved around, free from regulation. In 1997, the proposal was leaked to Public Citizen, a Washington-based public interest group founded by Ralph Nader, and then immediately published on the Internet. As a result, interested groups came together to share information about the agreement and to form a high-level campaign to stop the agreement.

The MAI aimed to institute three principles for international investment: non-discrimination of foreign investors; no entry restrictions for corporations; and the absence of special conditions for national companies. The agreement's aims were to create an equal playing field for international investment. However, objections were raised by NGOs and SMOs on a number of counts: conducting the negotiations in secret; the potential for corporations to override national and international labour and environmental standards; and the imbalance between corporations' rights (which were many) and corporations' responsibilities (which were few). The agreement was seen as a threat to democracy, economic development, human rights and the environment. The groups opposing the MAI claimed that the agreement would 'give corporations the "sovereign power to govern countries", make elected governments "their compliant puppets" and "radically limit our ability to promote social, economic and environmental justice"' (Kobrin, 1998, p.98).

For the public, NGOs and SMOs were the only source of information about this agreement. A transnational network of groups came together to lobby their own governments, to lobby OECD officials, and to launch a media campaign about the agreement. Information and mobilization were the key elements of this campaign, and the Internet was the essential medium, bringing groups together, and informing other groups about the agreement, in order that they could in turn join the lobby. The negotiations on the agreement were stopped shortly after this campaign began, as the following article describes.

Box 5.3 How the Net killed the MAI

From *The Globe & Mail*, Wednesday 29 April 1998

Grassroots groups used their own globalization to derail deal

By Madelaine Drohan

PARIS – High-powered politicians had reams of statistics and analysis on why a set of international investing rules would make the world a better place.

They were no match, however, for a global band of grassroots organizations, which, with little more than computers and access to the Internet, helped derail a deal. Indeed, international negotiations have been transformed after this week's successful rout of the Multilateral Agreement on Investment (MAI) by opposition groups, which – alarmed by the trend toward economic globalization – used some globalization of their own to fight back.

Using the Internet's capability to broadcast information instantly worldwide, groups such as the Council of Canadians and the Malaysia-based Third World Network have been able to keep each other informed of the latest developments and supply information gleaned in one country that may prove embarrassing to a government in another. By pooling their information they have broken through the wall of secrecy that traditionally surrounds international negotiations, forcing governments to deal with their complaints.

'We are in constant contact with our allies in other countries,' said Maude Barlow, the Council of Canadians' chairwoman. 'If a negotiator says something to someone over a glass of wine, we'll have it on the Internet within an hour, all over the world.' The success of that networking was clear this week

when ministers from the 29 countries in the Organisation for Economic Co-operation and Development admitted that the global wave of protest had swamped the deal.

'This is the first successful Internet campaign by non-governmental organizations,' said one diplomat involved in the negotiations. 'It's been very effective.' The OECD, which represents largely the major industrial economies, yesterday halted the negotiations aimed at developing international rules for foreign investment, similar to those for trade in goods. It is unclear when, or even if, the OECD will try again. The irony in this outcome is that the OECD, which has been an ardent advocate of globalization and has done much research into its effects, did not recognize that advocacy groups would use cyber-globalization to further their own ends.

OECD secretary-general Donald Johnston conceded that the OECD was caught flat-footed: 'It's clear we needed a strategy on information, communication and explication,' he told a press conference. The OECD's efforts to harness the Internet have not caught up in colour, content and consumer friendliness to those of the advocacy groups.

For example, the OECD report released this week on the benefits of opening markets to trade and investment is a compilation of statistics and analysis written in language more readily understood by economists than by the average person. Instead of finding examples of real people who have benefited

235

from globalization to help trade ministers make this case, the report repeats many of the same statistics on economic growth, investment and the dangers of protectionism. By comparison, hundreds of advocacy groups, in attempting to galvanize opposition to the MAI, used terms and examples that brought their message home to the public. Their sites on the Internet's World Wide Web are colourful and easy to use, offering primers on the MAI that anyone could understand.

Canadian Trade Minister Sergio Marchi has taken the OECD to task for its poor communications effort, although he agrees some of the blame must be shared by the member governments. He said the lesson he has learned is that 'civil society' – meaning public interest groups – should be engaged much sooner in a negotiating process, instead of governments trying to negotiate around them.

Ms Barlow of the Council of Canadians, which says it has more than 100 000 members, called the OECD report on the benefits of globalization 'pathetic.' In an interview in Paris, where she was taking part in a protest against the MAI, Ms Barlow said the immediacy of the Internet has changed the dynamics of advocacy campaigns. She is a veteran of the campaigns against the Canada–US free-trade agreement and the North American free-trade agreement. The Internet was not in widespread use when those campaigns were conducted.

Today, however, advocacy groups make sure useful information ends up in the right hands right away. 'If we know something that is sensitive to one government, we get it to our ally in that country instantly,' she said. 'I don't think governments will ever be able to do these kinds of secret trade negotiations again.' For example, when the Council of Canadians got its hands on a draft version of the MAI last year, it immediately posted it on its website and made sure allies around the world knew it was there through e-mail correspondence.

The Internet also provides a low-cost way for groups in the Third World to get their message out and keep on top of developments. 'All they need is one computer,' Ms Barlow said. The major Internet sites of these advocacy groups provide hyperlinks to others involved in the campaign, as well as phone numbers and e-mail addresses, and often bibliographies of relevant books. It adds up to a powerful tool that the advocacy groups are using to better effect than governments and the OECD at the moment. Ms Barlow predicts that this advantage may not last now that the OECD members have seen its potential. 'They'll be revving up their PR machines.'

But so are the advocacy groups. The next stage, she said, is to start making suggestions about what should be in trade agreements, rather than just opposing what the negotiators propose. Tony Clarke, director of the Canadian Polaris Institute, stresses that anti-MAI groups such as his are not against all aspects of globalization – their use of the Internet itself is proof of that. 'We're against this model of economic globalization,' he said, referring to the MAI. 'But the global village, the idea of coming together and working together, is a great dream.'

Through this case study, we have seen that the co-ordinated lobbying and campaigning of NGOs and SMOs on the MAI was one of the key reasons why the agreement failed to materialize. These groups came together to form a transnational network and utilized the Internet as the best medium available to collect and disseminate information on the agreement. They also used this medium to build solidarity amongst very different groups who might not necessarily have come together over such issues. While these NGOs and SMOs all lobbied and campaigned within their own countries, it was the co-ordinated effort of being part of a transnational campaign that gained them their success.

Summary of Section 5.4
■ Lobbying and campaigning have different styles, the former more negotiation oriented and subtle, requiring high-level skills; the latter more dependent upon clear identification of responsibility for injustice and popular support.
■ Both rely on a relatively loose form of organizational networking, but one where results benefit from harmonization of ambitions.
■ Global campaigns have emerged as a distinctive form of operation, facilitated by technological innovations (although as we noted earlier there are examples of effective campaigns dating from the nineteenth century) to challenge global regulations, conventionally set by negotiations amongst state actors.

5.5 Bridging levels

'Bridging' is the mechanism whereby a transnational network acts as an intermediary between the grass roots and international institutions. Such bridging allows for a strategic, multi-pronged approach to lobbying, and also increases the legitimacy of the organizations involved in international campaigns, by linking them firmly to their 'roots'.

An IFI's policy decision, made in Washington, New York or Geneva, for example, can have an impact on people all over the world. NGOs and SMOs have realized this, and, consequently, advocacy is now occurring at every level of NGO programme work, and as we have seen, a growing number of NGOs are becoming involved in operations based in the geographic centres of global power. These centres of power, as you may recall from Chapter 4 on City Futures, can be thought of as sites from which the global economy is co-ordinated and controlled. It follows that advocacy and lobbying activities need to be focused in those same sites. Places, or localities, which are affected by decisions taken by IFIs are also important to organizations as sources of support and legitimacy for their international work. It is because they are based in local struggles and have support in local and national contexts that organizations can claim the right to operate at an international scale. The phenomenon of bridging thus highlights two crucial ways in which *places* continue to matter in the context of transnational networking, first as sites where protests or lobbying can be concentrated in order to try to change policy, and second, as bases for organizational support and legitimacy.

5.5.1 Why bridging organizations?

Oxfam International was formed as a response to the globalization of development-related decision-making. While the different Oxfams are national agencies working at the grass roots level, in forming Oxfam International (OI) the members have bridged scales in order to better influence development issues, such as education and debt relief. Their rationale is captured in the following statement:

> [Because of] changes in international policy-making and international communications, the world is slowly becoming more globalized. Messages do not stop at national frontiers – the medium operates globally. It all moves very quickly – international policy-making is far more an international affair.
>
> (OI, 1998a)

Many NGOs and SMOs have responded to these changes by networking and organizing activities across national boundaries – the creation of transnational networks has increased the ability of NGOs and SMOs to participate in a political space outside that of local and national politics. However, these scaling-up efforts and the focus on advocacy have, perhaps ironically, brought a renewed recognition of the importance of being grounded at a grass roots level. If organizations lose their connection to their operational work – to the 'ground' – they lose their legitimacy, as well as their ability to run co-ordinated and 'multi-pronged' campaigns across different contexts. While not all NGOs take on both the operational and advocacy roles, it seems that those that do are in a stronger position with respect to their legitimacy to speak and be heard.

Transnational networks are increasingly being challenged on these issues by governments and IFIs. Mats Karlsson, the Vice President for External Affairs at the World Bank (1999–), recently attacked NGOs based in Washington, 'for their "weak accountability", "shallow democracy" and "precarious legitimacy" as actors in the global debate … [thus] NGOs are victims of their own success. Now that they have arrived as players on the world stage, the stakes are higher, and so is the temptation for their targets to fight back' (Edwards, 2000, p.3). Consequently, the concept of bridging has become vital in linking the various levels of their work. Being 'bridging organizations' is essential to how some of these groups are conceptualizing themselves.

As NGO and SMO members are unelected and they have no shareholders to report to, they must constantly strive to ensure that their actions are perceived as being 'legitimate'. Transnational networks have thus utilized their ability to bridge between levels as a means of establishing their legitimacy and authority. Bridging ensures that they are seen to be directly involved in the implementation of development interventions, and in this way as closer to the ground, and more able to represent the opinions of people around the world who are likely to be affected by IFI decisions.

Fox and Brown note the way in which transnational networks are gravitating towards an organizational bridging function, and emphasize the importance of trust in bridging:

> ...trust may be particularly important in bridging the gaps between grass roots social movements and international advocacy NGOs because both are organisational forms that are excruciatingly sensitive to differences in values and ideologies. Successful coalitions grow out of cycles of negotiation that bridge the gaps among their members – negotiations that deal with inevitable conflicts without destroying trust among the parties.
>
> (Fox and Brown, 1998, p.455)

Bridging enables network members to increase their level of influence in relation to a wide range of policy-makers, and to better co-ordinate their efforts to influence states and IFIs through participating in the increasingly deterritorialized process of governance. The 'multi-level' approach, where groups work in a co-ordinated manner, in various countries and at various levels of politics, is one that is a challenge for most NGOs, especially because of the time needed to co-ordinate these efforts and the transnational scope of this co-ordination.

In the case study of Oxfam International which follows the two key reasons for bridging will be discussed: bridging to increase legitimacy, and bridging to allow for a strategic, multi-pronged approach to lobbying.

5.5.2 Oxfam International

In this section, a number of informants from the NGO Oxfam International discuss their strategy and tactics in forming this transnational network (Yanacopulos, 2001). Oxfam International acts as a bridging organization on a number of levels. Primarily, it was set-up for the purpose of bringing together all of the national Oxfams for wider campaigns. It also bridges the Oxfams' operational work on the ground with their advocacy work in national capitals and centres of power. It also links national Oxfams, and partner organizations that Oxfam works with, to Oxfam International, enabling all of the groups to work on issues simultaneously, for greater effect. This multi-pronged approach to influencing is perhaps the most valuable feature of Oxfam International. The IFIs have increasingly become the focus of targeted lobbying, which is reflected in Oxfam International opening an office in Washington, DC.

During its debt cancellation campaigns, Oxfam International lobbied for a portion of Nicaragua's debt to be cancelled. An Oxfam International member reflected on the process:

> [Oxfam lobbyists] are basically going and meeting the people responsible in the IMF and the World Bank for Nicaragua – they're very country-focused or regional-focused. And that's because our strategy on debt is to take forward our debt work looking at maximizing the benefits

Figure 5.6 An Oxfam International leaflet, part of its 'Cut the Cost' campaign 2001.

for individual countries. So we're trying to gather information to produce a paper, then we'll lobby governments as Nicaragua goes through at the Board level.

(OI, 1998b)

An official of Oxfam International described the skill of lobbying as a combination of 'art' and 'science'. The science aspect refers to the ability to conduct and disseminate sound research, and 'influencing – now that's the art part. So you have your science and you have your art. And that's where [our lobbyists] are great artists' (Oxfam International, 1998a). While this member was referring to the professional Oxfam International lobbyists based in Washington, DC, he also contended that 'the representatives of all the Oxfams do this [lobby] with their government contacts, with their representatives in each of the countries' (OI, 1998a).

Another Oxfam International lobbyist explained that the Oxfam formula is that it is essential to have 'one or two very effective lobbyists with the right relationships and the right information flows to co-ordinate [the

NGO members]. So you walk in the right doors in a co-ordinated manner and you push on the players who push on each other' (OI, 1998c). This was reiterated by an Oxfam International member describing this process in the UK. She noted that Oxfam UK speaks to 'the Finance Ministry, to Clare Short*, to others, particularly before they're off to the World Bank and IMF meetings ... they'll have had discussions, and Gordon Brown* will have received materials about what we think about certain issues' (OI, 1998a). The advantage of bridging or transnational networking, then, is that this kind of lobbying on the same issue is undertaken simultaneously by all of the Oxfams in different places and at different levels.

*UK Labour Party MP and Secretary of State for International Development 1997–

*UK Labour MP and Chancellor of the Exchequer 1997–

Bridging means, then, that a number of governments can be lobbied concurrently. One member of Oxfam claimed, 'co-ordination is the key' (OI, 1999). The ability to co-ordinate different groups within the network is fundamental to their potential to influence policy outcomes. The increased benefit of belonging to a transnational network that utilizes the idea of bridging is that there is a co-ordinated effort on a number of different levels – a multi-pronged approach to collaborative advocacy.

> What adds a lot of the value is all of the Oxfams will go to their governments, we'll go to companies, we'll talk to ministers, we'll talk to representatives of international institutions – all about the same subject – and they act in co-ordination, all working on that subject. If it was [only our lobbyists, they would be] a small NGO which would be doing interesting things in Washington. Oxfam International working on advocacy means eleven organizations, each with their base in their country, acting in co-ordination and thereby making [a] much better advance.
>
> (OI, 1998a)

> You need to be able to lobby several countries and you need to be able to move, if you're not making progress in one or two of them, to other influencing opportunities. You need to be able to take advantage of the media in many places to localize the pressure ... All modern successful campaigns have to be international and in a way what we're doing is gearing up more to be able to do more international campaigning. But that doesn't mean that the national bits of it aren't key. It's just being able to do it all at once.
>
> (OI, 1998b)

Thus we see that it is through multi-level lobbying and co-ordination that development NGO networks increase their potential. A member of Oxfam International describes this process in the following statement:

> At the moment, the Oxfams do high-level lobbying and media work together. Really that's what we're talking about, advocacy – but all the Oxfams do major campaigns as well, which involves mobilizing their supporters and reaching out to the public ... So that's a way of going beyond lobbying, to mobilize all the resources the different Oxfams have within one campaign.
>
> (OI, 1998b)

An official of the World Bank also assessed Oxfam International's multi-level strategy concerning the debt relief campaign, which he summarized:

> ...sometimes there is lobbying within the country, sometimes it would be people like [Oxfam lobbyists] going to see executive directors here [Washington, DC] sometimes it would be getting articles in newspapers, the *FT* [*Financial Times*], *Washington Post*, whatever. I mean a whole variety of things that they did to build greater awareness [of debt relief] and to really make it into a much more political issue, rather than just a technocratic issue that would be buried away in a corner. And that's what distinguished debt from a number of other issues, that it became a much higher profile issue than others. And certainly NGOs were the key factor in that happening.
>
> (World Bank official, personal interview 1999)

This type of strategy moves beyond campaigning into highly organized and co-ordinated advocacy programmes. It means that NGOs and SMOs must be very familiar with the individual members and the processes of the institutions being targeted. A member of Oxfam International outlined that this type of knowledge is imperative:

> You don't influence the IMF and the World Bank by speaking to Camdessus [the IMF president at the time]. You influence it through its Board members. But being able to mobilize pressure on the Americans, the British, the Canadians and the Dutch [all national Oxfam countries] at the same time, around a key decision, that's happening internationally, is a way that you have more impact. And then if you can link that to the Southern partners lobbying their own governments, then you begin to see, the pressure is coming from lots of different angles. And you do it through lobbying, media pressure and mobilizing supporters and the public.
>
> (OI, 1998b)

Another level of bridging is between 'Northern' and 'Southern' NGOs. Oxfam International provides an example of this during the negotiation and implementation of the HIPC (Highly Indebted Poor Countries) initiative for Uganda, where there was a close relationship between the Ugandan government (the first country to receive debt relief) and Oxfam International.

> One of the key things was how long Uganda would have to wait before it got HIPC [status] ... So there was a lot of collaboration going on that meant that there was serious lobbying that worked very well ... [the Ugandan government sent a] letter to the FT, that's on the record that 'We'll guarantee that we'll use every penny in this way' [all funds from debt relief would be used for education]. So there was a combination of very good collaboration and then we were working very closely with the World Bank person responsible for Uganda ... So this combination of insiders in the Bank, NGO pressure linked with the Ugandan government and the few governments, like the British, and others,

really made sure it was an effective external insider. In the end Uganda probably got as good a deal as possible ... It also got a lot of the debt relief earlier than was envisioned, and larger amounts. Which has, in the end, funded this programme of 2 million kids going back to school.

(OI, 1998b)

This strategy would not be possible without the technological advances in ICT that have made multi-level tactics possible. An Oxfam International official stated that 'there are lots of ingredients of successful advocacy, but one of them is undoubtedly in a modern communications world, in terms of how decisions are made, the ability to mobilize pressure in many places at once, and be able to move from one target to the next' (OI, 1998b).

Summary of Section 5.5

■ The tension between the need to influence development policy at an international level, and the requirement to remain grounded in organizations with clear support at the grass roots level has led development agencies to work at bridging the levels or scales at which they work.

■ Effective advocacy at a transnational level depends on strong organizational links, but also on the legitimacy of grass roots support and on being able to influence decision-making in the centres of power.

■ The benefits of bridging are apparent both for locally based organizations and for international campaigns, as the example of Oxfam International demonstrates.

5.6 Conclusion

Through the three examples in Sections 5.3–5.5, we have explored how transnational networks of NGOs and SMOs have interacted and negotiated with IFIs and state actors both in and across territories.

■ The Zapatistas took advantage of scaling-up their efforts in order to influence not only their own government, but to also influence other governments and businesses dealing with Mexico.

■ Lobbying and campaigning are other essential features of transnational networks. Such efforts were illustrated through the anti-MAI campaign, where ICT was utilized to collect and disseminate information, and also to mobilize groups in various countries.

■ Oxfam International is an organization that is well placed to bridge grass roots work with international advocacy, thereby increasing its legitimacy as an organization, as well as mobilizing popular support behind its demands for changes in international regulations and policies.

The categorizations of different kinds of transnational networking which we have made here – scaling-up, campaigning and bridging – are not absolutes, and they often co-exist in the same networks. Although we have used these categories for the purposes of illustration, this does not mean that Oxfam, for example, does not utilize all of the above tactics, depending on the issue, the organizations targeted and the desired outcome. Transnational networks utilize whatever tactics are available to them or seem most likely to work.

Exploring transnational networks has allowed us to reconceptualize development action beyond the level of the state. These networks have revealed that development actions do not just take place within bounded spaces, but also within flows of information and networks of association across and beyond the scale of the state. As we discussed at the beginning of this chapter, networks are arguably displacing the state as the primary arena where development actions occur.

The conception of deterritorialized governance was introduced to explain these changes. Theories of governance do not discriminate between state, non-state or intergovernmental actors, as all are involved in a process of influencing the others. Moreover, as we have seen in this chapter, governance is not limited to territorialized political organizations (e.g. states, or local social movements) but rather includes social and political activities which cut across territories and places – it is deterritorialized. Neither is it limited to only one set of institutions or processes, such as 'the state' or 'the network', but helpfully incorporates both these arenas of action and considers how they interact. Using the concept of deterritorialized governance also allows us to speculate as to how development change is occurring, by examining the policy outcomes of certain actions, and also the broader social and political dynamics which cause these changes and their likely future impact.

Transnational networks challenge, influence and work between and across local areas or state territories. These flows and networks, we have suggested, represent the positive side of displacement. Groups forming transnational networks are not necessarily limited to negotiating with their own governments, but can utilize networks, aided by the availability of Information and Communication Technology, to influence decision-makers, mobilize other groups and individuals, and put external pressure on governments and international institutions to effect changes in development policy and practice. Bringing displacements into view in the field of development highlights the potential for new kinds of development alternatives to emerge and for new kinds of actors and associations to contribute to shaping future development interventions. We explore this further in the chapter which follows.

6 Conclusion
by Giles Mohan and Jenny Robinson

Contents

Displacement and development

This book has considered four examples of displacement and development: forced migration, diasporic communities, the flows which shape city futures, and the expansion of transnational networking amongst non-governmental organizations and social movements.

We suggest that together these examples of displacement encourage new ways of thinking about development, and thus promote a *reframing* of development thought and practice. Such scenarios offer opportunities for new types of development intervention and highlight emergent contests over what development ought to involve.

In this concluding chapter we will draw these ideas together, examining how considering displacements could make a difference to both the practice and conceptualization of development. The discussion is organized around four aspects of development:

- alternative forms of development;
- new agencies of development;
- new spaces of development;
- key development concepts.

Overall, then, this book presents some challenges to the usual definitions of 'development', and also questions the ways in which development issues are approached, both institutionally and spatially. In particular, we have emphasized that the conventional spatial and analytical categories around which development is organized – such as the 'national' and 'local' – are increasingly meaningless if we persist in seeing them as bounded 'containers' for development processes. Instead, we have argued that while places are crucial to development, they are best conceived of as products of wider networks and flows – or displacements. The case studies and examples that we have explored have shown how, through these wider networks and flows, alternative forms of development are emerging and new vehicles for implementing intentional development interventions can be identified. 'Displacements' also have consequences for some of the key concepts deployed in the field of development studies, and in the final section below, we consider specifically the ideas of 'social capital' and 'governance'.

6.1 Alternative forms of development

The ways in which alternative forms of development emerge is one of the key themes of this book. They can be expected to emerge not only in local places, in opposition to wider and sometimes more powerful influences – as Arturo Escobar (1995), for example, anticipates – but also in forms of 'globalization from below' and through wider networks of connections. This was examined most closely in Chapter 3 on diasporic community networks and Chapter 5 on networks of associations (NGOs and social movements).

In Chapter 5 we discussed the idea of the association revolution, involving the expanding networks of civil society actors, NGOs and social movements. In terms of opposing the downside of global development such types of association have a long history. We saw in Chapter 3 that anti-slavery movements in the eighteenth century and pan-African movements in the early twentieth century were active in a complex geopolitics which spanned the Atlantic, and this was highlighted by our extended discussion of Sierra Leone. However, the idea of a 'revolution' in transnational networking suggests a marked growth in the number and an intensification of the influence of these associations over the past 20 years.

Campaigns and protests, like the prominent 'Drop the Debt' and anti-globalization campaigns and protests, have been waged against the development agendas of powerful international agencies. Others have been organized around more localized issues, such as the Narmada Dam (also discussed in Chapter 2), but as this and the Zapatista example both showed, local protests not only benefit from international support, but link to and create a model for resistances elsewhere. While the specific issues of dam construction or land reform might be local, the campaigns often develop to draw upon transnational networks and organizations that defy the conventional territorialization of politics. These wider associations can in turn transform local struggles and shape the ways in which local communities see the scope of their conflicts and their own role in them (as David Turton discusses in relation to the Narmada Dam campaign in Chapter 2).

The balance of power at a 'global' scale might seem stacked against even internationally networked NGOs and community organizations. But as the series of anti-capitalist demonstrations throughout the late-1990s and early-2000s showed, it was possible for flexible deterritorialized networks to escape the surveillance and discipline of the state-based regulators who opposed such activity. Something of a paradox emerges in that these networks utilize the technologies of globalization, which have generally facilitated the powers of transnational corporations and international agencies, in order to influence, contest and resist globalization. The technologies employed in campaigning include the Internet, (which was originally a military creation), as well as corporation produced computers and software.

There are some sticky questions to address, however, about whether 'displacements', in this case in the form of transnational networks, are necessarily good or bad for development, and who benefits from them. In the case of economic globalization, for example, a consensus exists among International Financial Institutions (IFIs) and more powerful states that development requires the inward investment that 'footloose' transnational companies control. In this view transnational flows of finance and goods are crucial to economic growth, and thus anti-globalization movements are damaging to strong market-led development. In contrast, for anti-globalization campaigners, opening national borders to flows of global capital is disastrous for the goal of equitable and positive development. In theory, though, there is no intrinsic reason why flows of information, ideas and resources should either be fundamentally beneficial or harmful. Similarly, there is no guarantee that transnational campaigns or networks of organizations – any more than locally based organizations – will generate effective alternative forms of development.

For example, we saw in Chapter 3 that 'resistance' by Hindu nationalists to what they label Muslim oppression resulted in exclusionary forms of development intervention. For the Hindu nationalists their 'philanthropic' support of development projects is partial and partisan and forces us to question how different groups, even if they are 'networked', conceive of development. And paradoxically, some transnationally networked forms of alternative development may actually be too parochial. Many of the diasporic NGOs that we discussed in Chapter 3 concentrate their efforts on small-scale infrastructure projects, while the need for these interventions may have resulted from the withdrawal of state support for welfare during structural adjustment programmes. Supporting small-scale development work may simply be a case of putting 'Band Aids' on the wounds caused by neoliberal reform and authoritarian government. It may be that diasporic organizations could also use their position to lobby internationally for changes to these harsh political and economic policies.

Alternative forms of development may emerge in transnational networks which cut across the conventional territories of development studies. But these new forms of development still need critical interrogation, and are as strongly contested as 'local' or 'national' development strategies ever were.

6.2 New agencies of development

Another recurring theme of this book has been about the emergence of new agencies of development operating at a range of different scales. As Alan Thomas puts it, 'community and local organizations are here to stay alongside national governments and international organizations as agents of national development' (2000b, p.785). The different chapters in this book have all highlighted the potential for non-state agents to play a role in shaping development beyond the local or national scale. Scaling-up their activities through networking, and establishing new forms of organizational structure to facilitate lobbying and campaigning around issues usually reserved for states, these non-state organizations are by no means limited to the local, or community, level or even to influencing 'national' scale development interventions. We have emphasized how processes of deterritorialization have created new opportunities for individuals and (transnational) communities to improve their well-being and to resist certain negative aspects of globalization. Thinking about development through the lens of displacements helps to extend our understanding of the ways in which 'groups and individuals [can] be involved as agents of their own development' (Thomas, 2000b, p.782).

In Chapter 3 on diaspora and development, we considered the example of Congolese traders in Paris. The authors of a major study of these traders argued that:

> Globalization is generally thought of in terms of multi-national companies and the changing relations between nation states and peoples as they become enmeshed in the world economy. Our study … focuses instead on individuals operating in the interstices of these larger entities, and on how they manage to take advantage of the way the world economy now works.
>
> (MacGaffey and Bazenguissa-Ganga, 2000, p.3)

It is this spirit of taking developmental advantage of displacement that we wish to emphasize. One simple yet important dimension of this involves remittances. We have seen how economic migrants, as well as some people who have been forced to move, have used their enhanced earning power to support family back in their homelands. These flows of capital and commodities are often between members of the same family or kin group, as in the case of the African traders in Paris who migrated in response to the developmental crises in the Congo. Debate exists over the developmental impact of these financial flows back home, because the money may not be used in directly productive ways. Some have argued that the money is often spent on conspicuous consumption and not on longer-term investments in business. However, families also invest in basic requirements such as school fees and housing, which clearly do have longer-term implications for development and well-being, even if they are not blatantly entrepreneurial.

More collective support for local development initiatives is channelled through organizations which fund localized activities in the homelands of migrants, refugees and diasporic communities. In Chapter 3 we saw how one group of Mexican immigrants living in New York travelled back to their village to oversee a water-supply project. African NGOs, such as the Hometown Associations of the Nigerian diaspora, are increasingly active in sending money and equipment to support a wide-range of local projects. With the growth of global communications the ease with which such transfers can be made is likely to increase. In view of the increased polarization attendant upon globalization, the need for such creative and displaced solutions to uneven development will also increase. Hence, displacements – wider flows and networks – can be both a response, and a possible source of solutions, to developmental crises in different places.

Furthermore, not all flows are as concrete as financial or material assistance, but they nonetheless shape development. As Chapter 5 showed, many flows are political in that they consist of ideas, policies, campaigns and messages. The co-ordination of these flows has fallen on a range of non-state organizations including advocacy networks, campaign organizations and social movements. What is interesting and new is the impact such organizations have had on helping to set and, to an extent, circumscribe or resist the development agendas of powerful state-based and corporate actors. These associations and networks often contest the dispersed processes of globalization through equally deterritorialized forms of opposition. While quantifying the impact is difficult, in Chapter 5 we noted some examples of successful political activity. Campaigning through these transnational non-state organizations is arguably one of the most effective means of enabling action to contest the flows and displacement of globalization.

Many of the agents of development brought more clearly into view through the lens of displacement are associated with deterritorializations (like diasporic communities or networked NGOs). But the case of the city highlights an increasingly important development agent: territorially based city governments. Perhaps paradoxically, just as the world's economy has come to be strongly associated with globalization and deterritorialization, cities are increasingly playing a crucial role in facilitating economic development. Cities assemble and enable the co-ordination and management of the extended social networks which comprise economic activity. We have argued that this is as true for those cities whose economic activities have quite modest reaches into a regional or national hinterland as it is for cities which host the headquarters of powerful 'global' corporations, and the clusters of activities which co-ordinate the complex transnational flows of the global economy. All cities, we have suggested, offer a range of opportunities for economic growth which can potentially be creatively managed to meet the urgent development needs of their poorest citizens.

The case of cities also reminds us that the 'places' relevant to development, like cities, or local communities, are sites and subjects of contestation and power struggles. New or alternative forms of development may be possible, but they are by no means inevitable, whether located in places, or in the networks and flows of globalization.

6.3 New spaces of development studies

Most generally, this book has argued that for a full understanding of development we need to pay attention to both place and displacement. Arturo Escobar observes that place and displacement (or what he calls non-place) 'are more than contrastive modalities. There are high cultural and political stakes in asserting one or the other' (2001, p.147). Stressing displacement over place, or global flows over local communities, for example, can lead to an over-emphasis on those powerful organizations (like transnational corporations, or IFIs such as the World Bank and the International Monetary Fund) whose reach enables them to operate at a global scale. It can mean less attention is paid to the creative energy which might be derived from the successful development efforts (or effective resistances to development) of local communities. In his early work (1995), Escobar saw places as positive repositories of resistance to wider, powerful forces of development. Nederveen Pieterse (1997, p.81) notes that many accounts of alternatives to dominant forms of development have portrayed local places as 'enclaves that provide shelter from the storm'.

However, the discussions in this book have also shown that there is a range of transnational and translocal actors with the ability to operate across the globe and shape development outcomes in today's globalizing society and economy. This includes what was described in Chapter 3 as 'globalization from below'. Thus it is not only powerful global corporations and international agencies which operate at a global or national scale. So while proponents of alternative development like Escobar are perhaps rightly concerned that losing sight of local places might mean that emergent alternative visions of development drop out of view, we suggest that there is a need for an approach to development which fully acknowledges the significance of both places and displacements. More than this, we have argued that places and displacements are closely inter-related. On this basis we suggest that a more hopeful (and accurate) version of the potential for change and development in an increasingly interconnected world might be realized if *both* places *and* displacements are kept in view.

Thus there is an emerging criticism, which this book has contributed to, of the idea that local places should be seen simply as sites of 'resistance' or as privileged repositories of alternative forms of development. In our view this fails to capture the complex ways in which people make a living and shape their futures in these increasingly global times. We have seen that many people do not simply defend the local, but also exploit networks and seek associations which stretch well beyond their local areas. Local people certainly contribute to 'place-making', shaping the futures of their local areas, but always in association with wider forces, as active and knowing agents in their own development. Escobar has also embraced this wider understanding of place, without losing sight of the potential for new practices and ideas to emerge in local areas. He writes: 'Theoretically, it is important to learn to see place-based cultural, ecological, and economic practices as important sources of alternative visions and strategies for reconstructing local and regional worlds, no matter how produced by "the global" they might also be' (2001, p.166).

We are suggesting that a vision for alternative forms of development can be more effectively mobilized if we hold the interconnectedness of places and displacements, territories and flows, in view. Places, then, are made what they are and their futures are shaped by the wider flows and connections which move through and settle in those places. As Bebbington demonstrated in the case of the Otavaleno traders in Ecuador (see Chapter 1), the development trajectories of local places are shaped as much by external forces as by local initiatives. Both, working together, co-produce the future of that place. What Massey has called a 'global sense of place' is one starting point to begin reframing development, moving beyond a dichotomy between places and displacement, or the local and the global. As she writes, 'what gives a place its specificity is not some long internalized history but the fact that it is constructed out of a particular constellation of social relations, meeting and weaving together at a particular locus' (1994, p.154).

Another starting point is to take Anna Tsing's advice, and explore the territorializing impacts of global flows. As she notes: 'these world-making flows, too, are not just interconnections, but also the recarving of channels and the remapping of the possibilities of geography' (2000, p.327). Flows take place along specific routes across the earth's surface, have points of origin and end points, and quite often require places from which to operate and be organized. The classic case of this, discussed in Chapter 4, is the concentration of the functions of co-ordinating and managing elements of the global economy in large cities, such as São Paolo or Sydney. The expansion of transnational economic flows has, perhaps paradoxically, required a re-territorialization of economic agents in small areas of major cities in order to facilitate their co-ordination. Even as the proponents of the existence of a truly global economy promote the idea of the deterritorialization of social and economic life, the re-territorialization of those processes is taking place. In fact, and to go back to the Escobar quote with which we started this section, place and non-place (or displacement) are not simply contrasting ways of being (or modalities) – they are each closely bound up with the production of the other.

This was most strikingly illustrated in Chapter 4, where the wider connections and flows which shape cities were seen as crucial to the future development of those places. But the city also emerged as a crucial territorialization of global economic flows, a place not only where the global economy takes place, but from where it is actively shaped by increasingly entrepreneurial urban managers and, hopefully, active citizens. And as the World Bank and related international agencies (such as the United Nations Development Programme or the UNCHS) take up the task of enabling cities to perform this new role in the global economy, this territorialization of development studies is being settled and fixed in place for the foreseeable future. In this case at least, to be effective development efforts need to engage with the productive potential of flows and networks; but they also need to grapple with what it means to operate at the scale of emerging territories like cities. Building the capacity to act at a city-wide scale is a challenge not only for disparate urban social movements but also for local governments themselves, many of which have little experience in promoting economic growth.

Similarly, while global networking may epitomize the significance of displacement for the future of development, transnational agencies, like Oxfam, have found that their voice within an international arena often rests on capacities and claims to represent local and national groups. As Chapter 5 explains, globally networked development actions have remained dependent upon these older territorial foundations.

All four of our examples in this book have demonstrated how flows and territories, places and displacements are not simply opposites, or contrasts, but are closely entwined with one another and usually produced together in any given social or economic field. Territories are cut across by flows and networks. And local places are tied through social, economic and political networks to regional hinterlands, other local areas and other regions of the world. With this approach, then, there is potential for alternative forms of development (and even alternatives to development) to emerge in places as well as in the networks and flows which make up the field of displacement studies.

6.4 Key development concepts

We turn finally to consider the implications of displacement for two key concepts which currently play a significant role in framing development interventions – governance and social capital.

(Deterritorialized) governance

As noted in Chapter 5 the promotion of good governance has become central to development practice. Governance is not just about governments. Instead, it relates to the prospects of creative partnerships amongst state and non-state actors, offering the scope for a networked and deterritorialized view of development interventions. Governance is usually explored on a territorial basis, for example, when city governments draw on NGOs, communities and business interests to facilitate city-wide urban development initiatives, as we saw in Chapter 4. But processes of governance can, and often do, involve a range of actors whose co-operation, negotiation and conflicts are forged across and beyond the territories of nation-states and local communities.

Currently, many developmental interventions work through long-standing political channels. Aid, for example, might be bilateral, linking two national governments, or multilateral, whereby an organization comprised of a group of states works through the government of a recipient country. These are largely state-based transfers and flows, but this book has shown that consideration of displacements renders the popular understanding of development processes, as territorialized around states, in need of reconfiguration.

Alongside intergovernmental organizations and globalizing economic processes we have seen important contributions to deterritorialized governance emerging from NGOs. An example was given in Chapter 2 concerning the set of laws, norms and institutional structures that make up the International Refugee Regime. The refugee 'problem' is arguably the most pressing instance of displacement challenging the territorially organized nation-state system, and NGOs and social movements have been active in oppositional resistance and campaigning activity which has served to constrain and shape the agendas of national and international state-based organizations. Similarly, in relation to forced resettlement within nation-states, NGO and social movement campaigns have drawn attention to some of the worst impacts of grand development schemes, and shaped forms of regulation to ameliorate their consequences. However, small-scale NGOs on their own are relatively powerless to do much more than provide basic welfare provision or to lobby local or national governments. Contributing to global governance or international regulation, such as the International Refugee Regime, or challenging state-based human rights, requires creative and complex networks of agencies, institutions and actors. Chapter 5 explored in some detail the role of different kinds of networked associations in contesting and shaping global governance and economic and political regulation.

These emergent transnational networks and practices are crucial in the search for an alternative to limited and divisive state-based conceptualizations of citizenship and rights. A commitment to alternative transnational communities beyond the state requires a notion of global citizenship, linked to growing calls for human-rights based development in which 'Individuals have certain rights by virtue of their humanity, not the basis of their citizenship' (UNDP, 2000, p.25). This clearly has important implications for the rights of non-citizens – migrants, refugees and stateless people. The very fact of displacement generates the need for increasingly deterritorialized governance which can mirror and work with these complex processes.

The challenge for development practice, then, is to respond to this new terrain. Clearly, much has already been done, especially by the relatively nimble NGO sector as well as astute entrepreneurs. However, the problem with deterritorialized governance is precisely the legacy that David Turton identified in Chapter 2: that the largely state-centred system in which we still operate gives legitimacy to the territorial and the fixed, rather than to the mobile and the deterritorialized. Since much of the development industry is centred on states, anything which challenges this supremacy is likely to be resisted by these institutions which presently control and benefit from the system. The challenge, then, is to persuade states and international agencies of the potential of deterritorialized governance, and that for development to be viable and effective in the new millennium they need to embrace rather than ignore emergent transnational networks and associations. Such issues come to the fore in the case of the African diaspora NGOs identified in Chapter 3, as one activist noted:

> 'Development' has now become a top-down, professionalised and impersonal service that concentrates too much power in the hands of various agencies in the developed Northern countries, including the UK. This paradigm needs to shift to working with diaspora groups – based on their network of relations, trust and commitment – to empower local communities in Africa to make decisions about their own development … All agencies need to work towards open-ended visions that allow room for other perspectives.
>
> (Ndofor-Tah, 2000, p.13)

Such a recommendation goes to the heart of new approaches to developmental governance by addressing questions of power and trusteeship and change (cf. Thomas, 2000b). It also raises questions about how these complex alliances, collaborations and networks might be sustained in the longer term so that they can effectively shape broader development agendas.

Social capital (out of place)

It is all very well to say that new configurations of actors working between sites and across space are becoming the norm, but it still not clear how such networks might function in practice. A key problem is how to effect the collaboration necessary for shared perspectives and joint decision-making. It is here that the idea of social capital could be important. Social capital is described by one of its main protagonists as 'features of social organization, such as networks, norms and trust, that facilitate co-ordination and co-operation for mutual benefit' (Putnam, 1993, p.36). Such capital is usually conceived of in localized terms, pertaining to the regional or community level, and can explain different degrees of local success in response to a wider policy environment. For Putnam, social capital fosters reciprocity, facilitates information flows for mutual benefit and trust, and once it exists tends to be self-generating as successive generations are socialized into the localized norms which create success. In Putnam's words 'stocks of social capital … tend to be self-reinforcing and cumulative'. In this way theorists of social capital have argued that regions and localities are locked into a 'path dependency' whereby their initial stocks of social capital, wherever they come from, inculcate a self-fulfilling cycle of prosperity.

However, Fox (1996) argues that increases in social capital can result from a broad range of forces, both local and external. This could include the state's willingness and capacity to encourage or dismantle social capital, the contextual strategies of local political actors, and the effect of other local and non-local organizations in enabling or disabling collective action. Together these causal processes explain variations from place to place in the 'thickness' of civil society, the density of social capital and the ability to 'scale-up' activity beyond the local. The lesson is that social capital is not a fixed local endowment but can be destroyed (and created) by external actions. For example, the Zapatista uprising described in Chapter 5 showed high levels of localized trust and reciprocity. But, as discussed in Chapter 1, local social capital in this case was initially fostered by a range of external interventions from national and international institutions such as the church, the state and NGOs (Fox, 1996). Through communication technologies this movement managed to create links with like-minded organizations across the world, evidence that local social capital can be influenced by wider connections.

We have also explored ways in which social capital is not only *built up* in local areas, but can also be *created* in more dispersed social networks which tie people from one locality or country to another. The links which the Zapatistas created with supporters and organizations across the world to some extent depended upon building links of trust and reciprocity far beyond their local area of operation.

At various points in this book, then, we have seen examples of social capital being created in networks which stretch beyond the bounds of the local area. The embedded ethnic firms discussed in Chapter 3 operated through kinship and other affective ties which linked their local livelihoods to co-members of their group who may have been quite distant. Similarly, refugees and resettlers operate politically and economically through complex networks held together across space by pre-existing relations, or through new social ties forged in foreign places in the collective experience of dislocation. All these cases demonstrate that social capital, like the other processes described in this book, operates within places but also extends beyond them through translocal networks.

Thus social capital can be built outside of local places and can exist in wider networks and associations. Alliances, coalitions and campaigns such as those discussed in Chapter 5 all rely on trust and reciprocity between actors and organizations stretched across space. It is here that the idea of social capital 'out of place' could extend our understanding of how deterritorialized governance might work more effectively. Rather than seeing social capital as binding only localized communities, often through face-to-face interactions, it could be stretched or deterritorialized to encompass the networks of actors outlined above. Certainly, the concerted anti-Multilateral Agreement on Investments campaign discussed in Chapter 5 showed that collaboration and solidarity can be effective in a 'virtual' campaign. More generally, if the key to effective and participatory development both in places and through networking is dialogue and collaboration amongst multiple actors, then building social capital must be a key priority.

However, we must be wary of treating social capital as a unilateral 'magic bullet' because networks of collaboration, if cemented and rigid, can also become exclusionary and divisive. We saw with the Hindu nationalists in Chapter 3 that there was a great deal of trust and reciprocity within this global community, but it also served to exclude those groups not considered worthy of assistance. Where social capital fosters divisive and exclusionary behaviour it has been labelled negative or 'perverse' social capital. A classic case is the Mafia, which has lots of internal reciprocity, but could hardly be seen as acting in the interest of the common good.

Deterritorializing the concept of social capital, then, extends thinking about development in at least two ways. Firstly, if social capital is an important component of effective development strategies, then building it through supportive external interventions is a real possibility. A conceptualization of social capital as deterritorialized is crucial if we are to avoid a pessimistic view of local places as 'locked in' to certain development paths. Secondly, the concept of social capital can be stretched to consider the consolidated links of trust and collaboration in transnational networks.

6.5 Reframing development

We started this book by highlighting a set of problems associated with forced displacement and associated humanitarian emergencies, which have become a significant component of the work of many development agencies. Not least, at the time of writing, is the looming humanitarian crisis in the Afghanistan region as the attacks by Western nations exacerbate a desperate refugee situation. Development teaching and students motivated by the impulse to ameliorate the desperate conditions of poor people around the world are increasingly shadowed by the condition of displacement. And yet development studies has few intellectual resources to analyse these problems, or assess whether or how they might be of a similar or different order of experience from all the other mobilities which shape contemporary global society. This is a difficult intellectual task – and one which can be uncomfortable: what can the traumatic experience of being a refugee possibly have in common with the pleasures of cosmopolitan consumerism?

But once we start to explore the condition of forced displacement, its meaning is indeed shown to be closely bound up with other kinds of flows and movements which are capturing the imagination and delineating the experiences of much of the world's population at the beginning of the twenty-first century. In this light the authors of this book have drawn together a range of conditions of mobility – of people, and of resources and ideas – in our attempt to excavate their implications for development.

Our most overarching conclusion is that development studies – both in theoretical analysis and in practice – needs to address the profoundly territorialized nature of its interventions and conceptualizations. In short, the architecture of development studies' imagination needs to change. It needs to draw on emergent associations and networks which are challenging dominant forms of development, creating new opportunities for livelihoods, and prefiguring the potential for a more globally inclusive form of citizenship. It also needs to spend far more resources and energies than it has to date addressing the needs of cities. Far from being the privileged recipients of too much government investment and development aid (as an earlier wisdom regarding urban bias suggested), cities are now urgently in need of the best creative efforts of citizens and observers if life in these places is to be improved in a sustainable way. A view of the city and the countryside as interconnected, bound up in circulations and interactions which stretch across the nation, or even stretch transnationally, is urgently needed to refresh the relevance of development's endeavours at the end of the twenty-first century.

This book has also contributed to shifts within the field of development which argue that it has become less meaningful to talk of broad divisions between the 'developed North' and 'developing South' (Allen and Thomas, 2000, p.vii). As poverty rises in wealthy nations, and inequality deepens in poorer regions, the boundaries which divided a wealthy 'North' from an impoverished 'South' are no longer (and probably never really were) so valid. More importantly, as the dynamics of economy and society are transnationalized, the motors of both poverty and development are not necessarily nationally or even locally organized. The world is connected up across the borders of nation-states (and as David Turton pointed out in Chapter 2, at least partly because of the territorial nature of states), which must have consequences for how and where development is conceived and implemented.

Closely related to this is the question of global interconnectedness and moral responsibility. If distant lives are connected in ways which we can hardly imagine, Stuart Corbridge (1993) has argued that this means that moral responsibility, too, is necessarily stretched as 'our' and 'their' lives (or the lives of 'others' more generally) are increasingly interlinked. Hence, development is not just a problem 'out there' (whether in another part of the country, or city, or in another part of the world), but, given the interconnectedness of the global economy, 'development' everywhere is actively made or undermined by our actions and those of our organizations, communities and governments, wherever we are.

Finally, we suggest that thinking about place and displacement is central to discussions of citizenship and human rights. Citizenship is usually thought of as being nation-state based, but if, following David Turton, we take a more communitarian view (and one which stretches the 'community' across space) then being a citizen with rights could extend both beyond and below the nation-state. Wherever local or diasporic groups are self-governing we could call it a form of citizenship. Human rights concerns put the emphasis on universality and, in theory at least, these rights should apply to all humans, regardless of social position or spatial location. In this sense, the human rights discourse challenges the traditional spatialization of political representation and economic redistribution. All of this arguably places pressures on states who still seek to police their borders, defend their wealth and welfare regimes and maintain the sanctity of their territory.

It is precisely these territorially defined and defended inequalities which development studies has always been concerned to address. But by grounding its own practices on these very territories, perhaps it has ironically reinforced the capacities of states and supported the territorial ordering of society. We hope that in emphasizing the dynamics of displacements, we have brought into view a range of agents and opportunities for development which might prefigure the emergent tracks of alternatives to these territorial foundations.

References

Abdullah, I. (1998) 'Rethinking African labour and working-class history: the artisan origins of the Sierra Leonean working class', *Social History*, vol.23, no.1, pp.80–96.

Ackah, W. (1999) *Pan-Africanism: Exploring the Contradictions*, Ashgate, Aldershot.

Adelman, H. (1999) 'Modernity, globalization, refugees and displacement', in Ager, A. (ed.) *Refugees: Perspectives on the Experience of Forced Migration*, Pinter, London and New York.

AFFORD (2000) *Globalisation and Development: A Diaspora Dimension*, submission from the African Foundation for Development to the Department for International Development, London, p.10.

Afriline website, http://www.afriline.net/ [accessed December 2001].

Al-Ali, N., Black, R. and Koser, K. (1999) *Mobilisation and participation of transnational exile communities in post-conflict reconstruction, 1989–1999*, report to Economic and Social Research Council.

Allen, J. (1999) 'Cities of power and influence: settled formations' in Allen, J., Massey, D. and Pryke, M. (eds) *Unsettling Cities*, Routledge, London, pp.181–228.

Allen, T. (2000) 'Taking culture seriously' in Allen, T. and Thomas, A. (eds) *Poverty and Development in the 21st Century*, Oxford University Press, Oxford, in association with the Open University, Milton Keynes, pp.443–466.

Allen, T. and Eade, J. (2000) 'The new politics of identity' in Allen, T. and Thomas, A. (eds), *Poverty and Development into the 21st Century*, Oxford University Press, Oxford, in association with the Open University, Milton Keynes, pp.486–496.

Allen, T. and Thomas, A. (2000) (eds) 'Preface' in *Poverty and Development into the 21st Century*, Oxford University Press, Oxford, in association with the Open University, Milton Keynes, pp.vii–ix.

Amin, A. and Graham, S. (1997) 'The ordinary city', *Transactions of the Institute of British Geographers*, vol.22, pp.411–429.

Amnesty International Online (2001), 'About AI', http://www.web.amnesty.org/web/aboutai.nsf [accessed November 2001].

Appiah, K. (1993) *In My Father's House: Africa in the Philosophy of Culture*, Oxford University Press, Oxford, p.26.

Arthur, J. (2000) *Invisible Sojourners: African Immigrant Diaspora in the United States*, Praeger, Connecticut.

Ashcroft, B., Griffiths, G. and Tiffin, H. (1998) *Key Concepts in Post-Colonial Studies*, Routledge, London.

Auclair, C. (1998) 'The city product', *Urban Age*, World Bank, Washington, DC.

Banton, M. (1957) *West African City: A Study of Tribal Life in Freetown*, Oxford University Press, London.

Barutciski, M. (2000) *Addressing legal constraints and improving outcomes in development-induced development projects*, ESCOR Project No.R7305, Department for International Development, Refugee Studies Centre, University of Oxford, p.6.

Bastide, R. (1978) *The African Religions of Brazil*, Johns Hopkins University Press, Baltimore.

Bauer, P.T. (1954) *West African Trade. A Study of Competition, Oligopoly and Monopoly in a Changing Economy*, Cambridge University Press, Cambridge, p.164.

Bauman, Z. (1998) 'Europe of strangers', paper delivered to the ESRC Transnational Communities Programme, University of Oxford.

Beall, J. (2000) 'Life in the cities', in Allen, T. and Thomas, A. (eds) *Poverty and Development into the 21st Century,* Oxford University Press, Oxford, in association with the Open University, Milton Keynes, pp.425–443.

Beall, J., Crankshaw, O. and Parnell, S. (2000) 'Local government, poverty reduction and inequality in Johannesburg', *Environment and Urbanization*, vol.11, no.2, pp.107–122.

Bebbington, A. (2000) 'Re-encountering development: livelihood transitions and place transformations in the Andes', *Annals of the Association of American Geographers*, vol.90, no.3, pp.495–520.

Benjamin, S. (2000) 'Governance, economic settings and poverty in Bangalore', *Environment and Urbanization*, vol.12, no.1, pp.35–56.

Bhabha, H. (1994) *The Location of Culture*, Routledge, London.

Bharutiya Janata Party website, 'Mindutva: the great nationalist ideology', http://www.bjp.org [accessed December 2001].

Blyden, E.W. (1967) *Christianity, Islam and the Negro Race*, Edinburgh University Press, Edinburgh, p.368 [first published in 1888].

Borton, J. (1996) 'An account of co-ordination mechanisms for humanitarian assistance during the international response to the 1994 crisis in Rwanda', *Disasters*, vol.20, no.4, pp.305–323.

Bourdieu, P. (1987) *Distinction: The Social Judgement of Taste*, Harvard University Press, Cambridge, Massachusetts.

Brah, A. (1996) *Cartographies of Diaspora: Contesting Identities*, Routledge, London, p.182.

Brenner, N. (1998) 'Global cities, global states: global city formation and state territorial restructuring in contemporary Europe', *Review of International Political Economy*, vol.5, no.1, pp.1–37.

Burgess, R., Carmona, M. and Kolstee, T. (eds) (1997) *The Challenge of Sustainable Cities: Neo-Liberalism and Urban Strategies in Developing Countries*, Zed Books, London.

Campbell, T. (1999) 'The changing prospects for cities in development – the case of Vietnam', *Business Briefing: World Urban Economic Development*, official briefing for World Competitive Cities Congress, World Bank, Washington, DC, pp.16–19.

Cardoso, A. and Lago, L.C. (1993) 'Pobreza urbana e condições habitacionais na periferia metropolitana do Rio de Janeiro', *Cadernos IPPUR/UFRJ*, anoVII no.2 set., pp.67–78.

Castells, M. (1996) *The Information Age: Economy, Society and Culture, Volume I: The Rise of the Network Society*, Blackwell, Oxford.

Castells, M. (1997) *The Information Age: Economy, Society and Culture, Volume II: The Power of Identity*, Blackwell, Oxford.

Castells, M. (1998) *The Information Age: Economy, Society and Culture, Volume III: End of Millennium*, Blackwell, Oxford.

Castles, S. and Miller, M.J. (1998) *The Age of Migration: International Population Movements in the Modern World*, Macmillan Press, Basingstoke.

Cernea, M. (1996) 'Understanding and preventing impoverishment from displacement – reflections on the state of knowledge', in McDowell, C. (ed.) *Understanding Impoverishment: The Consequences of Development-Induced Displacement*, Berghahn Books, Providence, RI.

Cernea, M. (2000) 'Risks, safeguards, and reconstruction: a model for population displacement and resettlement' in Cernea, M. and McDowell, C. (eds) *Risks and Reconstruction: Experiences of Resettlers and Refugees*, The World Bank, Washington, DC.

Cernea, M. and McDowell, C. (eds) (2000) *Risks and Reconstruction: Experiences of Resettlers and Refugees*, World Bank, Washington, DC, p.2.

Chambers, R. (1998) 'Paradigm shifts and the practice of participatory research and development' in Nelson, N. and Wright, S. (eds) *Power and Participatory Development*, Intermediate Technology Publications, London, pp.30–42.

Chimni, B.S. (2000) *International Refugee Law: A Reader*, Sage Publications, Thousand Oaks, CA, pp.408–410.

Chinkin, C. (1998) 'International law and human rights', in Evans, T. (ed.) *Human Rights Fifty Years On: A Reappraisal*, Manchester University Press, Manchester.

Chukwu-Emeka Chikezie-Fergusson, P. (2000) 'Africans help their homelands', *West Africa*, 13–19 November, pp.12–14.

Clark, J. (1992) 'Policy influence, lobbying and advocacy', in Edwards, M. and Hulme, D. (eds) *Making a Difference: NGOs and Development in a Changing World*, Earthscan, London, p.197.

Clifford, J. (1994) 'Diasporas', *Cultural Anthropology*, vol.9, no.3, pp.302–338.

Cohen, M.A. (1996) 'The hypothesis of urban convergence: are cities in the North and South becoming more alike in an age of globalization?' in Cohen, M.A., Ruble, B.A., Tulchin, J.S. and Garland, A.M. (eds) *Preparing for the Urban Future: Global Pressures and Local Forces*, Woodrow Wilson Center Press, Washington, DC, p.25.

Cohen, R. (1997) *Global Diasporas: An Introduction*, UCL Press, London.

Colchester, M. (1999) Introduction in 'Dams, indigenous peoples and ethnic minorities', *Indigenous Affairs*, International Work Group on Indigenous Affairs, vol.3–4, p.13.

Collinson, S. (1999) 'Globalisation and the dynamics of international migration: implications for the refugee regime', *New Issues in Refugee Research*, working paper no.1, UNHCR.

Colson, E. (1971) *The Social Consequences of Resettlement: The Impact of the Kariba Resettlement on the Gwembe Tonga*, Manchester University Press, Manchester.

Congress of South Africa Trade Unions website, http://www.cosatu.org.za/samwu/igolimain.htm [accessed December 2001].

Connolly, W. (1991) 'Democracy and territoriality', *Millennium: Journal of International Studies*, vol.20, no.3, pp.463–484.

Coopers and Lybrand (1996) *New York New Media Industry Survey*, Coopers and Lybrand, New York.

Coopers and Lybrand (1997) *Second New York New Media Industry Survey*, Coopers and Lybrand, New York.

Corbridge, S. (1993) 'Marxisms, modernitites and moralitites: development praxis and the claims of distant strangers', *Environment and Planning D: Society and Space*, vol.11, no.4, pp.449–472.

Cox, K. and Mair, A. (1988) 'Locality and community in the politics of local economic development', *Annals of the Association of American Geographers*, vol.78, pp.307–325.

Crang, P. (1997) 'Cultural turns and the (re)constitution of economic geography', in Lee, R. and Will, J. (eds) *Geographies of Economies*, Arnold, London, pp.3–15.

Crisp, J. (1999) 'Policy challenges of the new diasporas: migrant networks and their impact on asylum flows and regimes', *New Issues in Refugee Research*, working paper no.7, UNHCR, p.4.

Crisp, J. (2000) 'Managing forced migration: evolving international responses to the refugee problem', paper presented at the Conference on International Migration and Foreign Policy, Wilton Park, UK, 4 October 2000, unpublished.

Curtin, P. (1984) *Cross-Cultural Trade in World History*, Cambridge University Press, Cambridge, pp.2–3.

De Boeck, F. (1996) 'Postcolonialism, power and identity: local and global perspectives from Zaire' in Webner, R. and Ranger, T. (eds) *Postcolonial Identities in Africa*, Zed Books, London, p.95.

de Wet, C. (2001) 'Can everybody win? Economic development and population displacement', paper presented at the 10th Conference of the International Rural Sociology Association, Rio de Janeiro, October 1999, unpublished.

Dirlik, A. (1997) 'Critical reflections on "Chinese capitalism" as paradigm', *Identities*, vol.3, no.3, pp.303–330.

Douglas, M. (1966) *Purity and Danger: An Analysis of Concepts of Pollution and Taboo*, Routledge, London.

Edwards, M. (1993) 'Does the doormat influence the boot? Critical thoughts on UK NGOs and international advocacy', *Development and Practice*, vol.3, no.3, p.163.

Edwards, M. (2000) *NGO Rights and Responsibilities: A New Deal for Global Governance*, Foreign Policy Centre, London, p.3

Escobar, A. (1995) *Encountering Development: The Making and Unmaking of the Third World*, Princeton University Press, Princeton, NJ.

Escobar, A. (2001) 'Culture sits in places: reflections on globalism and subaltern strategies of localization', *Political Geography*, vol.20, pp.139–174.

Feeney, P. (1998) *Accountable Aid: Local Participation in Major Projects*, Oxfam Publications, Oxford.

Ferguson, J. (1999) *Expectations of Modernity: Myths and Meanings of Urban Life on the Zambian Copperbelt*, University of California Press, Berkeley.

Fine, B. (1999) 'The developmental state is dead – long live social capital?', *Development and Change*, vol.30, no.1, pp.1–19.

Finkelstein, L.S. (1995) 'What is global governance?', *Global Governance,* vol.1, no.1, p.267.

Firman, T. (1999) 'From "global city" to "city of crisis": Jakarta metropolitan region under economic turmoil', *Habitat International*, vol.23, no.4, pp.447–466.

Fowler, A. (1997) *Striking a Balance*, Earthscan, London.

Fox, J.A. (1996) 'How does civil society thicken? The political construction of social capital in rural Mexico', *World Development*, vol.24, no.6, pp.1089–1105.

Fox, J.A. (2000) 'When does reform policy influence practice? Lessons from the bank-wide resettlement review', in Fox, J.A and Brown, L.D. (eds) *The Struggle for Accountability: The World Bank, NGOs and Grassroots Movements*, MIT Press, Cambridge, Massachusetts.

Fox, J.A. and Brown, L.D. (1998) *The Struggle for Accountability: The World Bank, NGOs and Grassroots Movements*, MIT Press, Cambridge, Massachusetts, p.455.

Fox, J.A. and Brown, L.D. (2000) 'Introduction', in *The Struggle for Accountability: The World Bank, NGOs and Grassroots Movements*, MIT Press, Cambridge, Massachusetts, p.23.

Frelick, W. (1993) 'Closing ranks: the North locks arms against refugees', in Bennis, P. and Moushabeck, M. (eds) *Altered States: A Reader in the New World Order*, Olive Branch, New York, p.442.

Friends of River Narmada website, http://www.narmada.org [accessed November 2001].

Fryer, P. (1984) *Staying Power: The History of Black People in Britain*, Pluto Press, London.

Fukuyama, F. (1995) *Trust: The Social Virtues and the Creation of Prosperity*, Penguin, London, p.10.

Galtung, J. (1998) 'The Third World and human rights in the post-1989 world order', in Evans, T. (ed.) *Human Rights Fifty Years On: A Reappraisal*, Manchester University Press, Manchester, p.212.

Ghosh, B. (1998) *Huddled Masses and Uncertain Shores: Insights into Irregular Migration*, International Organisation for Migration, Martinius Nighoff Publishers, The Hague, p.35.

Gibney, M. (2000a) 'Between control and humanitarianism: temporary protection in contemporary Europe', *Georgetown Immigration Law Journal*, vol.14, no.3, pp.689–707.

Gibney, M. (2000b) 'Kosovo and beyond: popular and unpopular refugees', *Forced Migration Review*, Refugee Studies Centre, Oxford, vol.5, pp.28–30.

Gibney, M. (2002) *The Politics and Ethics of Asylum*, Cambridge University Press, Cambridge, in press.

Giddens, A. (1990) *The Consequences of Modernity*, Polity Press, Cambridge, in association with Blackwell, Oxford.

Gilbert, R. (1995) 'Rio de Janeiro: the make up of a modern mega-city', *Habitat International*, vol.19, no.1, pp.91–122.

Gilroy, P. (1987) *There Ain't No Black in the Union Jack: The Cultural Politics of Race and Nation*, Unwin Hyman, London.

Gilroy, P. (1993a) *Small Acts: Thoughts on the Politics of Black Cultures*, Serpent's Tail, London.

Gilroy, P. (1993b) *The Black Atlantic: Modernity and Double Consciousness*, Verso, London.

Goodwin-Gill, G. (1999) 'Refugee identity and protection's fading prospect' in Nicholson, F. and Twomey P. (eds), *Refugee Rights and Realities: Evolving International Concepts and Regimes*, Cambridge University Press, Cambridge, p.237.

Government of the Republic of Zambia (1972) *Second national development plan, 1972–1976,* Ministry of Development Planning and National Guidance, Lusaka, pp.145–149.

Gray, A. (1996) 'Understanding impoverishment: the consequences of development-induced displacement', *Indigenous Resistance to Involuntary Relocation*, Berghahn Books, Oxford, pp.99–122.

Gray, A. (2000) 'Development policy – development protest: the World Bank, indigenous peoples, and NGOs' in Fox, J.A. and Brown, L.D. (eds) *The Struggle for Accountability: The World Bank, NGOs and Grassroots Movements*, MIT Press, Cambridge, Massachusetts.

Greater Johannesburg Metropolitan Council (2000) *iGoli 2002: making the city work.*

Greater Johannesburg Metropolitan Council (2001) *City development plan 2001/ 2002*, p.29.

Halfani, M. (1996) 'Marginality and dynamism: prospects for the sub-Saharan African city' in Cohen, M.A., Ruble, B.A., Tulchin, J.S. and Garland, A.M. (eds) *Preparing for the Urban Future: Global Pressures and Local Forces*, Woodrow Wilson Centre Press, Washington, DC, Chapter 5.

Hall, S. (1990) 'Cultural identity and diaspora', in Rutherford, J. (ed.) *Identity: Community, Culture, Difference*, Lawrence & Wishart, London, pp.222–237.

Hall, S. (1991) 'The local and the global: globalization and ethnicity', in King, A. (ed.) *Culture, Globalization and the World System*, Macmillan, London, pp.19–39.

Hall, S. (1994) 'Cultural identity and diaspora' in Williams, P. and Chrisman, L. (eds) *Colonial Discourse and Post-Colonial Theory*, Columbia University Press, New York, pp.392–403.

Hall, S. (1995) 'New cultures for old', in Massey, D. and Jess, P. (eds) *A Place in the World? Places, Cultures and Globalization*, Oxford University Press, Oxford, in association with the Open University, Milton Keynes, pp.175–213.

Hannerz, U. (1997) 'Flows, boundaries and hybrids: keywords in transnational anthropology', ESRC Transnational Communities Project, Working Paper WPTC-2K-02, http://www.transcomm.ox.ac.uk/working_papers.htm [accessed November 2001].

Hansen, K. (1994) 'Dealing with used clothing: *salaula* and the construction of identity in Zambia's third republic', *Public Culture*, vol.6, pp.503–523.

Harris, N. (1992) *Cities in the 1990s*, UCL Press, London.

Harriss, J. (2000) 'The second "great transformation"? Capitalism at the end of the twentieth century', in Thomas, A. and Allen, T. (eds) *Poverty and Development into the 21st Century*, Oxford University Press, Oxford, in association with the Open University, Milton Keynes, pp.325–342.

Harvey, D. (1989a) *The Condition of Postmodernity*, Blackwell, New York, pp.147–159.

Harvey, D. (1989b) 'From managerialism to entrepreneurialism: the transformation of urban governance in late capitalism', *Geografiska Annaler*.

Harvey, D. (2000) *Spaces of Hope*, Edinburgh University Press, Edinburgh, pp.138–141.

Hewitt, T. (2000) 'Half a century of development' in Allan, T. and Thomas, A. (eds) *Poverty and Development into the 21st Century*, Oxford University Press, Oxford, in association with the Open University, Milton Keynes, pp.289–308.

Hill, R.C and Kim, J. W. (2000) 'Global cities and developmental states: New York, Tokyo and Seoul', *Urban Studies*, vol.37, no.12, pp.2167–2195.

Hirst, P. (2001) 'Politics: territorial or non-territorial?', http://www.theglobalsite.ac.uk/press/104hirst.htm [accessed November 2001].

Hirst, P. and Thompson, G. (1996) *Globalization in Question: The International Economy and the Possibilities of Governance*, Polity Press, Cambridge.

Hope-Simpson, J. (1939) *The Refugee Problem: Report of a Survey*, Oxford University Press, London, pp.3–4.

Howe, S. (1998) *Afrocentrism: Mythical Pasts and Imagined Homes*, Verso, London.

Hulme, D. and Edwards, M. (1997) 'NGOs, states and donors: an overview', in Hulme, D and Edwards, M. (eds) *NGOs, States and Donors: Too Close for Comfort?*, Macmillan Press, Basingstoke, pp.6–7.

Huxham, C. (ed.) (1996) *Creating Collaborative Advantage*, Sage, London.

Ilisu Dam Campaign website, http://www.ilisu.org.uk/ [accessed November 2001].

James, C.L.R. (1963) *The Black Jacobins*, Vintage Books, New York, p.397.

Jessop, B. and Sum, N. (2000) 'An entrepreneurial city in action: Hong Kong's emerging strategies in and for (inter)urban competition', *Urban Studies*, vol.37, no.12, pp.2287–2313.

Joppke, C. (1998) 'Immigration challenges to the nation-state', in Joppke, C. (ed.) *Challenge to the Nation-State: Immigration in Western Europe and the United States*, Oxford University Press, Oxford.

Jordan, L. and Van Tuijl, P. (1998) *Political Responsibility in NGO Advocacy*, The Hague, NOVIB.

Kahn, H. (1979) *World Economic Development: 1979 and Beyond*, Morrow Quill, New York, p.128.

Keck, M. and Sikkink, K. (1998) *Activists Beyond Borders*, Cornell University Press, Ithaca.

Kelly, P.F. (2000) *Landscapes of Globalization. Human Geographies of Economic Change in the Philippines*, Routledge, London.

Khapre, S. (2000) 'BJP pledges to strengthen bond with NRIs', Overseas Friends of the BJP website, http://www.ofbjp.org/news/0800/20.html [accessed November 2001].

Kibreab, G. (1999) 'Revisiting the debate on people, place, identity and displacement', *Journal of Refugee Studies*, vol.12, no.4, pp.384–410.

King, A. (1995) 'Re-presenting world cities: cultural theory/social practice' in Knox, P. and Taylor, P. (eds) *World Cities in a World-System*, Cambridge University Press, Cambridge, pp.215–231.

Klein, N. (2000) *No Logo*, Picador, New York, NY.

Kobrin, S.J. (1998) 'Globalization at work – the MAI and the clash of globalizations', *Foreign Policy*, no.112, pp.97–109.

Koenig, D. (2000) *Toward local development and mitigating impoverishment in development-induced displacement and resettlement*, final report for ESCOR Grant R7644, Department for International Development, Refugee Studies Centre, University of Oxford, p.14.

Koser, K. (1997) 'Negotiating entry into Fortress Europe: the migration strategies of "spontaneous" asylum seekers', in Muus, P. (ed.) *The Exclusion and Inclusion of Refugees in Contemporary Europe*, ECRCOMER, Utrecht.

Krasner, S. (1995) 'Power politics, institutions, and transnational relations' in Risse-Kappen, T. (ed.) *Bringing Transnational Relations Back in Non-State Actors, Domestic Structures and International Institutions*, Cambridge University Press, Cambridge, p.279.

Kymlicka, W. (1995) *Multicultural Citizenship*, Clarendon Press, Oxford.

Lago, L.C. (1992) 'Política urbana e a questão habitacional: novas tendencias face à crise econõmica basilerira', *Cadernos IPPUR/UFRJ*, anoVI, no.1 dez, pp.41–47.

Lavie, S. and Swedenburg, T. (1996) *Displacement, Diaspora and Geographies of Identity*, Duke University Press, Durham, NC, p.14.

League of Nations, (1921) 'Memorandum from the Comité International de la Croix-Rouge at Geneva to the Council of the League of Nations', *Official Journal*, March–April, p.225–229.

Lewis, R. (1954) *Sierra Leone: A Modern Portrait*, Her Majesty's Stationery Office, London, p.32.

Lipton, M. (1977) *Why Poor People Stay Poor: A Study of Urban Bias in World Development*, Temple Smith, London.

Loescher, G. (1993) *Beyond Charity: International Co-operation and the Global Refugee Crisis*, Oxford University Press, New York.

London Development Agency (2001) *Economic Development Strategy*, http://www.lda.gov.uk/pdfs/Economic_Dev_Strategy.pdf, [accessed January 2002].

Loomba, A. (1998) *Colonialism/Postcolonialism*, Routledge, London.

Lumsden, D.P. (1973) 'The Volta river project: village resettlement and attempted rural animation', *Canadian Journal of African Studies*, vol.7, no.1, pp.115–132.

MacGaffey, J. and Bazenguissa-Ganga, R. (2000) *Congo–Paris: Transnational Traders on the Margins of the Law*, James Currey, Oxford.

MacIver, D. (1999) 'Introduction: states and ethnic pluralism', in MacIver, D. (ed.) *The Politics of Multinational States*, Macmillan Press, Basingstoke.

Magubane, B. (1987) *The Ties that Bind: African-American Consciousness of Africa*, Africa World Press, Trenton, NY.

Malkki, L. (1992) 'National geographic: the rooting of peoples and the territorialization of the national identity among scholars and refugees', *Cultural Anthropology*, vol.7, no.1, pp.24–44.

Malkki, L. (1997) 'National geographic: the rooting of peoples and the territorialization of national identity among scholars and refugees' in Gupta, A. and Ferguson, J. (eds) *Culture, Power, Place: Explorations in Critical Anthropology*, Duke University Press, Durham, NC, pp.52–74.

Mandaville, P. (1999) 'Territory and translocality: discrepant idioms of political identity', *Millennium, Journal of International Studies*, vol.28, no.3.

Martin, B. (1998) 'Waiting for Oprah and the new US constituency for Africa', *Review of African Political Economy*, vol.75, pp.8–24.

Martin, S. (2000) 'Forced migration and the evolving humanitarian regime', *New Issues in Refugee Research*, working paper no.20, UNHCR, p.22.

Martinussen, J. (1999) *Society, State and Market: A Guide to Competing Theories of Development*, Zed Books, New York, p.332.

Massey, D. (1994) *Space, Place and Gender*, Polity Press, Cambridge.

Massey D. (1995) 'The conceptualization of place', in Massey, D. and Jess, P.M. (eds) *A Place in the World? Places, Cultures and Globalization*, Oxford University Press, Oxford, in association with the Open University, Milton Keynes.

Massey, D., Allen, J. and Pile, S. (1999) *City Worlds*, Routledge, London, in association with the Open University, Milton Keynes.

Mazumdar, S. (1995) 'Women on the march: right-wing mobilization in contemporary India', *Feminist Review*, vol.49, pp.1–28.

McDowell, C. (1996) 'Introduction' in *Understanding Impoverishment: The Consequences of Development-Induced Displacement*, Berghahn Books, Providence, RI, p.4.

McGee, T. (1989) 'Urbanisasi or kotadesasi? Evolving patterns of urbanisation in Asia' in Costa, F., Dutt, A., Ma, L. and Noble, A. (eds) *Urbanisation in Asia. Spatial Dimensions and Policy Issues*, University of Hawaii Press, Honolulu, pp.93–94.

McGrew, A. (2000) 'Sustainable globalization? The global politics of development and exclusion in the new world order' in Allen, T. and Thomas, A. (eds) *Poverty and Development into the 21st Century*, Oxford University Press, Oxford, in association with the Open University, Milton Keynes, pp.345–364.

Meghani, M, 'Hindutva: the great nationalist ideology', Bharatiya Janata Party website, http://www.bjp.org/history/htvintro-mm.html [accessed November 2001].

Mertus, J. (1998) 'The state and the post-Cold War refugee regime: new models, new questions', *International Journal of Refugee Law*, vol.10, no.3, pp.321–348.

Mitchell, K. (1997) 'Different diasporas and the hype of hybridity', *Environment and Planning D: Society and Space*, vol.15, pp.533–553.

Mohan, G. and Stokke, K. (2000) 'Participatory development and empowerment: the dangers of localism', *Third World Quarterly*, vol.21, no.2, pp.247–268.

Monitor Group (2001) *Towards a strategy for building Johannesburg into a world-class city*, Monitor Group, Johannesburg.

Morrison, J. and Crosland, B. (2001) 'The trafficking and smuggling of refugees: the end game in European asylum policy?', *New Issues in Refugee Research*, working paper no.39, UNHCR.

Morsink, H. (1996) 'Preface' in Allen, T. (ed.) *In Search of Cool Ground: War, Flight and Homecoming in Northeast Africa*, UNRISD, Geneva, in association with J. Curry, London, and Africa World Press, Trenton.

Moser, C. (1998) 'The asset vulnerability framework: reassessing urban poverty reduction strategies', *World Development*, vol.26, no.1, pp.1–19.

Mudimbe, V. (1988) *The Invention of Africa: Gnosis, Philosophy, and the Order of Knowledge*, Indiana University Press, Bloomington, p.103.

Ndofor-Tah, C. (2000) *Diaspora and development: contributions by African organisations in the UK to Africa's development*, report commissioned by AFFORD as part of Africa21 Project, African Foundation for Development, London.

Nederveen Pieterse, J. (1997) 'Globalisation and emancipation: from local empowerment to global reform', *New Political Economy*, vol.2, no.1, pp.79–92.

O'Neill, O. (1986) *Faces of Hunger. An Essay on Poverty, Justice and Development*, Allen Unwin, London.

Oliver-Smith, A. (1996) 'Fighting for a place: the policy implications of resistance to development-induced resettlement', in McDowell, C. (ed.) *Understanding Impoverishment: The Consequences of Development-Induced Displacement*, Berghahn Books, Providence, RI, p.78.

Oliver-Smith, A. (2001) *Displacement, resistance and the critique of development: from the grassroots to the global*, final report for ESCOR Grant R7644, Department of International Development, Refugees Studies Centre, University of Oxford, p.98.

Ong, A. (1992) 'Limits to cultural accumulation: Chinese capitalists and cultural citizenship in California', *New York Academy of Sciences*, vol.645, pp.124–145.

Ong, A. (1993) 'On the edge of empires: flexible citizenship among Chinese in diaspora', *Positions*, vol.1, no.3, pp.745–778.

Oxfam International 1998a, personal interview conducted by H. Yanacopulos, Oxford, UK, 30 September 1998.

Oxfam International 1998b, personal interview conducted by H. Yanacopulos, Washington, DC, 8 July 1998.

Oxfam International 1998c, personal interview conducted by H. Yanacopulos, Boston, US, 25 June 1998.

Oxfam International 1999, personal interview conducted by H. Yanacopulos, Washington, DC, 16 February 1999.

Padmore, G. (1971) *Pan-Africanism or Communism*, Doubleday, New York, p.283 [first published 1953].

Peterson, J. (1968) 'The Enlightenment and the founding of Freetown: an introduction to Sierra Leone history, 1787–1816', in Fyfe, C. and Jones, E. (eds) *Freetown: A Symposium*, Sierra Leone University Press, Freetown, pp.9–23.

Portes, A. (1997) 'Globalization from below: the rise of transnational communities', ESRC Transnational Communities Project, Working Paper WPTC-98-01, http://www.transcomm.ox.ac.uk/working_papers.htm [accessed November 2001].

Portes, A. and Jensen, L. (1987) 'What's an ethnic enclave? The case for conceptual clarity', *American Sociological Review*, vol.52, pp.768–771.

Portes, A. and Sensenbrenner, J. (1993) 'Embeddedness and immigration: notes on the social determinants of economic action', *American Journal of Sociology*, vol.98, no.6, pp.1320–1350.

Posner, R. (1995) 'The most primitive nation', *Times Literary Supplement*, no.4822, 1 September 1995.

Potts (1999) 'The impact of structural adjustment on welfare and livelihoods: an assessment by people in Horare, Zimbabwe' in Jones, S. and Nelson, N. (eds) *Poverty in Africa: From Understanding to Alleviation*, Intermediate Technology Publications, London.

Pratt, A. (2000) 'New Media, the new economy and new spaces', *Geoforum*, vol.31, no.4, pp.425–436.

Putnam, R. (1993) 'The prosperous community: social capital and public life', *The American Prospect*, vol.13, pp.35–42.

Rakodi, C. (1988) 'Upgrading in Chawama, Lusaka: displacement or differentiation?', *Urban Studies*, vol.25, no.4, pp.297–318.

Ramansara, A. (2000) 'Indonesia: the struggle of the people of Kedung Ombo', in Fox, J.A and Brown, L.D. (eds) *The Struggle for Accountability: The World Bank, NGOs, and Grassroots Movements*, MIT Press, Massachusetts.

Rashtriya Swayamsevak Sangh website, 'The story of the Sangh', http://www.rss.org/rssstor.htm [accessed November 2001].

Reisman, M.W. (1990) 'Sovereignty and human rights in contemporary international law', *American Journal of International Law*, vol.84.

Reno, W. (1995) *Corruption and State Politics in Sierra Leone*, Cambridge University Press, Cambridge.

Reno, W. (1996) 'Ironies of post-Cold War structural adjustment in Sierra Leone', *Review of African Political Economy*, vol.67, pp.7–18.

Riddell, J. (1970) *The Spatial Dynamics of Modernization in Sierra Leone: Structure, Diffusion and Response*, Northwestern University Press, Evanston.

Riley, E., Fiori, J. and Ramirez, R. (2001) 'Favela Bairro and a new generation of housing programmes for the urban poor', *Geoforum*, vol.32, no.4, pp.521–532.

Robins, K. and Aksoy, A. (1996) 'Istanbul between civilisation and discontent', *City*, vol.5–6, pp.6–33.

Rogerson, C. (1999) 'Local economic development and urban poverty alleviation: the experience of post-apartheid South Africa', *Habitat International*, vol.23, no.4, pp.511–534.

Rorty, R. (1996) 'Moral universalism and economic triage', *The Second UNESCO Philosophy Forum*, http://www.unesco.org/phiweb/uk/2rpu/rort/rort.html [accessed November 2001].

Rose, G. (1995) 'Place and identity: a sense of place', in Massey, D. and Jess, P. (eds) *A Place in the World? Places, Cultures and Globalization*, Oxford University Press, Oxford, in association with the Open University, Milton Keynes, pp.87–132.

Rosenau, J. (1990) *Turbulence in World Politics*, New Jersey, Princeton University Press.

Rosenau, J. (1995) 'Governance in the twenty-first century', *Global Governance*, vol.1, no.1, p.14.

Rosenau, J. (1997) *Along the Domestic–Foreign Frontier. Exploring Governance in a Turbulent World*, Cambridge, Cambridge University Press, p.10.

Rosenau, J. and Czempiel, E.-O. (1992) *Governance Without Government: Order and Change in World Politics*, Cambridge University Press, Cambridge, p.4.

Routledge, P. (1998) 'Going globile: spatiality, embodiment, and mediation in the Zapatista Insurgency' in Dalby, S. and O'Tuathail, G. (eds) *Rethinking Geopolitics*, Routledge, London, pp.240–260.

Routledge P. (2002) '"Our resistance will be as transnational as capital": convergence space and strategy in globalising resistance' *GeoJournal*, in press.

Rowlands, D. (1998) 'Poverty and environmental degradation as root causes of international migration: a critical assessment', paper presented at the Technical Symposium on International Migration and Development, The Hague, Netherlands.

Roy, A. (1999) 'The greater common good', *The Cost of Living*, The Modern Library, New York.

Rutinwa, B. (1999) 'The end of asylum? The changing nature of refugee policies in Africa', *New Issues in Refugee Research*, working paper no.5, UNHCR.

Safran, W. (1991) 'Diasporas in modern societies: myths of homeland and return', *Diaspora*, vol.1, pp.83–99.

Salamon, L. (1994) 'The rise of the nonprofit sector', *Foreign Affairs*, vol.73, no.4, p.109.

Sassen, S. (1994) *Cities in a World Economy*, Pine Forge Press, Thousand Oaks, California.

Sassen, S. (1995) in Knox, P. and Taylor, P. (eds) *World Cities in a World-System*, Routledge, London.

Scholte, J. (1996) 'The geography of collective identities in a globalizing world', *Review of International Political Economy*, vol.3, no.4, pp.565–607.

Scholte, J.A. (1997) 'Global capitalism and the state', *International Affairs*, vol.73, no.1, pp.427–452.

Schumpeter, J. (1953) 'Die sozialen Klassen im ethnisch homogenen Milieu', in Schumpeter, J. (ed.), *Aufsatze zur Soziologie*, Mohr, Tübingen [first published in 1927].

Scudder, T. (1993) 'Development-induced relocation and refugee studies: 37 years of change and continuity among Zambia's Gwembe Tonga', *Journal of Refugee Studies*, vol.6, no.2, pp.123–152.

Segal, R. (1998) 'Globalisation and the black diaspora', ESRC Transnational Communities Project, Working Paper WPTC-98-15, http://www.transcomm.ox.ac.uk/working_papers.htm [accessed November 2001].

Simai, M. (1994) *The Future of Global Governance – Managing Risk and Change in the International System*, United States Institute of Peace Press, Washington, p.348.

Simone, A. (1998) 'Globalization and the identity of African urban practices' in Judin, H. and Vladislavic, I. (eds) *Blank____: Architecture, Apartheid and After*, D8.

Smith, R. (1992) *Los ausentes siempre presentes: the imagining, making and politics of a transnational community between New York City and Ticuani, Puebla*, Institute for Latin American and Iberian Studies, Columbia University, New York.

Soguk, N. (1999) *States and Strangers: Refugees and Displacements of Statecraft*, University of Minnesota Press, Minneapolis.

Stark, O. and Taylor, J.E. (1991) 'Migration incentives, migration types: the role of relative deprivation', *Economic Journal*, vol.101, no.408, pp.1163–1178.

Storper, M. (1995) 'Territorial development in the global learning economy: the challenge to developing counties', *Review of International Political Economy*, vol.2, pp.394–424.

Storper, M. (1997) *The Regional World: Territorial Development in a Global Economy*, Guilford Press, New York.

Strange, S. (1996a) 'The retreat of the state: the diffusion of power in the world economy', *Cambridge Studies in International Relations*, no.49, Cambridge University Press, Cambridge.

Strange, S. (1996b) *The Retreat of the State*, Cambridge University Press, Cambridge.

Tekeli, İ. (1994), 'Geleceğin İstanbul'u', *İstanbul*, vol.8, pp.114–116.

Telekon, S. (1999) 'It's a long way to … harmonization', *Refugees Magazine*, vol.113.

Teson, F. (1988) *Humanitarian Intervention: An Enquiry into Law and Morality*, Transnational Publishers, Dobbs Ferry.

The National Summit on Africa website, 'Mission and objectives', http://www.africasummit.org/about/mission.htm [accessed November 2001].

Third World Network, personal interview conducted by H. Yanacopulos, 5 May 1998.

Thomas, A. (2000a) 'Meanings and views of development', in *Poverty and Development into the 21st Century*, Oxford University Press, Oxford, in association with the Open University, Milton Keynes, pp.23–48.

Thomas, A. (2000b) 'Development as practice in a liberal capitalist world', *Journal of International Development*, vol.12, pp.773–787.

Thomas, A. and Allen, T. (2000) 'Agencies of development', in *Poverty and Development into the 21st Century*, Oxford University Press, Oxford, in association with the Open University, Milton Keynes, pp.189–216.

Tsing, A. (2000) 'The global situation', *Cultural Anthropology*, vol.15, no.3, pp.327–360.

Tyner, J.A. (2000) 'Global cities and circuits of global labour: the case of Manila, Philippines', *Professional Geographer*, vol.52, pp.61–74.

Udall (2000) 'The World Bank and public accountability: has anything changed?' in Fox, J.A. and Brown, L.D. (eds) *The Struggle for Accountability: The World Bank, NGOs and Grassroots Movements*, MIT Press, Cambridge, Massachusetts.

UNCHS (2000) 'The state of the world's cities', *Global Urban Observatory and Statistics*, United Nations Centre for Human Settlements (Habitat) website, http://www.urbanobservatory.org [accessed March 2000].

UNCHS (2001) *Cities in a Globalising World: Global Report on Human Settlements 2001*, Earthscan, London.

UNDP (1996) *Human Development Report 1996*, Oxford University Press, Oxford.

UNDP (2000) *The Human Development Report: Human Rights and Human Development*, UNDP, New York, in association with Oxford University Press, Oxford.

UNHCR (2000) *The State of the World's Refugees: Fifty Years of Humanitarian Action*, UNHCR and Oxford University Press, Oxford.

Uvin, P. (1995) 'Scaling up the grass roots and scaling down the summit: the relations between Third World non-governmental organisations and the United Nations', *Third World Quarterly*, vol.16, no.3, p.495.

Uvin, P., Jain, P, and Brown, D. (2000) 'Think large and act small: toward a new paradigm for NGO scaling-up', *World Development*, vol.28, no.8, p.1411.

Uvin, P. and Miller, D. (1996) 'Paths to scaling-up: alternative strategies for local non-governmental organizations', *Human Organization*, vol.55, no.3, p.348.

Van Kessel, G. (2001) 'Global migration and asylum', *Forced Migration Review*, Department for International Development, Refugee Studies Centre, University of Oxford, vol.10, pp.10–13.

Waldinger, R. (1995) 'The "other side" of embeddedness: a case-study of the interplay of economy and ethnicity', *Ethnic and Racial Studies*, vol.18, no.3, p.555–580.

Warner, D. (1997) 'Migration and refugees: a challenge for the 21st century', in Carlier, J.-Y. and Vanheule, D. (eds) *Europe and Refugees: A Challenge?*, Kluwer Law International, The Hague, p.60.

Warner, D. (1999) 'The refugee state and state protection' in Nicholson, F. and Twomey P. (eds) *Refugee Rights and Realities: Evolving International Concepts and Regimes*, Cambridge University Press, Cambridge, p.261.

Warner, M. (ed) (1995) 'Organisational networks', *International Encyclopedia of Business and Management*, Routledge, London.

Weber, M. (1989) *The Protestant Ethic and the Spirit of Capitalism*, Unwin Hyman, London [first published in 1922].

Weiss, T. and Gordenker, L. (1996) *NGOs, the UN, and Global Governance*, Boulder, CO, Lynne Rienner Publishers, p.25.

Wirth, D. (2000) 'Partnership advocacy in World Bank environmental reform', in Fox, J.A. and Brown, L.D. (eds) *The Struggle for Accountability: The World Bank, NGOs and Grassroots Movements*, MIT Press, Massachusetts.

Wolfensohn, J. (1999) 'Foreword from the World Bank', *Business Briefing: World Urban Economic Development*, official briefing for World Competitive Cities Congress, World Bank, Washington, DC.

Woodhouse, P. (2000) 'Environmental degradation and sustainability', in Allen, T. and Thomas, A. (eds) *Poverty and Development into the 21st Century*, Oxford University Press, Oxford, in association with the Open University, pp.141–162.

World Bank (1991) 'Urban policy and economic development: an agenda for the 1990s: a World Bank policy paper', World Bank, Washington, DC.

World Bank (1994) 'Resettlement and development: the bankwide review of projects involving involuntary resettlement, 1986–1993', World Bank, Washington, DC.

World Bank (2000) *Cities in Transition: World Bank and Local Government Strategy*, World Bank, Washington, DC.

World Commission on Dams (2000) *Dams and Development: A New Framework for Decision Making*, report of the World Commission on Dams, Earthscan Publications, London and Sterling, VA.

Yanacopulos, H. (2001) 'The dynamics of governance: the role of development NGO coalitions in world politics', PhD Dissertation, University of Cambridge, Cambridge.

Zack-Williams, A. (1990) 'Sierra Leone: crisis and despair', *Review of African Political Economy*, vol.49, pp.22–33.

Zolberg, A.R., Suhrke, A. and Aguayo, S. (1989) *Escape from Violence: Conflict and the Refugee Crisis in the Developing World*, Oxford University Press, Oxford.

Zukin, S. and DiMaggio, P. (1990) 'Introduction' in Zukin, S. and DiMaggio, P. (eds) *Structures of Capital: The Social Organization of the Economy*, Cambridge University Press, Cambridge, pp.1–36.

Acknowledgements

Grateful acknowledgement is made to the following sources for permission to reproduce material within this book:

Cover

Main cover image: Panos Pictures; cover montage, left to right: Howard Davies/Exile Images, Jonathan Yee, Howard Davies/Exile Images, J.C. Tordai/Panos Pictures.

Figures

Figure 1.1: Glacco Pivozz/Panos Pictures; *Figure 1.2*: Armstrong, 1997 for the Tanganyika Christian Refugee Service; *Figure 1.3*: Howard Davies/Exile Images; *Figure 1.4*: Dag Jenssen; *Figure 2.1(a)*: Courtesy of UNHCR/A. Hollman; *Figure 2.1(b)*: Howard Davies/Exile Images; *Figure 2.2(a)*: Courtesy of UNHCR; *Figure 2.2(b)*: Courtesy of UNHCR/L. Astrom; *Figure 2.2(c)*: Courtesy of UNHCR/A. Hollman; *Figure 2.3(a)*: Associated Press; *Figure 2.3(b)*: Associated Press/Jassim Mohammed; *Figure 2.4*: Panos Pictures/Howard Davies; *Figure 2.5*: Courtesy of Dr Henry Madsen, Bilharziasis Library; *Figure 2.6*: Panos Pictures; *Figure 3.1*: Mary Evans Picture Library; *Figure 3.2*: National Maritime Museum; *Figure 3.3*: Mary Evans Picture Library; *Figure 3.5*: Based on Fyfe, C. and Jones, E. (1968) 'The foundings of Freetown', *Freetown: A Symposium*, Sierra Leone University Press; *Figure 3.6*: Collection Ghassan Salhab/AIF, © Arab Image Foundation; *Figure 3.7 left*: Jonathan Yee; *Figure 3.7 right*: http://www.britainonview; *Figure 3.8*: Hulton Getty Picture Collection; *Figure 3.9*: Courtesy of Western Union; *Figure 4.2*: Rakodi, C. (1998) 'Upgrading in Chawama, Lusaka: displacement or differentiation?', *Urban Studies*, vol.25, pp.297–318, Carfax. Taylor & Francis Limited, PO Box 25, Abingdon, Oxfordshire, OX14 3UE; *Figure 4.3*: Mark Edwards/Still Pictures; *Figure 4.4*: Knox, P.L. and Taylor, P.J. (1995) *World Cities in a World-System*, Cambridge University Press; *Figure 4.7*: Ron Giling/Still Pictures; *Figure 4.8*: The Lowdown; *Figure 4.9*: Chris Powers/Panos Pictures; *Figure 4.11*: Greater Johannesburg Metropolitan Council; *Figure 4.12(a)*: Philip Schedler/ Link Picture Library; *Figure 4.12(b) & (c)*: Les Bush/Link Picture Library; *Figure 5.1*: Associated Press; *Figure 5.2*: Panos Pictures; *Figure 5.3*: Panos Pictures; *Figure 5.5*: Panos Pictures/Clive Shirley; *Figure 5.6*: Courtesy of Oxfam.

Text

Box 2.2: UNHCR (2000) *The State of the World's Refugees 2000: Fifty Years of Humanitarian Action*, by permission of Oxford University Press; *Box 3.6*: Ong, A. (1993) 'On the edge of empires: flexible citizenship among Chinese in diaspora', *Positions*, vol.1, no.3. Copyright 1993, Duke University Press. All Rights Reserved. Reprinted with permission; *Box 4.2*: Riley *et al.* (2001) 'Favela Barrio and a new housing generation', *Geoforum*, vol.32, no.4. Reproduced by permission of the authors; *Box 4.5*: Benjamin, S. (2000) 'Governance, economic settings and poverty in Bangalore', *Environment and Urbanization*, vol.12, no.1, IIED, reproduced with permission; *Box 5.3*: Reprinted with permission from *The Globe & Mail*.

Table

Table 3.1: Al-Ali, N., Black, R. and Koser, K. (1999) *Mobilisation and participation of transnational communities in post-conflict reconstruction, 1989–1999,* ESRC Transnational Communities Research Programme.

Indexing by Isobel McLean